D0152732

SCIENCE AND TECHNOLOGY IN

NINETEENTH-CENTURY AMERICA

The Greenwood Press "Daily Life Through History" Series

SCIENCE AND TECHNOLOGY IN

NINETEENTH-CENTURY AMERICA

TODD TIMMONS

The Greenwood Press "Daily Life Through History" Series

GREENWOOD PRESS
Westport, Connecticut • London

Library of Congress Cataloging-in-Publication Data

Timmons, Todd.
   Science and technology in nineteenth-century America / Todd Timmons.
      p. cm. — (Greenwood Press "Daily life through history" series, ISSN 1080–4749)
   Includes bibliographical references and index.
   ISBN 0-313-33161-8 (alk. paper)
   1. Technology—United States—History—19th century. 2. Science--United States—
History—19th century. I. Title: Science and technology in 19th-century America. II. Title.
III. Series.
T21.T56   2005
509'.73'09034—dc22   2005020063

British Library Cataloguing in Publication Data is available.

Library of Congress Catalog Card Number: 2005020063
ISBN: 0–313–33161–8
ISSN: 1080–4749

First published in 2005

Greenwood Press, 88 Post Road West, Westport, CT 06881
An imprint of Greenwood Publishing Group, Inc.
www.greenwood.com

Printed in the United States of America

The paper used in this book complies with the
Permanent Paper Standard issued by the National
Information Standards Organization (Z39.48–1984).

10 9 8 7 6 5 4 3 2 1

Contents

Acknowledgments

Even when a book shows the name of a single author, it is truly the result of a team effort. Thank you to everyone on my "team." Special thanks go to the librarians at the University of Arkansas—Fort Smith, who treat me as if I am their only patron. Thank you to my wife, who not only encourages me but serves as editor, sounding board, and personal technical advisor when the computer doesn't do what I want it to do!

Introduction

To Americans living in the twenty-first century, the influences of science and technology are evident. We travel by car or airplane at speeds unimaginable to our great-grandparents. If we wish to talk with someone across town, across the state, or across the nation, we pick up a telephone—most likely a cell phone—and are instantly connected. Farmers use incredibly sophisticated machinery to ensure that we have a wide variety of fresh foods available at the supermarket; and when we arrive home from our shopping trip, we have microwave ovens to cook our food and televisions to entertain us after (or as) we eat. Very few of us can avoid science and technology in the workplace. We operate machinery, we employ sophisticated communication devices, and we are surrounded at work and at home by a myriad of electronic gadgets (including the computer, which allows me to correct my errors instantaneously as I write this). When we are sick, science often supplies the cure or technology provides the machine or instrument required to make us well again. Whereas a century ago, nobody had ever traveled into space or to the ocean floor, today both trips are almost commonplace for modern-day explorers. Our children are taught science in high school and college laboratories filled with equipment of which professional scientists once never dreamed. In our modern culture, it is usually accepted without debate that science and technology will continue to improve our lives.

This book is about a time when the intersection of science and technology with everyday life was still in its infant stages. It was in the nineteenth century that Americans first found that science might play a role in their lives and that technology would certainly change the way they lived. The role of science and technology in the everyday life of most Americans, essentially off the radar when the nineteenth century began, became a reality by the end of the century. The following pages chronicle some of these monumental changes.

Chronology

1800 Benjamin Waterhouse begins smallpox vaccination in the United States.

1801 Eli Whitney demonstrates interchangeable parts in firearms to John Adams and Thomas Jefferson.

1802 United States Military Academy is established at West Point.

1804 Lewis and Clark expedition begins.

1807 Robert Fulton launches his first steamboat.

United States Coast Survey is established by Congress.

1816 Baltimore becomes the first American city to install gas street-lights.

1824 Franklin Institute is formed.

1825 Erie Canal opens.

John Stevens lays out a small experimental railroad track on his own estate to demonstrate the feasibility of rail travel.

1826 Baltimore and Ohio Railroad is established.

1830 Joseph Henry demonstrates the power of the electromagnet—forerunner of the telegraph.

1835   Samuel Colt obtains his first patent for a revolving pistol.

1839   Harvard Observatory opens.

1842   Thomas Woodward patents the forerunner of the modern safety pin.

Crawford Long begins administering ether to patients undergoing surgery.

1844   Samuel Morse sends the message "What hath God wrought?" over a telegraph line strung between Baltimore and Washington, D.C.

Dentist Horace Wells begins administering nitrous oxide to his patients.

United States Naval Observatory is formed.

1845   Elias Howe receives a patent for his sewing machine.

1846   American Medical Association (AMA) is formed.

Smithsonian Institution is founded.

Sheffield Scientific School opens at Yale.

1847   Lawrence Scientific School opens at Harvard.

1848   The American Association for the Advancement of Science is created.

1849   Elizabeth Blackwell becomes the first woman to receive a medical degree from an American college.

1851   Crystal Palace exhibition opens in London.

1855   Niagara Suspension Bridge opens.

1859   Edwin Drake discovers oil in Pennsylvania.

1861   Western Union completes the first transcontinental telegraph.

1862   President Abraham Lincoln creates the United States Department of Agriculture.

Congress passes the Morrill Act.

1863   National Academy of Sciences (NAS) is formed.

1866   The first successful trans-Atlantic telegraph cable is laid.

1869   Transcontinental railroad is completed.

1873   Eli Janney patents his automatic coupling device for railcars.

First cable car line opens in San Francisco.

1874 Eads Bridge opens connecting St. Louis to East St. Louis over the Mississippi River.

1876 Centennial Exhibition opens in Philadelphia.

First elevated railroad opens in New York City.

Alexander Graham Bell utters the famous words "Watson, come here. I need you," and the telephone is born.

Johns Hopkins University is established.

1879 United States Geological Survey is established.

1881 The first long-distance telephone service established, between Boston and Providence.

1882 Edison opens the Pearl Street Station in New York City.

1883 Brooklyn Bridge opens.

1884 Coney Island opens its first roller coaster.

1893 Columbian Exposition opens in Chicago.

The Duryea brothers build their first automobile.

1

Science and Technology in Nineteenth-Century America: An Overview

Never in history had humankind experienced such revolutionary changes in everyday life as was experienced in the nineteenth century. In 1800, horses were the fastest mode of both transportation and communication; in 1900, railroads and steamships traveled at speeds unimaginable a century earlier, and communication was made instantaneous with the telegraph and telephone. At the beginning of the nineteenth century, the farmer worked his small fields with hand implements very similar to those used by many generations of his ancestors, and his wife made the family's clothing and preserved all of the family's food for the winter; by the end of the century, that same farmer's grandchildren drove mechanical reapers capable of harvesting endless acres of grain ready to be sold and transported by rail or steamship, and the family used the profits from the harvests to purchase ready-made clothing and a variety of foods unknown to their ancestors. Most Americans in 1900 lived a life so fundamentally different that it would have been unimaginable to people of only a few generations earlier—and advances in science and technology fueled these changes. These phenomenal changes in everyday life make the growth of nineteenth-century science and technology a fascinating historical study.

One of the problems inherent in an attempt to address science *and* technology in the nineteenth century is that—unlike the twentieth century—there was no well-established basis for connecting technology with science:

Until sometime in the nineteenth century, science and technology led separate careers. There were several reasons for this. The most obvious was that before the nineteenth century, science had, for the most part, not produced generalizations that were of any clear use to industry. The history of science is replete with examples of scientific investigations which ultimately explained a long-practiced technology. Brewing, for example, was an ancient and much-appreciated art; yet scientists did not understand the processes involved until Pasteur's investigations into yeast in the 1860's. Factors other than the lag of scientific knowledge help explain this separation. Class differences were also involved. Science was the product of a literate, educated aristocracy; technology belonged to the lower and middle classes. Class barriers were often difficult to cross, particularly when the educated aristocracies often disdained handicrafts and ignored the utilitarian. (Birr, 36)

The United States in the nineteenth century, even more than European countries, was a society of a pronounced utilitarian leaning. Tocqueville observed, "Those in democracies who study sciences are always afraid of getting lost in utopias" (Tocqueville, 459). He continued his analysis of the practice of science in the uniquely American democracy:

In America the purely practical side of science is cultivated admirably, and trouble is taken about the theoretical side immediately necessary to application. On this side the Americans always display a clear, free, original, and creative turn of mind. But hardly anyone in the United States devotes himself to the essentially theoretical and abstract side of human knowledge. (Tocqueville, 460)

Tocqueville even offered a reason for this peculiarly American tendency toward utilitarianism: "Everyone is on the move, some in quest of power, others of gain. In the midst of this universal tumult, this incessant conflict of jarring interests, this endless chase for wealth, where is one to find the calm for the profound researches of the intellect?" (Tocqueville, 460).

So the story of nineteenth-century American science and technology is necessarily heavy on technology and the application of science to technology. Until the second half of the century, few Americans were concerned with anything approaching pure science, and certainly very few common people cared. To fully grasp the impact of science and technology on everyday life, however, one must consider the changing attitudes toward science as the century progressed. As Americans slowly embraced science, for both its usefulness in applications and its inherent value as a human intellectual pursuit, it began to play a larger role in the lives of more and more Americans.

The Industrial Revolution transformed life around the world, beginning in England and spreading to other European countries. There is, however, no clearer picture of the impact of the Industrial Revolution than the incredible changes appearing in American society in the nineteenth century. Transforming itself from an isolated agrarian nation with little international presence in science, technology, trade, or politics, the United States emerged from the century as a world power. Much of this dramatic change can be traced to how Americans embraced science and technology—from the politicians and powerful industrialists who controlled the country to the everyday people who adopted technology to fit their own needs and improve their lives.

Advances in technology, the growth in the manufacturing sector, and the burgeoning need for natural resources such as timber and minerals resulted in a snowball effect, as expressed by Charles L. Smith:

In the early nineteenth century the technology and capital that flowed into the new nation, and the manufacturing infrastructure it subsequently created, rapidly gained momentum. In many instances this growth fed upon itself, setting a cycle in motion. Profitable manufacturing enterprises required larger and more sophisticated industrial technology. New technologies increased the need for natural resources. Increased extraction of resources (water, coal, iron, timber) spurred further industrial activity, which in turn required more land and material to support it. Viewed in this light, there was always a symbiotic relationship between the "industrial East" and the agrarian "frontier West." (Smith, 389)

At the turn of the century, America counted little manufacturing in its gross domestic product. By 1860, the United States ranked fourth in the world in manufacturing; by the 1890s, America emerged as the world leader (Billington, 214).

Technological innovations, from the steam engine to electricity and everything in between, completely changed the face of American society. From a small start in New England, industry grew at a staggering rate until, by the end of the century, American manufacturing corporations had created a new kind of America. Industrialists became a new class of rich and powerful people, as did the bankers, newspaper publishers, land speculators, and other ancillary professions fed by technological advances. In the meantime, a new working class emerged as the country turned from its agrarian roots and required an ever increasing number of factory workers.

The nineteenth century found the accelerated urbanization of America. This trend was both a factor of and a contributor to technological advances. Faster, cheaper, and more comfortable modes of transportation made the "suburbs" a desirable place to live for the emerging middle class. As this phenomenon continued, suburbs of large cities, such as New York and Chicago, were subsequently swallowed up by the growing urban sprawl, and new suburbs sprang up to repeat the process. In the ultimate manifestation of this phenomenon, New York City consolidated with suburban Brooklyn, Queens, the Bronx, and Staten Island in 1889 to create the nation's largest city (Bain, 236). Perhaps the most important phenomenon of the century, however, was the emergence of an entirely new system of manufacturing, a system uniquely American that became the envy of the rest of the world.

The term "American System," coined in the nineteenth century, referred to the perception of many Americans that their country needed an industrial identity different than—and superior to—the European system. In fact, the term itself was first used by a British commission created to investigate the success of American inventions and technology—in particular the Colt revolver and the McCormick reaper—at the famous Crystal Palace Exhibition in London in 1851. Driven almost to a patriotic frenzy by Henry Clay and other orators, promoters of this new system pointed to every conceivable segment of the manufacturing industries, from its workforce to its manufacturing methods.

The meaning of the American System of manufactures evolved through the nineteenth century to denote specifically the production of interchangeable parts for various items, from farm machinery to the sewing machine. The prototype of the American System of manufactures, however, was the firearms industry. Working around the turn of the century, Eli Whitney dreamed of producing firearms with interchangeable parts but was only partially successful. What Whitney did succeed in doing was convincing the American government that such a system could work and should be implemented. In 1801, Whitney staged a demonstration in front of President John Adams and President-elect Thomas Jefferson in which he, "using only a screwdriver, assemble[d] ten different locks to the same musket" (Hounshell, 31). Although the lock parts were not truly interchangeable—only the entire locks themselves—Whitney opened up the possibility of producing firearms using this unique system. By the 1830s, muskets using interchangeable parts were produced at the United States Armory in Springfield, Massachusetts (Hounshell, 44). This is the birth of what became known as "high armory practice," in which specially designed machines were used to produce standard, interchangeable parts.

The idea of an American system of manufacturing became an important theme in the evolving social and cultural atmosphere of nineteenth-century America. The belief that the United States had developed a system different, and far better, than that of any other country was a source of pride for a nation still struggling to establish itself in the international community. This patriotic theme in technology began to manifest itself in American culture even before the beginning of the century. In *The Young Mill-Wright and Miller's Guide*, published in 1795, authors Oliver Evans and Thomas Ellicott envisioned a country of endless opportunities in manufacturing offering the "idea that technology in America would foster almost inconceivable material prosperity" (Marcus and Segal, 53). This optimism pervaded American society for most of the nineteenth century, from the political and industrial leaders down to the farmer, artisan, and factory workers.

Uniform agriculture was an important manifestation of the American system. Technology encouraged new practices on the farm, such as uniform rows of corn or stands of wheat; faster and more efficient planting, cultivating, and harvesting; and faster and more efficient methods for transporting agricultural products to the market. Americans saw these practices as proof that their system not only meant that American manufacturing was superior to that of Europe, but also that American farming and American farmers were superior to their European counterparts.

Americans viewed the use of technology to harness nature in the same light as the Manifest Destiny: It was the inevitable right of Americans to possess the land and to shape it into a more usable and profitable form. Historian David Nye finds that, "for most Americans of the middle of the nineteenth century, the river was waiting to be dammed; similarly, the prairie was waiting to be farmed, the woodlands to be cut down, and the desert to be irrigated" (Nye 2003, 10). If scientific and technological knowledge contributed to the conquest of the rivers, prairies, and woodlands, so much the better.

Americans in the nineteenth century embraced progress through science and technology almost as if it were a religion. In fact, evangelical Christians viewed progress and technology as "not only integral but justifying elements in the widely accepted vision of America's higher moral order" (Rosenberg 1997, 140). America's newfound leadership in technology was understood to be a direct consequence of the country's superior religious and moral standing. The technological advances were thought to represent superiority in the American political system, and much like the natural wonders found on the new continent, "mechanical triumphs like the Erie Canal were said to elevate the moral character of the people" (Nye 1994, 39). Many dreamed of a classless, almost utopian society in which the "noble mechanic" replaced the "noble savage" as the American ideal. Leaders of American science and industry held that "the skillful use of scientific knowledge was the way to eliminate social distinctions" (Sinclair, 138). Furthermore, technological progress provided wealth and a higher standard of living for Americans. Horace Greeley, he of "Go west, young man" fame, argued:

In our discoveries in science, by our applications of these discoveries to practical art, by the enormous increase of mechanical power consequent upon mechanical invention, industry and skill, we have made them a common possession of the people; and given to Society at large—to almost the meanest member of it—the enjoyments, the luxury, the elegance, which in former times were the exclusive privilege of kings and nobles. (cited in Nye 2003, 18)

The artisan and the mechanic who possessed appropriate scientific knowledge were more apt to produce the advanced products expected from a nation founded on democratic ideas. In this way, Americans—educated and uneducated, rich and poor, urban and rural—embraced science and technology as a panacea for all that ailed the world.

Celebrations marking the completion of major technological projects involved everyone from local dignitaries to the workers responsible for the project to the citizenry affected by the new technology. For instance, in 1825 the parade marking the opening of the Erie Canal included firemen,

THE PROGRESS OF THE CENTURY.
THE LIGHTNING STEAM PRESS.   THE ELECTRIC TELEGRAPH.   THE LOCOMOTIVE.   THE STEAMBOAT.

A lithograph titled "The Progress of the Century," circa 1876. Note the utopian theme, as evidenced by the message being printed by the telegraph. Library of Congress.

carpenters, millwrights, merchants, militiamen, cabinetmakers, and many other types of workers (Nye 1994, 65). Three years later, a similar parade celebrating the completion of the Baltimore and Ohio railroad included more than 5,000 people. Along with the dignitaries, participants included "farmers, gardeners, plough makers, millers, bakers, victuallers, brewers, tailors, blacksmiths, steam engine makers, weavers and dyers, carpenters and joiners, stone cutters, masons and bricklayers, painters, glaziers, and twenty more [professions]" (Nye 1994, 65–66). Common people from all walks of American life realized the significance of these technological innovations and wanted to participate in the historic moments.

Another avenue for celebrating technological innovation was the exhibition. World's fairs became popular throughout the world in the nineteenth century. From the Crystal Palace Exhibition in London in 1851 to the Paris World's Fair of 1889—for which the Eiffel Tower was constructed— European nations took the opportunity to show the world their cultural and technological best. In the United States, the first large world's fair occurred in Philadelphia in 1876. Known, appropriately enough, as the Centennial Exhibition, American organizers embraced the opportunity to show the world just how far their country had come, especially in science and technology.

The Centennial Exhibition covered more than 450 acres and included exhibits in education and the arts. The exhibits pertaining to science and technology, however, were the focal point for the more than 10 million visitors who attended the six-month long exhibition. The most impressive building was Machinery Hall; and central to Machinery Hall was the incredible Corliss steam engine. Built specifically to power the maze of machinery throughout the Hall, the 1,500-horsepower engine was the a major attraction as visitors not yet accustomed to the new industrial age marveled at its size, not to mention the incredible array of motions and noises emanating from the engine. The Corliss engine provided the only power to the large assortment of machines in the great building: printing presses, sewing machines, elevators, locomotives, electric lights, and countless other marvels of technology. Also in Machinery Hall, visitors were amazed at the first typewriter and the first telephone, as well as innovative telegraphs and calculators.

Visitors to the Centennial Exhibition also showed great interest in the natural history displays. In particular, Horticulture Hall displayed thousands of samples of the flora native to America and to other locales. Other exhibits displayed fish and animal life, including some species rarely seen by Americans, such as polar bears and sharks. There were displays of ores, minerals, and other natural resources, as well as agricultural and textile products. All of these exhibits served to show the richness of the country and the cleverness and skills of its inhabitants. After the exhibition closed, so many of the machines, plant and animal specimens, and other artifacts were donated to the Smithsonian Institution (a major organizer of the Centennial Exhibition) that new buildings were required to house the suddenly overflowing museum.

The last major world's fair of the century in the United States was held in Chicago in 1893. Called the Columbian Exposition, in honor of the 400th anniversary of Columbus's landing in America (the start of the fair was delayed from its planned 1892 starting date), the Chicago World's Fair was, like the Centennial Exhibition 17 years earlier, a celebration of American invention and ingenuity. Perhaps the most noted attraction was the first Ferris Wheel, named after its designer and builder, George Ferris. Ferris modeled his invention on the water wheels used to haul buckets of water to troughs that he observed as a boy growing up in a Nevada mining district (J. Adams, 31). His ride was an engineering and technological masterpiece, no doubt the first time "technology had been harnessed so purely for the purpose of creating a pleasure machine" (J. Adams, 31). By the end of the exposition, almost 1.5 million visitors had paid their $0.50 to ride the Ferris Wheel (J. Adams, 32).

Everywhere fairgoers went, technology was evident. Nearly 27 million visitors from around the world traveled to the fair, many by train or by steamship. Once at the fair, visitors could move within the grounds themselves by taking an elevated railway or numerous electric launches through the interconnecting canals and man-made lagoons. Like the Centennial Exhibition, one of the central attractions in the Columbian Exposition was Machinery Hall. Whereas the power for the Philadelphia event was all supplied by a single, albeit gargantuan, Corliss engine, the fair at Chicago was powered by more than 40 steam engines and three times as many dynamos, all providing the electricity to operate the various machinery and incredible number of electric lights. There were also buildings displaying America's manufactured products, as well as its animal, plant, and mineral diversity.

It was electricity, though, that was the star of the Columbian Exposition. For many fairgoers, this would be their first real experience with electricity, a mysterious and, to some, dangerous phenomena. The Electricity Building displayed exhibits of products already gaining familiarity around the country; electric lights, phonographs, and sewing machines were among the numerous items on display. In addition, the organizers exhibited futuristic electrical appliances such as moving sidewalks and Edison's new kinetoscope. All of the displays were meant to show the progress that Americans had already made and the promise of more technological advances in the future. Although many people came away with a better understanding of technology, leading to less anxiety about the approach of a new world, some, like nineteenth-century historian Henry Adams, came away confused as to their place in this new world.

One reason for the confusion was that scientific and technological advances did not always result in improved lives. The change from an agrarian economy, in which each person was essentially self-sufficient, to a manufacturing economy had many drawbacks; Labor unrest, economic dysfunction, and a general upheaval of the traditional social order were only a few of the challenges facing an industrializing America.

The result was that the industrialization resulting from advances in science and technology was not universally praised. The "march of progress" was derided by philosophers and intellectuals as well as by many common people trampled in the process:

Men generally were questioning the trend of their age. They were ill-attuned to the song of the machine—or it was ill-attuned to them. They saw the powers of the air, steam, and water, performing work that would have required the labor of thousands; labor-saving devices so-called that had not lightened the labor, but had succeeded only in adding to the profits of the owners of the machine, "while those who labor are not only required to toil longer than before, but, compared with their employers, are as a class sinking day by day to a still deeper degradation." (Ware, 20)

If life in the United States at the beginning of the nineteenth century was slow-paced and agrarian in nature, where the individual was generally self-reliant, by the end of the century science and technology had spurred a tremendous change. In 1900,

The dense crowds hurrying through the streets of the great cities, the breakneck pace of workers in Pittsburgh feeding the massive blast furnaces at the Edgar Thompson Steel Works or bottling fifty-seven varieties of ketchup at the Heinz factory, Great Northern locomotives running a hundred miles an hour full throttle across the prairies carrying settlers into North Dakota and Montana, the turbines churning at Niagara Falls, the chaotic hurly-burly at the stock exchanges—all seemed to spell the coming of a qualitatively different civilization, open to imagination and defiant of limits (Kent, 17).

Life had indeed changed both quantitatively and qualitatively, and science and technology were at the center of the changes.

2

Transportation

In 1800, transportation in the United States was not much different than it had been throughout the world for hundreds, if not thousands, of years. Although improvements to sailing ships over the centuries had made travel and transportation of goods easier and faster between coastal cities, inland transportation continued to depend primarily on horses or horse-drawn vehicles and boats propelled by man power (paddles, poles, etc.). For most Americans, walking continued to be the most common mode of travel.

Horse-drawn carriages, wagons, or stagecoaches usually followed animal or Indian trails. Even well-traveled routes between population centers could only charitably be called roads. Various improvements were attempted, such as the so-called corduroy roads, built with a foundation of logs parallel to the path layered with smaller logs perpendicular. These logs were often covered with sand and dirt in an attempt—usually quite futile—to smooth out the ride. Later roads made of tarred planks provided a slight improvement to the comfort of a traveler (Lacour-Gayet, 49). The appearance of toll roads in some parts of the country made overland travel somewhat faster and marginally more comfortable. These roads connected towns and, in the process, provided rural Americans increased opportunity for social interactions with neighbors and townsfolk.

The decisions as to where roads would be built (and later, where railroads would be built) affected settlement patterns. Immigrants settled along main roads and railroads, while established towns bypassed by the new transportation systems often shrunk in population and sometimes disappeared altogether. A grand plan to build the National, or Cumberland,

Road connecting the east to the interior of the country was begun in 1802 but not completed until 1852. However, by 1818 the road had connected the eastern United States to the Ohio River, and as new sections opened it became a main artery for settlers traveling west and for western farm products moving east. Needless to say, the difficulties facing a traveler in the United States contributed greatly to the fact that the country was still a thin strip of settled area along the Atlantic Coast in 1800.

A myriad of technical innovations in the nineteenth century combined to forever change the way Americans would look at travel and transportation. The perfection of steam engines allowed great improvements in transportation both overland and on the water. New methods developed to harness the power of electricity led to wondrous machines that changed the face of urban transportation. By the end of the century, the rapid development of the first automobiles formed a punctuation mark for a century of transportation advances never before seen.

THE RISE OF THE STEAMBOAT

As the nineteenth century approached, the steamboat represented the most promising advance in transportation since humans first domesticated horses. It gave rise to a new era in travel and in transportation of goods across the country and across the world. Although the steamboat eventually gave way to the railroad as the fastest and most convenient mode of transportation, its importance remains as America's initial foray into the applications of technology to transportation.

Robert Fulton did not invent the steamboat. Fulton's name is forever attached to the steamboat, however, because the American visionary was the first man to fully utilize its capabilities and to take economic advantage of those capabilities. The first Americans to build working steamboats were James Rumsey and John Fitch in the 1780s. Rumsey successfully tested a steamboat driven by jet propulsion on the Potomac River in 1786. Fitch experimented with several types of steamboats, using both paddle wheels and screw propellers for propulsion. Fitch attempted to capitalize commercially from his invention, using one of his vessels to carry passengers and freight on the Delaware River between Philadelphia and Burlington, New Jersey.

Fitch and Rumsey, along with other early steamboat builders, were technical innovators who were never successful in establishing their steamboats as viable commercial enterprises. That honor falls to Fulton and his partner Robert Livingston. After years of unsuccessfully attempting to sell his ideas on steamboats, submarines, torpedoes, and other inventions to the British, the French, and the Americans, Fulton finally built and launched his steamboat in 1807. Although the vessel is called the *Clermont* by history books, Kirkpatrick Sale, in his book *The Fire of His Genius: Robert Fulton and the American Dream*, points out that Fulton actually registered his boat as the

Robert Fulton. Library of Congress.

"North River Steamboat of Clermont," and referred to the boat as the *North River*. Calling the boat the *Clermont* is an historical inaccuracy that has, over a period of time, embedded itself in American history.

Fulton's steamboat was an instant success. Not only had he surpassed his predecessors in his technical knowledge of steamboat design, but, with the help of a monopoly obtained by Livingston from the State of New York guaranteeing sole rights to steamboat navigation on the Hudson, Fulton's new steamboat proved a financial success.

To Fulton and Livingston, along with a third partner, Nicholas J. Roosevelt, also goes the credit for operating the first steamboat on the Mississippi River, the *New Orleans*, launched from Pittsburgh in 1811. The ship made it to New Orleans and operated on the lower Mississippi for some time. After several setbacks, however, the partners withdrew from the Mississippi and were replaced by, among others, Henry Miller

Shreve. Shreve's steamboats, and others like them, made the Mississippi the busy waterway that Americans had envisioned it would some day become. Before the appearance of the steamboat on the Mississippi and its tributaries, passengers and goods were carried down the river on various types of boats that were built to float *downstream* but, unfortunately, were not very efficient for the trip back *upstream*. Some boats, like the keelboat, could be propelled upstream by poling or by pulling on ropes from the bank. Both methods, of course, were very slow and difficult modes of travel. Other boats were specifically built for the trip downstream and turned into scrap lumber upon arrival at their destination. The steamboat was a tremendous improvement to either of these systems.

Although not as famous as his competitor, John Stevens probably contributed more to the technical advancement of steamboats than did Fulton. The list of innovations by Stevens and his sons, particularly Robert L. Stevens, is long. From experiments with propeller-driven steamboats to advances based on a solid understanding of the science of hydrodynamics, the Stevens family designed and built the vessels that were to become synonymous with American steamboat lore. After his father's death, Robert made many important improvements to the design of steamboat hulls and boilers. His most important contribution, however, may have been his introduction of the use of coal instead of wood to feed the boilers of his new ship, *The Philadelphia*.

An important improvement to the basic steam engine design came from an American named Oliver Evans. In 1803 Evans invented a high-pressure, double-acting steam engine. It was this new kind of steam engine

Samuel Hollyer's 1907 portrayal of the first trip of Fulton's steamboat. Library of Congress.

that powered steamboats later in the century. Fulton used a Watts-type engine in the *Clermont*, but the more powerful Evans engine was needed for Western rivers. In 1816, riverboats began using an Evans engine in the horizontal, rather than vertical, position. At first the piston was attached to a flywheel that turned the steamboat paddle wheels, but soon designers found they could attach the piston directly to the paddle wheels (de la Pedraja, 224).

The first decades of steamboat travel, especially in the West, provided a "rough democracy of accommodations" (Larkin, 226):

There were no staterooms, and passengers bedded down on berths that folded down from the walls of the cabin. Female travelers simply slept behind a curtain. When boats became overcrowded passengers "took part in a sort of lottery" every night to determine who got the berths and who would be allotted "chairs, benches and tables" to sleep on in descending order of their desirability. On Thomas Hamilton's first night on a Mississippi steamboat, "fortune fixed me on the table, and there I lay with the knee of one man thrust directly into my stomach, and with my feet resting on the head of another." (Larkin, 226–27)

Life aboard a Western steamboat was generally, "heterogeneous and disorderly" with "incessant card playing" by, as a traveling minister described them, a crowd of "profane swearers, drunkards, gamblers, fiddlers, and dancers" (Larkin, 227).

The first steamboats were not only crude and uncomfortable for passenger travel; they often proved dangerous to the passengers. Fires, accidents involving boiler explosions, and hulls damaged by river obstacles frequently resulted in injury or death. The race to build faster steamboats and then to run them "all out" led to many careless and senseless accidents. It was not until the 1850s that the government began to regulate steamboats and their boilers in an attempt to make the vessels safer. Shreve, seeing the need to improve safety on his steamboats, designed and built a snag boat to deal with underwater obstructions. His steamboat, equipped with a specially designed bow, cleared navigation paths along the Mississippi and important tributaries, making river travel safer for everyone.

It did not take long for steamboat owners to realize the economic advantages of offering comfortable, even luxurious, accommodations to its passengers. Shreve designed and built the *Washington* for service on the Mississippi, employing for the first time the philosophy that passengers could travel on steamboats in an opulent setting unlike any they had experienced. From a humble beginning just after the turn of the century, when the first steamboats carried a few passengers on hot, loud and dangerous journeys, the steamboat quickly advanced until, in 1857, the *New World* could transport 1,000 passengers in comfort between New York City and Albany. By the 1870s thousands of steamboats carried passengers and cargo on Eastern rivers, on the Mississippi, and on the Great Lakes. In addition, people were able to make the Atlantic crossing in a matter of days rather than the weeks that sailing ships took for the same trip.

Although steamboats were viewed primarily as passenger transportation vessels, they also contributed to burgeoning trade along the river (and later canal) routes in the United States. Utilized to tow barges packed with agricultural products and mined resources such as coal, steamboats grew in size to handle increased demands for these products. Yet, in spite of the importance of faster transportation and more efficient hauling of goods, the most important long-term consequence of the steamboat actually occurred on dry land. There, settlements appeared where once there had been none, and small towns grew to become important cities flourishing on the trade supplied by the steamboats.

CANAL BUILDING: ERIE TO PANAMA

In the early nineteenth century, canals quickly became vital arteries for commerce in the fledgling United States of America. With overland travel being difficult at best, American politicians, civic and business leaders, and engineers turned to canals to transport crops and raw materials east and manufactured goods west. Canals also became a preferred mode of travel for many Americans looking for a more comfortable journey than could be had over rough inland terrain. In the process, the canals came to symbolize nationalistic feelings of pride and accomplishment for a country that was only beginning to make its place in a new and changing world.

Canals have a long history, dating back to the ancient Egyptians more than three millennia B.C. Canals played an important role in Chinese and in European commerce and transportation long before the United States came into existence. In the eighteenth century, small canals began to appear in America, the first of which were used to help transport coal from mines in Pennsylvania to cities such as New York, Philadelphia, and Boston. Canal planners often sought funding from the local, state, and federal governments, but this was a time in America's history when many national leaders believed the constitution forbade such actions by the federal government. Therefore, early canals were usually financed by a combination of private investment and state funding. The most famous and most important canal built in the United States, the Erie Canal, was built using this financial model.

Suggestions for a canal across the state of New York, to connect the Hudson River with Lake Erie, first arose during Colonial times. Later, such luminaries as George Washington and Robert Fulton became proponents of such a plan. It was not until 1817, however, that ground was actually broken for the long dreamed-of canal. Over the next eight years work continued on the canal, and sections were opened for use as they were completed. Finally, in 1825, the full length of the Erie Canal was opened to traffic. Stretching across 363 miles of wilderness, the Erie Canal was 40 feet wide and 4 feet deep. Much of the credit for the canal is given to the governor of New York, DeWitt Clinton, whose vision for a canal across his state was instrumental in its completion. Often derisively referred to during construction as "Clinton's Ditch," the governor and his supporters were vindicated when the canal was completed and immediately began to turn a profit.

The Erie Canal represented the largest construction project undertaken in the United States up to that time. American engineers, previously trained in Europe, learned their craft on the Erie project under the direction of its chief engineer, Benjamin Wright. These newly trained engineers then fanned out across the nation to build other canals and public works projects. These engineers made numerous innovations in canal building, including the design and construction of scores of locks, many with improvements made over previous designs. American engineers designed other modes of moving boats from one elevation to another on the canals. Some used lifts, operating much like an elevator, and others designed inclined planes along which the boats were pulled to the next level. A surveyor and engineer named Canvass White patented a new kind of cement vital to the building of the canal. Presaging the use of immigrants on the massive railway projects later in the century, the canals employed European, most particularly Irish, immigrants working under extreme conditions for very low wages. Thousands of laborers were used on the massive project, and many died from malaria, cholera, and other diseases.

The importation of these laborers to dig the canal, and later to handle the unskilled, low-paying jobs operating the canal, led to difficulties all along the canal's length. From offending the local communities by working on Sundays to living in dirty, often temporary shantytowns, the hard-drinking canal workers—in 1835 one could find a tavern or grog shop an average of every quarter mile along its entire length—provided a multitude of threats to the middle-class inhabitants of the local towns and countryside (Nye 2003, 184).

The Erie Canal was enlarged several times over its life as more and larger vessels sought to carry goods up and down its length. It played a key role in the growth of New York cities such as Syracuse, Rochester, and Buffalo, and helped make New York City the most important port in the world. Rochester experienced such phenomenal growth after completion of the canal that a visitor described the scene as a mass of confusion where the "very streets seemed to be starting up of their own accord" and the "half-finished, whole-finished, and embryo streets were crowded with people, carts, stages, cattle, pigs, far beyond the reach of numbers" (Nye 2003, 151–52). In Rochester, as in other towns in the path of the monumental canal, everyday life was forever changed.

Before the Erie Canal, it took 20 days and cost $100 a ton to move freight from Buffalo to New York City; after completion of the canal, the time and cost was reduced to 8 days and $10 a ton (Lacour-Gayet, 52). By 1854, 83 percent of the nation's entire shipment of grain moved through the Erie Canal (Bauer, 140). By 1871, as the railroad began to take over as the nation's most important mode of transportation, this number had fallen to only 30 percent. However, the Erie Canal continued service well into the twentieth century.

Other major canals followed on the heels of the much ballyhooed Erie Canal. In fact, sections of the country entered into a decades-long race to build canals with the expectation of the economic impact they would have on the local areas. A long-planned canal connecting the Susquehanna and Ohio rivers was completed in 1834 and later linked to the Erie Canal. Whereas the Erie Canal had helped make New York City the most important port on the Eastern seaboard, another manmade waterway, the Illinois & Michigan Canal, provided access to the Mississippi River from Lake Michigan and began the tremendous explosion of growth of Chicago, where the canal entered the lake. Later, railroads contributed further to

West Shore Railroad and Erie Canal at Little Falls, New York. William Henry Jackson, circa 1890. Library of Congress.

Chicago's rise as the nation's "second city." When a canal was completed in 1830 bypassing rapids in the Ohio River near Louisville, navigation became possible all the way from Pittsburgh to New Orleans. The network of canals connecting the Mississippi Valley to the Great Lakes also helped cities such as Detroit and Cleveland become major centers of trade and population. Just as railroads were to do a few decades later, the location of major canals played a crucial factor in the development of population centers in the United States.

Canals became more than just modes of transportation; they became symbols of progress. They also became tourist attractions. Families came to marvel at the engineering feats exhibited at canals throughout the country:

The citizen who contemplated such public improvements [as canals] became aware of the power of democracy and saw himself as part of the moral vanguard, leading the world toward universal democracy. These man-made objects became national symbols. Traveling to America's natural wonders and great public works became the act of a good citizen, just as a pilgrimage to Jerusalem was the sign of a good Christian. (Nye 1994, 36)

Parades, fireworks, and other celebrations accompanied the opening of new canals as community leaders and local workers alike reveled in their accomplishments. Canals became "one of the first icons of the [American] technological sublime" (Nye 1994, 34).

While canals helped form many of the major cities in the United States, this increasing population promoted more travel along the canals themselves. The canals brought people, news, and ideas to the Western settlements, in the process connecting the country in a way that many had thought impossible. The travel was not fast by today's standards. The 400-mile trip from Philadelphia to Pittsburgh took 6 1/2 days and cost about $6. If the traveler continued on to Saint Louis, the trip took 13 days and cost $13 (Lacour-Gayet, 53). Unlike the steamboats that plied the major rivers in later decades, the canal boats were small and cramped, providing sparse, dirty, and unpleasant accommodations for the canal traveler. One magazine correspondent traveling on the Erie Canal complained of poor food, overcrowding, and unbearable mosquitoes—not a particularly pleasant way to travel (Nye 2003, 177).

One story of a pioneer family in 1834, related by William Chauncy Langdon in his book *Everyday Things in American Life*, serves to illustrate the importance of canals to common families in the United States and also relates a certain degree of "American ingenuity" when it came to getting things done:

A man, a Pennsylvanian, living on the Lackawanna River, whose name is lost to fame, decided, as many others did, to take his family and move out West, beyond the Mississippi. So, as the others did, he built himself a boat; it was like a small-sized flatboat. He put his family and all he owned aboard, and floated down the Lackawanna River....

They floated down the Lackawanna to the Susquehanna and down the Susquehanna to Columbia and the Pennsylvania Canal. He got his flatboat transferred to the Canal and went on by the smooth canal and up the 108 locks through the mountains (sometimes called foothills) to Hollidaysburg. Here the Lackawanna man knew he must give up his boat, sell it as lumber, and go on over the mountains, "hiring" his way from others. He probably, in looking for a purchaser for his lumber, expressed his regret at having to sell. But the canal people there at Hollidaysburg were not asleep.... So they made a proposition to him. Would he take a chance on letting them try to rig up a car that would carry his boat and take it in "as is" condition up the five inclined planes and down the other five inclined planes over the mountain to Johnstown? There he could slip it off the car into the canal again and he could go on without extra expense to Pittsburgh, and on a thousand miles more in his own boat down the Ohio River to St. Louis or wherever he wanted to go. The Lackawanna man said he would take the chance. He did; they did. (Langdon, 123–124)

In spite of the vagaries surrounding this story of the Lackawanna man, this sort of travel was common to Americans during the age of canals. It inspired the canal authorities of that region to modify their equipment so that any canal boat could be "lifted out of the water, divided into sections, put on wheels, and rolled along their way over the mountain, with reverse action and reassembling at the other place" (Langdon, 125). This use of inclined planes became a common method for lifting boats over higher ground to other sections of a canal.

The Great Lakes region of the country experienced perhaps the most notable gains from being connected to the Eastern population centers for the first time. In the meantime, the trend started by the canals to connect the Ohio Valley and Great Lakes region to the Northeastern parts of the country helped to isolate the South both socially and economically from the rest of the nation and became one of the causes for the rifts developing along North–South lines. Canals had become the first in a series of improved modes of transportation that were recognized as crucial if the expanding territories of the country were to come together as a cohesive nation.

A new excitement for canal building began to take hold of the American imagination later in the nineteenth century. When the French engineer and visionary, Ferdinand de Lesseps, began the Suez Canal in 1859 (completed in 1869), American merchants and politicians joined with others around the world in their belief that a long-held dream of building a canal across Central America was possible. After de Lesseps and the French failed in their attempt to build such a canal, it became apparent to many that the job could and should be done by Americans. Plans for such an American canal began in the last years of the century, finally concluding with the opening of the Panama Canal in 1914.

Canals were primarily nineteenth-century phenomena in the United States. From the beginning of the century, when there were only about 100 miles of canals in the country, until the end of the century, when more than 4,000 miles were in use, canals provided much-needed links to important waterways on the North American continent. The canals, useful though they were, did present certain disadvantages, especially in comparison to the coming railroads. They were limited by location, speed, and the volume of commercial and human cargo they could carry. The railroads, in contrast, could go where canals could not, at much higher speeds and with a much larger carrying capacity. By the middle of the nineteenth century the railroad had already begun the process of overtaking canals and inland waterways as the most important form of transportation in the United States.

THE RAILROADS

The coming of the railroads had, quite possibly, the most profound effect of all technological innovations on everyday life in nineteenth-century America. Steamboat travel was a boon to those living on or nearby major waterways, but for the growing population of Americans living in the interior of the country, far away from the ocean and from major rivers, the railroad represented the first real opportunity to travel faster and farther than their feet or horses could take them. Before rail travel, the 90-mile trip between Philadelphia and New York was accomplished partially by boat and partially overland. At best it was an arduous and sometimes dangerous trip taking an entire day to accomplish (Douglas, 1–3). When the railroad began connecting major cities, such trips were reduced to a matter of hours, with the added benefits of increased comfort and convenience.

Even before the steam locomotive, rails were built utilizing cars pulled by horses or mules, or even outfitted with sails and propelled by the wind. Of course, the dream of rail travel did not become a reality until the appearance of the first practical steam locomotives. Although the steam locomotive was not invented in America (that claim goes to the English engineer Richard Trevithick), this newest form of locomotion was enthusiastically adopted by Americans and quickly adapted to the needs of the vast country. Amazingly, although the first steam locomotive did not appear in the United States until the second quarter of the century, by the end of the third quarter railroads literally crisscrossed the entire country. From its start in the 1830s, the railroad industry grew to more than 30,000 miles of track in 1860 and to more than 200,000 miles of track by the turn of the twentieth century. Such phenomenal growth forever changed life in America.

One of the first Americans to envision the endless possibilities of rail travel was John Stevens, who had already contributed so much to the evolution of the steamboat. Stevens concentrated his later efforts on convincing the American government and investors of the importance of rail travel. In 1825, after years of writing letters and lobbying for his vision of modern travel, Stevens, already an old man of 76 years, laid out on his own estate a small section of track, demonstrating its effectiveness with a crudely built steam locomotive.

John Stevens imported the first steam locomotives from England, most notably the *John Bull*, and adapted them to run effectively on American rails. Soon, however, American railroaders found that their own country presented problems not seen in England and began to develop their own track and locomotive technology. Because of the annoying and dangerous tendency exhibited by other locomotives of running off the tracks, an American inventor, John Jervis, designed an eight-wheel locomotive that handled relatively sharp curves. By the time American rails were being built over steep grades and long distances, other advances in locomotives and track construction were paving the way toward a continental system of railroads.

In the late 1820s and early 1830s, railroad companies began to spring up across the Atlantic seaboard. One of the first, and even today one of the best-known, of these railroad companies was the Baltimore and Ohio (known as the B&O to Monopoly players around the world), established in 1827. The first railroads provided very limited comfort to the weary traveler. Crowded into wooden wagons connected by chains, sitting on hard seats without backs, an early trip on a railroad was sure to be uncomfortable. Add to this the fact that cars often had no windows, and it becomes apparent that railcars were not a pleasant place to be on a hot summer afternoon. Worse yet, if the car did have windows and open doors, dust, soot, and sparks from the locomotive provided for a more unpleasant, even dangerous, trip. One magazine article complained about the hard seats, the overcrowding, and the poor ventilation, calling the typical railroad car "a moving stable" (Nye 2003, 177). Throw into this volatile mix other factors—a lack of reliable schedules, frequent accidents, fires started from the locomotive, washed-out bridges, breakdowns, robberies, and constant changes of cars due to nonuniform rails—and one can see that early travel on railroads could often be a very disagreeable experience.

This fact was not lost on famous visitors to the United States. In his influential book *American Notes*, Charles Dickens chronicled his travels in America. In one section, he wrote about his first experience with an American railroad:

There are no first and second class carriages as with us [in England]; but there is a gentlemen's car and a ladies' car: the main distinction between which is that in the first everybody smokes; and in the second nobody does. There is a great deal of jolting, a great deal of noise, a great deal of wall, not much window, a locomotive engine, a shriek, and a bell.

The cars are like shabby omnibuses, but larger: holding thirty, forty, fifty people. The seats are placed crosswise, a narrow passage up the middle, and a door at both ends. In the centre of the carriage there is usually a stove, fed with charcoal or anthracite coal; which is for the most part red-hot. It is insufferably close.

In the ladies' car there are a great many gentlemen who have ladies with them. There are also a great many ladies who have nobody with them: for any lady may travel alone from one end of the United States to the other and be certain of the most courteous and considerate treatment everywhere. If a lady take a fancy to any male passenger's seat, the gentleman who accompanies her gives him notice of the fact, and he immediately vacates it with great politeness.

The conductor or check-taker or guard, or whatever he may be, wears no uniform. He walks up and down the car, and in and out of it, as his fancy dictates; leans against the door with his hands in his pockets and stares at you, if you chance to be a stranger; or enters into conversation with the passengers about him. A great many newspapers are pulled out, and a few of them are read. Everybody talks to you, or to anybody else who hits his fancy. Politics are much discussed, so are banks, so is cotton. Quiet people avoid the question of the Presidency, for there will be a new election in three years and a half, and party feeling runs very high: the great constitutional feature of this institution being that directly after the acrimony of the last election is over the acrimony of the next one begins.

Except when a branch road joins the main one, there is seldom more than one track of rails; so that the road is very narrow. The character of the scenery is always the same. Mile after mile of stunted trees: some hewn down by the axe, some blown down by the wind, some half fallen and resting on their neighbors. Now you emerge for a few brief moments on an open country, glittering with some bright lake or pool; now catch hasty glimpses of a distant town with its clean white houses and their cool piazzas, its prim New England church and schoolhouse; when whir-r-r-r! almost before you have seen them comes the same dark screen: the stunted trees, the stumps, the logs. It rushes across the turnpike road, where there is no gate, no policeman, no signal, nothing but a rough wooden arch, on which is painted WHEN THE BELL RINGS, LOOK OUT FOR THE LOCOMOTIVE. On it whirls headlong, dives through the woods again, emerges in the light, clatters over frail arches, rumbles upon the heavy ground, shoots beneath a wooden bridge which intercepts the light for a second like a wink, suddenly awakens all the slumbering echoes in the main street of a large town, and dashes on haphazard, pell-mell, neck-or-nothing, down the middle of the road. (cited in Langdon, 353–55)

Dickens' amusing and romantic description of a trip on an American railroad portrayed what many Americans must have felt during their first trips over the rails.

A serious problem developed for American railroads as competing inventors and companies struggled to establish a foothold in the lucrative new business. As rails went up across the country, it became clear that a lack of uniformity in the railway gage would cause increasingly difficult problems for travelers and cargo. It was not unusual in the early history of railroads for a journey to necessitate several changes of trains to accommodate different track gages. For the weary traveler, this caused frustrating delays.

For the farmers, manufacturers, and other businesses that were becoming increasingly dependent on the railroads for transporting their goods across the country, the delays meant loss of product and loss of profit. The problem finally came to a head when the federal government agreed to subsidize the building of a transcontinental railroad. The question of what gage rail to use was crucial, as it would have been entirely unacceptable to embark on such a building project without a standard size for all involved. After much political maneuvering by the myriad of railroad companies, Congress settled upon 4 feet 8.5 inches as the gage of choice, effectively making that size the future standard for American railways.

One of the most celebrated achievements in American history was the completion of the transcontinental railroad. First conceived several decades earlier, this marvel of American persistence had both a real and a psychological impact on the country. In 1863, work began on the railway from the east at Omaha, Nebraska, and from the west at Sacramento, California. After more than half a decade of engineering problems, political infighting, financial woes, and backbreaking work, the Union Pacific Railroad, building from Omaha, and the Central Pacific Railroad, building from Sacramento, finally met at Promontory, Utah, in 1869. The completion of the transcontinental railroad symbolized the fulfillment of Manifest Destiny, which had driven Americans for decades.

The importance of the transcontinental railroad to millions of Americans cannot be overstated. Of course, the most directly affected were the thousands of workers who built the railroad. Using the cheap labor of immigrants, primarily the Chinese by the Central Pacific and the Irish by the Union Pacific, the two companies often exploited and discriminated against their own employees. These men led hard, impoverished lives marked by disease and violence. As David Nye writes, "The predominant forms of recreation [for the railroad workers] were drinking, gambling, whoring, and fighting" (Nye 2003, 185). Of course, such behavior virtually guaranteed that these railroad workers would conflict with the local, middle-class residents with whom they came into contact.

After the transcontinental railroad was completed, travelers could take advantage of the first real opportunity for fast and easy travel across the continent. To travel from one coast to another before the completion of the railroad was an arduous trip of many months fraught with danger and expense. The first passengers on the transcontinental railroad, in contrast, made the trip in relative comfort (especially those who could afford first class) in about a week and at an expense ranging from $70 for third class to $150 for first class (Ambrose, 369). Railroads, canals, and steamboats meant that a vacation became part of the yearly routine of many middle-class Americans. From visiting natural wonders such as Niagara Falls, the oceanfront, or even the mountains of the West, to sightseeing through the man-made wonders of the cities, faster and cheaper transportation meant more opportunities for vacationing Americans.

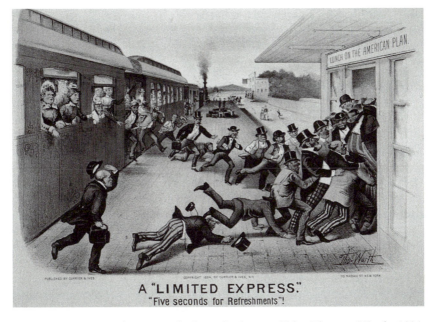

"A limited express: five seconds for refreshments!" by Thomas Worth, 1884. Library of Congress.

A combination of things contributed to a marked increase in leisure travel late in the nineteenth century. A rising middle class with leisure time and more disposable income meant more Americans were looking for entertainment. Much of this entertainment dollar was spent on leisure travel on the new transportation modes, which were well established by the end of the century. Railroads and steamship lines recognized this growing market and advertised their services. "Glossy advertisements" commonly appeared "in popular magazines read by the more comfortably middle class" (Kent, 23). Rail companies such as the Northern Pacific advertised trips to the Columbia River and Mount Hood; or they began "to tease cold northerners with the momentous question: 'Why endure disagreeable weather when California is reached by so quick and comfortable a journey?'" (Kent, 23) The Atchison, Topeka, and Santa Fe promoted California as "a land of sunshine, more delightful in the winter than the Mediterranean"; and the Burlington enticed passengers from Chicago and St. Louis with trips to Colorado (Kent, 23), home of what some advertisers called "the American Alps."

Not to be outdone, steamship lines aggressively advertised their own vacations:

The upscale White Star Steamship Line made frequent passages to Southampton, while the Hamburg American Line was offering "A Cruise Around the World," and various lines took passengers to the Caribbean and "the battlefields of the Spanish-American War." Staterooms in the best ships were hard to come by during the summer of 1900 as tourists crossed the Atlantic to see the glitzy Paris Exposition on the banks of the Seine. At West Palm Beach and other spots along the Florida coast, Standard Oil partner Henry Flagler was opening luxury hotels and sparking the original Florida land boom (Kent, 23).

Of course, without faster, cheaper, and more comfortable travel, visits to Paris or to luxury hotels in Florida would have been impossible, except for a very few. As the century drew to a close, more and more upper-class and upper-middle-class families found that they could afford such luxuries.

The impact on freight delivery was perhaps even more dramatic than that on the delivery of human cargo. Farm products and raw materials from the West were "shipped" East in a fraction of the time and at a fraction of the cost. In turn, manufactured goods were available for the first time at a reasonable cost to settlers in the West. Many Western towns, where forests were nonexistent, were literally built using the wood, nails, and other supplies delivered by the railroads. Later in the century, it was not uncommon for settlers in frontier towns to order prefabricated houses from the Sears or Montgomery Ward catalogs. Of course, these ready-to-build symbols of civilization were delivered by the railroad. In Cheyenne, Wyoming, one observer noted that "Houses arrive by the hundreds from Chicago, already made" (Nye 2003, 165). The exchange of mail, magazines, and other items of popular culture finally linked the vast continent into a single nation.

Coast-to-coast communication received a tremendous boost when railroads began delivering the mail in 1838. Although not as romantic as the fabled Pony Express, the railroads delivered mail quickly, efficiently, and inexpensively all over the country. Special cars were built in which mail clerks sorted the mail as the train moved; the mail was then either left at destinations along the way or sent on to distribution centers.

Interestingly, although the railroad connected vast sections of the country, it did not bring equal prosperity to each area it touched. Quite the contrary, improved transportation meant that certain areas of the country would grow and prosper as raw materials for manufacturing and food for workers became easier to obtain. As the railroad "encouraged regional economic specialization" (Nye 1994, 71), the gap between the industrialized North and the agrarian South grew. Instead of developing its own industries, the South shipped its agricultural products—particularly tobacco, sugar, and cotton—to the North for processing (Nye 1994, 71). Everyday life in the North was affected by technological improvements in transportation, whereas the South (and, for the most part, the West) remained close to its agrarian roots.

Advances in railroad technology made rail travel safer and more comfortable for the American public, as well as for railworkers. A serious problem hampering early rail travel was the absence of an effective braking system. An alarming death rate caused by accidents, as well as the loss of valuable freight, plagued the industry. The first braking systems consisted of hand brakes on each car operated by a brakeman. A young New Yorker, George Westinghouse, developed an alternative to this slow, ineffective, and dangerous system. Westinghouse conceived of a braking system that employed compressed air to operate a piston that in turn applied the brakes. This system was much faster, safer, and very reliable, and in the long run cheaper than employing dozens of brakemen for each train. In spite of its obvious advantages, the air brake did not become standard equipment on all trains until 1893, when Congress passed the U.S. Railroad Safety Appliance Act. Westinghouse's air brakes became standard equipment on trains all over the world. In addition to the air brake, Westinghouse built a device for restoring derailed railroad cars to the track and made a mark in the burgeoning natural gas and electricity industries.

Workers on nineteenth-century railroads experienced many hazards to their safety and their lives. Before the general adoption of Westinghouse's new braking system late in the century, railroad brakemen were particularly susceptible to accidents. One veteran brakeman described the hazards of the job during inclement weather to a Congressional committee in 1890:

Say, for instance, it is a bad night—what we call a blind night on the road— sleeting, raining, snowing, etc. We hear the call for "down brakes." Of course we cannot always be on top of the train [from where the brakes were operated]. During cold weather we go into the caboose occasionally to warm ourselves. We are called out by a signal "down brakes." We get out on top on the train. We find that the top of the cars are completely covered with sleet. In attempting to get at those brakes a great many brakemen lose their lives, slip off the cars and again, even if they do reach the brakes, it is more often the case than it is not that they find that the brakes are frozen up, and they cannot twist them. That again occasions danger. They cannot set the brakes at all, cannot set the dog, cannot twist the brake. What we call the dog is the little piece of iron which catches onto the ratchet wheel. As no brakes are set, all will depend on the engine to stop the train, and if the train was going with any speed it would take some time to stop it. (cited in Licht 1983, 183)

The rail workers also experienced dangers in coupling the cars by hand; the loss of fingers was often the least severe consequence of accidents.

Two other innovations, one that improved safety for rail workers and one that improved comfort for rail travelers, made lasting impacts on the railroad industry. In 1873, Eli Janney patented an automatic coupling device that alleviated the need for rail workers to manually couple rail cars. Janney's invention not only reduced the time for connecting the cars, it also reduced the injuries related to manual coupling, a dangerous process requiring the rail worker to stand between the cars and insert a link as the engineer backed the engine toward the car. The second invention, a sleeping car built and marketed by George Pullman, greatly increased the comfort of long-distance travel. The Pullman sleeping car, and later a dining car built by Pullman's company, came to represent the luxury of rail travel in the late nineteenth century.

The big railroad companies often set the standard for the development of the American business model—for example, technological innovation, labor relations, government relations, and the national scope of business. The railroad companies' choices concerning the location of the new lines and of the terminals had ramifications of a scope unimagined at the time. In addition to connecting already populated areas, railways were often built into vast unsettled areas *before* populations arrived, thus making the railroads incredibly influential in determining where settlement occurred. The famous newspaperman Horace Greeley wrote, "Railroads in Europe are built to connect centers of population; but in the West the railroad itself builds cities. Pushing boldly out into the wilderness, along its iron track villages, towns, and cities spring into existence, and are strung together into a consistent whole by its lines of rails, as beads are upon a silken thread" (Nye 2003, 157). From this one could infer that it is not so much a matter of railroads *affecting* everyday life in America as *dictating* it.

Once settlement began, the railroad depot invariably became the center of activity for the township. Townspeople gathered at the depot for arrivals with the expectation of mail, news, goods, and visitors. The depot was usually the site of the town telegraph office, another important source of news and information. Even when no trains were in the station, the depot was a central gathering place for townspeople and day visitors from outlying areas.

The railroads were probably the single most important factor in the astonishingly rapid settlement of the American West. With the coming of the railroad, settlers were no longer isolated from the rest of the country. Mail, news, and supplies, which had previously taken weeks or even months to reach their destination, now could reach locations across the country in a matter of days. Moreover, the very future of a Western settlement often depended on the route decided upon by the railroad. The railroad brought farmers and manufacturers closer to their markets and information in a timely manner to the entire country. What canals had begun the railroads brought near completion; by connecting the country, the nation was united both geographically and culturally.

The success of the free market experiment conducted as part of American democracy depended in part on the transportation infrastructure created in the nineteenth century. Not only did this infrastructure provide a means for farmers to move their product to markets and manufacturers to ship their goods around the country and around the world, but the new forms of transportation also meant that Americans could import everything from European manufactured goods to South American coffee. And it wasn't only the urbanites and East Coast residents who benefited. Many of these imported goods made their way inland, sometimes reaching as far as the frontier was settled.

Another, possibly unintended, consequence of the new transportation infrastructure was an increase in land values—sometimes an explosive increase—along the routes of railroads, canals, and major rivers. As important as transportation was to agricultural concerns, it "became central in determining the value of land and in creating wealth" (Nye 2003, 34). The land speculation fueled by the westward expansion of the railroads was a unique circumstance in the United States' history. Often the inflated land values caused by such speculation had an effect opposite of that intended; high costs actually tended to dampen settlement opportunities. As the railroads themselves, along with wealthy investors, obtained possession of the land around new rail lines, the dream of cheap land for the average American disappeared in many places. In fact, in many cases the coming of the railroad to Western locales "did not bring free-market development and prosperity; it brought immediate economic disaster for some, feverish land speculation, and long-term economic control for all" (Nye 2003, 179). Finally, after years of protest and outrage from Americans in all walks of life, Congress discontinued the land grant policy for railroads in 1871 (Nye 2003, 183).

Yet another unintended consequence of the explosive growth of the railroads was its contribution to the deforestation of large sections of the country. The statistics are staggering: In 1870 in Ohio alone, the railroads accounted for 15 million rail ties, 10 miles of trestles, 16 miles of bridges, and 10,000 miles of fence, all built of wood (Nye 2003, 193). Of course, all of these required periodic replacement as the wood rotted. As the railroads expanded into the prairie states, where wood was not to be had, logging interests in Michigan, Wisconsin, and Minnesota helped supply the almost half million acres of timber needed per year just to keep up with track maintenance and replacement (Nye 2003, 193). Combine this with an alarming increase in forest fires caused by the sparks of the engine, and many Americans feared that the railroads would eventually lead to the complete deforestation of America.

By the later part of the century, many Americans began to notice the abuses stemming from the seemingly uncontrolled growth of the large railroad lines. Writers, politicians, and other public figures began to question the wisdom of allowing—even encouraging—the immense wealth and power of these corporations. Even the towns that owed their very existence (or at least their phenomenal growth) to the railroad began to question, and attack, the companies, as indicated from this description of the chaos surrounding one nationwide event:

During the nationwide [railroad] strikes of 1877, most railroad towns sided with the strikers, and angry crowds attacked and burned railroad property in major rail centers such as Baltimore and Pittsburgh. Animosity toward the railroads was often greater among ordinary citizens in cities such as Albany, Syracuse, and Buffalo than among the workers themselves, and in some cases strikers actually protected railway property from an inflamed public. (Nye 2003, 186)

These "ordinary citizens" were angry for many reasons: dangerous railroad crossings that regularly accounted for injuries, deaths, and destruction of personal property; a perceived disruption of traditional social and moral values; fear of the ever-increasing power of the railroad companies; and dismay over the choking, smoky pollution spewed by the passing engines (Nye 2003, 186–187). All of these factors, and many more, caused an increasingly irate public to demand something be done about the powerful railroads.

If the townspeople of the Eastern United States were becoming increasingly disenchanted with the railroads, the farmers of the central plains were finding much more to hate about them. Unfair business practices, such as overcharging for freight whenever lack of competition permitted, caused great consternation in the Western states.

Before moving on to other innovations in American transportation, one should note that the advent of the railroads, steamboats, and canals did not all at once make travel in the United States what might today be considered modern and convenient. Incongruities abound that continued to delay cross-country travel in the nineteenth century. Railroads did not reach every destination, nor did canals or steamboats. Even those locales served by one or more of these "modern" transportation systems were often reached only through a series of travel options. A typical traveler in antebellum America might encounter a journey such as: "from New Jersey to Cincinnati—a journey of 450 miles . . . [a traveler] took a train from South Amboy to Philadelphia, where he changed to another train for Columbia; there he boarded a horse-drawn canal barge as far as Pittsburgh; finally, an Ohio steamer carried him to his destination" (Lacour-Gayet, 47). Of course, the same trip, embarked upon a half century earlier, would have been primarily completed on horseback and flatboat, an itinerary much longer and more difficult than the one described.

Perhaps, though, things are not as different today as they might first appear. A look at modern travel reveals a similar need to change modes of transportation several times: a recent trip from Fort Smith, Arkansas, to Baltimore, Maryland, involved an automobile ride to the airport in Fort Smith, where an airplane departed for Dallas, Texas; a change of planes was required, much like the change in trains for our nineteenth century traveler. Upon arrival in Baltimore, the twenty-first century traveler finds a shuttle bus to finally complete the journey. Although the distance covered is much greater and the time required much less, the similarities are striking. Doubtless, a twenty-third century traveler will look back at travel in the twenty-first century and think it quite slow and cumbersome.

BRIDGES

Wagon roads, railroads, and later automobile roads would find limited usefulness if they were not capable of crossing the great rivers and valleys of the United States. American engineers became master bridge builders in the nineteenth century as roads of all types pushed their way deeper into the interior of the country. From wooden bridges, whose design had changed little for centuries, to the mighty steel bridges that appeared late in the century, bridges became as much a part of American folklore as American engineering.

Advances made by Americans in material science and in bridge engineering contributed greatly to the increased ease with which farmers, merchants, and travelers of all sorts could move about the country. A series of American engineers developed better and stronger trusses, by far the most common bridge design. Throughout the nineteenth century, one can find patents for the Howe truss, the Pratt truss, the Whipple-Murphy truss, and many others, all named after their respective American designers.

The first bridges in the United States were simple designs made of wood. Wood was the material of choice for several reasons: It was plentiful and easy to work with, and the engineering of wood bridges was already well developed. Iron bridges later played an important, but rather short-lived, role in America. Similar in design to the wooden truss bridges, these iron bridges dotted the Eastern landscape, allowing railroads to cross rivers, canals, and ravines. A Massachusetts engineer by the name of Squire Whipple designed and constructed so many of these bridges that he became known as the "father of iron bridges" in America. Whipple's book, *A Work on Bridge Building*, was the first major American work to analyze the science and mechanics of bridges.

One of the first bridge improvements related to the use of iron was the suspension bridge. The first suspension bridges in the United States were built in the last decade of the eighteenth century and played a vital role in the development of railroad transportation a few decades later. A bridge using wire rope, first developed by a German immigrant named John A. Roebling, became the first suspension bridge to carry a railroad when the Niagara Suspension Bridge opened in 1855. This beautiful bridge "became almost as great a tourist attraction as the falls themselves" (Nye 1994, 78) and was only one of many important suspension bridges designed by Roebling.

It didn't take long for most engineers to realize the advantages of steel—its strength, durability, and other metallurgical qualities made steel ideal for building bridges. By the last quarter of the century great steel bridges were built over waterways across the country. Two of the most famous of these were the Eads Bridge (named after its designer, James Buchanan Eads) and the Brooklyn Bridge. Eads was a prolific builder and inventor who, in addition to his work building bridges, invented a diving bell used to help clear snags from the Mississippi, built a small fleet of ironclad river warships that contributed to the Union's victories on the Mississippi during the Civil War, and built jetties that formed an important ship channel on the river at New Orleans.

The triple-arch Eads Bridge, built across the Mississippi River to connect Saint Louis to East Saint Louis, Illinois, opened in 1874 and continues in service today. Eads employed several radical ideas to the design and construction of his bridge, including the use of a pneumatic caisson, a device that allowed workers to work on the foundation below water level on the river bed. One unfortunate result of this new technique was that the workers became ill with "the bends," a painful and dangerous affliction familiar to deep sea divers of the following century. This illness killed 14 workers and crippled many others (Nye 1994, 80). The construction of the Eads Bridge was followed with interest by an entire country. It was the first of the large steel cantilever bridges and became a national symbol and popular tourist site (Nye 1994, 79–80).

Because of the novelty of the design and many of the construction techniques, critics predicted the bridge would fail and fall into the Mississippi River. After completion, the bridge was tested with increasing loads until it was declared safe for both foot traffic and railroad traffic. The grand opening, on July 4, 1874, was marked by a great celebration that included workmen representing many trades, from plasterers to printers (Nye 1994, 82).

The most famous bridge in America, the Brooklyn Bridge, was completed in 1883 amidst much fanfare. It was the longest suspension bridge ever built and the first to use steel cables. When the bridge opened, it was already a tourist attraction, drawing thousands of sightseers. The Brooklyn Bridge, designed by John Roebling and completed by his son, Washington Roebling, dramatically changed the everyday life of thousands, if not millions, of New Yorkers. Note the opening paragraph of an article from *Harper's Monthly* celebrating the opening of the bridge:

People who seventeen years ago divided an amphibious existence between New York and Brooklyn will long remember their artic voyages in the East River during the severe winter of 1866–7. There were days in that season when passengers from New York to Albany [a distance of 150 miles] arrived earlier than those who set out the same morning from their breakfast tables in Brooklyn for their desks in New York. The newspapers were filled for weeks with reports of ice gorges, and with vehement demand for and discussion of the bridge, which all agreed must be built at once from New York to Brooklyn. (*Harper's Monthly*, 1)

The completion of the Brooklyn Bridge in 1883 paved the way for the eventual unification of various boroughs into present-day New York City. It connected New York City and Brooklyn with foot traffic, with carriage and wagon roads, with a specially designed cable car, and eventually with an urban rail system and, of course, automobile traffic, making commerce between the two cities seamless. But just as importantly, the Brooklyn Bridge became a symbol to New Yorkers, and perhaps all Americans, of the technological progress of the age. People of the 1890s as well as later visitors marveled at the engineering wonder:

Probably to the end of time thoughtful spectators unversed in the mysteries of engineering will pause, as they now do, before these gigantic towers, more wonderful than the Pyramids, with the everlasting sea beating their mighty bases, and will perplex themselves in vain to imagine by what means the granite masonry could have been laid so solid and true beneath not forty feet depth of rushing tides alone, but eighty feet below their surface, on the rock which those tides had not touched for untold ages. (*Harper's Monthly*, 9–10)

It wasn't only the technology, though, that produced reactions. The sheer immensity of the structure and the beauty of the architecture was awe inspiring. It was predicted that a pedestrian walking across the bridge would be in no hurry to get to the other side; rather,

He will linger to get the good of the splendid sweep of view about him, which his aesthetic self will admit pays wonderful interest on his investment of nothing. The bridge itself will be a remarkable sight, as he looks from his central path of vantage down upon the broad outer roadways, each with its tide of weighted wagons and carriages of his wealthier but not wiser brethren, and nearer the centre the two iron paths upon which the trains move silently and swiftly. (*Harper's Monthly*, 21)

The Brooklyn Bridge would take its place alongside the other architectural wonders of the world, becoming a "great landmark which characterizes and dominates the city as St. Peter's from across the Campagna dominates Rome, and the Arc de Triomphe the approach to Paris, and the Capitol on its height our own Washington—the double-tower bridge, whose massive masonry finds no parallel since the Pyramids" (*Harper's Monthly*, 21).

Beyond the bridge itself, New Yorkers and visitors alike could take in the sights of "a metropolis of nearly two million people—a population that will soon outgrow Paris, and have only London left to vie with" (*Harper's Monthly*, 20). The proud American pedestrian would see signs of a great nation, many of which were tied to the progress of technology: "Under him is the busy river, the two great cities now made one, . . . the Palisades walling the great Hudson; . . . the Bay, where the colossal Liberty will rise; at last the ocean, with its bridging ships" (*Harper's Monthly*, 21). Even accounting for the understandable hyperbole used by the author to mark the event, it is obvious that Americans were proud, and in their own eyes justifiably so, of the technological achievements they had made in their first full century of existence.

Advances in bridge building contributed as much to everyday life as did the railroads and automobiles designed to use the bridges. Aqueducts carried canal boats over rivers, viaducts carried trains over rivers and gullies, and tunnels were bored through mountains for both canals and railroads—each making significant contributions to faster and more efficient transportation. Whether connecting rural areas or connecting a number of islands to form present-day New York City, the bridge holds an important place in the history of American transportation.

TRANSPORTATION IN THE CITY

Mass transit plays an important role in modern America, especially in the cities. The idea of mass transit in the United States dates back to the early part of the nineteenth century, when several cities began using large horse-drawn coaches, called omnibuses, to transport passengers between predetermined locations. The first omnibus in America appeared in New York City in 1827. By building cars drawn by horses but riding on rails, the passengers in large metropolitan areas such as New York and New Orleans rode in greater comfort by the 1830s. This form of transportation continued to predominate in the major cities until relatively late in the century. However, technology had yet to change considerably the everyday transportation habits of urban Americans. People still depended on the horse for transportation in the city, even as the nation was beginning to build a network of railroads that would revolutionize transportation between population centers. Although railroad companies did build steam railroads connecting suburbs to the cities, including the first elevated railroad in New York City in 1876, the great revolution in urban transportation occurred when enterprising Americans developed new technologies to quickly, safely, and cheaply carry passengers within the city.

The first of these innovations was the cable car, patented by Andrew Hallidie in 1871. Hallidie constructed the first passenger cable car in San Francisco in 1873 and forever changed the face of urban transportation. Hallidie's system included a cable buried underground and pulled through a continuous loop powered by large steam engines. The cable car was outfitted with a device attached below street level that "gripped" the moving cable. By releasing the device (and applying a mechanical hand brake when necessary), the "gripman" controlled the movement of the car. The cable car soon spread to other major U.S. cities and for a few decades was a predominant form of urban transportation.

Less than 20 years after the cable car appeared in San Francisco, another technological innovation threatened to displace it as the choice of urban travelers. The basic idea for an electric trolley had been around since the early 1800s. Some inventors had little more than an idea, whereas others built actual working models. The first streetcar prototypes, unfortunately, ran on batteries—a power source much too bulky and inefficient to be practical (Nye 1990, 86). Early electric trolleys built in New Orleans and Montgomery, Alabama, among other places, incorporated several improvements important to the traveler:

All of these systems were attractive because they eliminated batteries and relied on improved dynamos. Collectively they solved problems of where to mount the motor (under the car), how to transmit electricity to it (overhead wires, using a troller), and what kinds of brakes, driving mechanisms, and operator controls worked. Nevertheless, most of these systems soon went out of operation because no one had combined all these elements in a single system, and because none of the existing systems had a satisfactory motor. (Nye 1990, 88)

The first commercially successful electric streetcar, or trolley, began service in Richmond, Virginia, in the late 1880s. Frank Sprague, the inventor, designer, and builder of this first successful trolley, was a former assistant to Thomas Edison and contributed scores of other inventions to nineteenth-century America, including electric locomotives, electric elevators, and numerous improvements to other electrical devices.

Sprague solved many of the problems associated with electric trolleys, including improving the direct current motor and discovering a better way to mount the motor (Nye 1990, 88). Sprague's success led to a buyout offer from Edison General Electric Company, and by 1890 two hundred cities had built or were in the process of building trolley systems, with about 90 percent based on Sprague's patents (Nye 1990, 89).

The first electric streetcars received their power from two rails fed with currents of opposite polarity. The dangers of such a system were evident as accidents regularly occurred when people (or horses) touched both rails simultaneously. The problem was rectified by the installation of the now-familiar overhead wires to which a "troller" (hence the word *trolley*) was attached from the car.

The cable car did not seriously challenge the electric trolley for preeminence in American cities primarily because of the cost—in 1890 the cost for installing a cable car was more than twice that of an electric trolley (Nye 1990, 90). Also faster and more efficient than the cable car, the trolley soon spread across the country. It was relatively easy for a city with a horse trolley system to string power lines above the rails and convert the whole system to an electric trolley. The growth of electric trolleys was staggering: The number of electric streetcars in the United States went from 130 in 1888 to more than 8,000 in 1892 (Marcus and Segal, 155). To sustain this growth, the amount of street-railway track in the cities that was electrified went from 16 percent in 1890, to more than 60 percent in 1893, and an amazing 98 percent by 1903 (Marcus and Segal, 155). Perhaps no other innovation in transportation affected Americans, especially urban Americans, as quickly as the electric streetcar.

Powered by large electric generators turned by steam engines, these electric trolleys, along with cable cars and in a smaller way the steam railroads, changed dramatically the face of urban America. No longer restricted to the city due to proximity to jobs, first the wealthy, and later the middle class, began moving to suburbs and took advantage of fast and inexpensive transportation into the city. These electric trains, connecting urban centers with rural areas and with other cities, came to be known as interurbans. The American commuter was born.

The electric trolley presented advantages over previous modes of transportation, from the horse-drawn trolleys of the past to steam locomotives used at that time. The trolleys provided a means of transportation that was affordable to a wide variety of customers. Electric trolleys were able to start and stop much more quickly than steam locomotives, allowing for more stops without great delays to the passengers already aboard. By 1902, trolleys in America registered 5.8 billion riders for the year (Rowsome, 11). The incredible popularity of the trolleys near the turn of the century, along with an American public that found itself with more and more leisure time, led to a rather unexpected change in everyday life for many people in or near the cities served by trolleys. The trolley companies began to build entertainment venues, especially amusement parks, along or at the end of their lines. Riding a trolley to such venues became

A sightseeing trolley parked in front of the Brown Palace Hotel in Denver around the turn of the century. Denver Public Library, Western History Collection, Call No.: X-18279.

a popular pastime for Americans hungry for entertainment and yielded a financial bonanza for the trolley companies.

Interurban transportation sparked recreational travel for all classes of American urbanites:

On a summer weekend day, Brooklyn trolleys and boats from the Battery might carry (heavily immigrant) crowds of 150,000 and more to the spit of sand called Coney Island to bathe in the sea and enjoy the shooting galleries, ferris wheels, bowling alleys, variety theaters, the fantasy and escape of Steeplechase park. Picking up dates for the day was a ritualized art form. Other ventures into the new modernistic mass culture—Cleveland's Euclid Beach, Chicago's Chettenham Beach, and Revere Beach in Boston—boasted amusement parks, pavilions, dance halls, and vaudeville shows. Fans hailed their favorite baseball players, Honus Wagner, Nap LaJoie, or Ohio farmboy turned great pitcher Cy Young, as they walked in full uniform from hotels to the ballparks. That such spectacles were urban helped speed the exodus out of the country. (Kent, 24)

Of course, entertainment for the urban masses was not always of the wholesome variety:

It was the factory workers, secretaries, cashiers, and tradesmen lining up for music halls and vaudeville, porno penny arcades and burlesque shows, and the ethnic theatres of the immigrant ghettos, who were in the vanguard of the revolt against the late nineteenth-century American Victorian façade of genteel respectability and relentless moralizing. Couples danced sensuously in the noisy, smoky concert saloons. (Kent, 24)

Without the new forms of transportation—fast, cheap, and readily available—the spectacle of thousands of people gathering at an amusement park or at a ball game would have been unthinkable. The transportation revolution changed American leisure every bit as much as it changed American agriculture and American industry.

The spread of streetcars in American cities had wide-ranging affects on industry, the economy, and everyday life. The impact on industry and on local economies was obvious in many ways:

Street railways purchased thousands of miles of steel rails and overhead copper wires. They created new business for producers of railway cars and plate glass, and in every community they spent money on line construction and on permanent jobs. By 1902, tens of thousands of people worked for the more than eight hundred railways.... The streetcar also played a central role in developing larger electrical-generation plants in most American cities.... Across the nation ... local utilities ... expand[ed] their power stations, thereby lowering electrical rates for traction companies and for the rest of their customers. (Nye 1990, 92–93)

Although known primarily for moving passengers, the trolleys also transported crops from outlying farms directly to the marketplace at the center of the city. Trolleys became so popular near the end of the century that cities began to look at ways of alleviating congestion on city streets. This problem eventually led (in the early twentieth century) to the emergence of the subway as an important means of transportation in large metropolises.

The last form of urban transportation to be discussed is not one that normally comes to mind when discussing transportation. It doesn't travel very far or very fast, but its impact on everyday life in the city was immense. It is the elevator. Elevators are what make cities possible, with their skyscrapers compressing more people into less space. Two American inventors contributed invaluable advances to the design and construction of elevators.

Elisha Otis made the use of elevators safe with his invention of the elevator "brake." Actually, Otis's brake was simply a series of notches, or teeth, built into the elevator shaft that caught the elevator should the cable break. This simple invention inspired the public confidence that was needed before cities could build taller and taller buildings accessed by elevators. Whereas Otis's first elevators were steam powered, another American inventor, Alexander Miles, patented an electric elevator that improved the system to power the elevators and also improved the methods for automatically opening and closing the elevator doors. The inventions of Otis and Miles made elevators the safe and efficient means of transportation that we see today in all multistory buildings.

BICYCLES

Today, most people think of bicycles as children's toys or as exercise machines for adults. In the last decades of the nineteenth century, however, a bicycle craze made the two-wheeler much more than a toy or a exercise machine for hundreds of thousands—even millions—of Americans. The craze peaked in the last two decades of the century, so that by the middle of the 1890s, more than 300 American companies produced more than a million bicycles per year (Hounshell, 192). The development of the bicycle was important not only for its immediate impact on everyday life in America but also for its role in the development of manufacturing practices that would lay the groundwork for the automobile and aviation industries of the next century.

In the early nineteenth century the forerunner of the modern bicycle was introduced by a German inventor, Baron Karl von Drais. His heavy, all wooden, two-wheeled machine had no pedals—the rider provided the propulsion by pushing with his feet on the ground. By the middle of the century, enterprising inventors had added pedals, and the bicycle craze spread throughout Europe and the United States. These first bicycles were heavy and had all metal or hard rubber tires, making them a very

Advertisement for a velocipede. Note the bloomers worn by the women, which came into style thanks in part to the popularity of the bicycle. Library of Congress.

rough ride; in fact, one of the earliest and most popular bicycles was aptly called the "Boneshaker." Early bicycles had another serious design flaw: The pedals attached directly to the front wheel. Designers soon found that the bigger the front wheel the faster the rider could propel the bike. Unfortunately, the huge front wheels also meant the rider sat so high above the ground serious injuries could occur from bicycle accidents. In spite of the hazards, and the cost of early bicycles, riding gained in popularity in the United States.

These early high-wheel bicycles, later referred to as "ordinaries," were first brought to the United States by Albert A. Pope. After importing English bicycles for a few years, Pope contracted with the Weed Sewing

Machine Company of Hartford, Connecticut, to begin manufacturing the Columbia bicycle in 1878 (Hounshell, 190). Pope's company would be a leader in bicycle manufacturing in the United States for the rest of the century. Building bicycles in existing manufacturing facilities became commonplace. In New England, bicycle manufacturing was often taken up by arms makers and sewing machine companies, whereas in the West bicycle companies often grew from carriage and wagon makers or agricultural implement makers (Hounshell, 208). Either way, the manufacture of bicycles was influenced by—and influenced—the manufacture of other machines in nineteenth-century America.

Two inventions, one by an Englishman and one by an Irishman, led to a yet faster rise in the popularity of the bicycle. In 1885, John Kemp Starley built the first device that the twenty-first century person would recognize as a modern bicycle. By using a chain-driven rear wheel and a front wheel of equal size, the "safety" bicycle made riding easier and safer for every rider. A few years later, Dr. J. B. Dunlop of Belfast, Ireland, designed the first pneumatic bicycle tire for his own son's tricycle. The new tire caught on quickly, and soon pneumatic tires were found on bicycles in the United States (Sloane, 356).

Bicycles became very popular in the United States in the late nineteenth century. Typical of American exuberance, the bicycle was seen as much more than a fad. An article in the *Atlantic Monthly* in 1898, titled "Fifty Years of American Science," placed the improvement and manufacture of bicycles in the United States in a lofty position:

A typical American device is the bicycle. Invented in France, it long remained a toy or a vain luxury. Redevised in this country, it inspired inventors and captivated manufacturers, and native genius made it a practical machine for the multitude; now its users number millions, and it is sold in every country. Typical, too, is the bicycle in its effect on national character. It first aroused invention, next stimulated commerce, and then developed individuality, judgment, and prompt decision on the part of its users more rapidly and completely than any other device; for although association with machines of any kind (absolutely straightforward and honest as they are all) develops character, the bicycle is the easy leader of other machines in shaping the mind of its rider, and transforming itself and its rider into a single thing. Better than other results is this: that the bicycle has broken the barrier of pernicious differentiation of the sexes and rent the bonds of fashion, and is daily impressing Spartan strength and grace, and more than Spartan intelligence, on the mothers of coming generations. So, weighed by its effect on body and mind as well as on material progress, this device must be classed as one of the world's great inventions. (cited in Hounshell, 190)

This rather embellished description of the bicycle and its effect on Americans does offer several points to consider. Although not invented in America, improvements made in this country led to the bicycle's practicality for everyone. Note also some of the most important ideas in the

American psyche: Americans are inventive and commercially oriented, yet also interested in personal and national improvement. Furthermore, the Industrial Age had produced a mindset in which machines were considered—unlike humans—to be "absolutely straightforward and honest," and by associating himself with a machine a man (and a women, in the case of the bicycle) develops character. Although there were scattered dissenting opinions, this was a typical reaction to industrialization and mechanization in America.

The bicycle had something to offer to everyone. For young people, the bicycle offered "a good way to get out from under the stern eye of their parents" (Sloane, 352). Women also enjoyed the newfound freedom that a bicycle offered; the style of women's clothing even changed to make bicycling easier (Sloane, 352). And for everyone, the bicycle was a means of transportation that was exciting and new:

At last man was free from the horse and wagon. A bicycle never needed daily cleaning and currying; it didn't eat, and it did not use an expensive harness that took time to put on and take off. One could jump on a bicycle and quickly be away from home. (Sloane, 352)

Riding clubs were formed, races organized, and everyone who could afford a bicycle wanted one. A national club, the League of American Wheelmen, counted thousands of enthusiasts as members. Periodicals supporting the new craze appeared, including *Bicycling World* and the *Wheelman*. Trade shows, later copied with great success by automobile manufacturers, were introduced by bicycle companies to advertise their new models. In 1896, the Chicago show drew more than 225 exhibitors and 100,000 admissions, and a similar show in New York drew 400 exhibitors and 120,000 admissions (Hounshell, 198). Bicycle races, from a few miles to across the country, captured the imagination of the American people. Multi-day bicycle races were held at Madison Square Garden in New York City and cross-country races and "tours" were common from the 1880s onward. In 1895 there were 600 professional cyclists competing for prize money in races across the United States (Sloane, 368).

By the waning years of the nineteenth century Americans were buying bicycles at an astounding rate; at the same time, spending on such things as jewelry, pianos, and books had fallen to an all-time low (Sloane, 357). An 1896 article in the magazine *Outing* sums up the popularity of bicycles in the United States:

The cycle trade is now one of the chief industries of the world. Its ramifications are beyond ordinary comprehension. Its prosperity contributes in no small degree to that of the steel, wire, rubber, and leather markets. Time was when the spider web monsters, now nearly extinct, were built in one story annexes to English and American machine shops; now a single patented type of a jointless wood rim, one of the minor parts of a modern bicycle, is the sole product of an English factory covering over two acres of ground. A decade ago the American steel tube industry was unprofitable. The production of this most essential part of cycle construction has, during the past two years, been unequal to the demand, and even now every high-grade tube mill in this country is working night and day on orders that will keep them busy throughout the year. Nearly every season since 1890 has witnessed a doubling of the number of our factories and a multiplication of the product of a large proportion of the older ones. Yet the supply from the opening of last season to mid-summer was unequal to the demand, and although preparations of astounding proportions have been and are being made to meet with a multiplicity of models of the most approved designs and best workmanship, the demands of '96, the prospects are that the field offers reasonable prosperity to all makers of high-grade products. The present prices are quite reasonable, considering the quality of material and workmanship involved. Prices will be very generally maintained, and the number of riders, of both sexes, will be at least doubled. (cited in Sloane, 359)

This article demonstrates the common belief that bicycling was not a fad and that it would continue to grow at accelerating rates. And if not for the appearance and eventual affordability of the automobile, this prophesy might have come true.

The bicycle craze and the industry it spawned in the United States had several unexpected consequences. As bicyclists organized themselves into clubs, they began to demand the right to use public roads. The League of American Wheelmen "waged legal battles in New York and other urban areas to get the bicycle classified as a transportation vehicle, a critical problem because cities like New York had prohibited bicycles on city streets" (Hounshell, 203). In addition, bicyclists organized to demand better roads. The success of the bicyclists "was crucial in the creation of both state and federal legislation resulting in a more extensive highway system in America" (Hounshell, 203). These roads would eventually be put to even better use with the appearance of automobiles.

Bicycle companies developed new manufacturing processes that played an important role in the bicycle industry and led to improved production techniques in other industries. The method of stamping or pressing was adopted by companies such as the Western Wheel Works (Hounshell, 209). By stamping aluminum parts for bicycles, American companies were able to bring mass production to the bicycle industry.

The bicycle industry served as a training ground for future transportation innovators. Charles Duryea and Henry Ford, pioneers in the automobile industry, were at one time involved in bicycle manufacturing. And many people know that the aviation pioneers, Wilbur and Orville Wright, were bicycle mechanics-turned-pilots. David Hounshell maintains that the bicycle industry was transitional for two reasons. First, "refined armory practice and well-developed stamping techniques provided the technical basis for automobile manufacturing in the early twentieth century." Second, the bicycle "led many an American—and not a few bicycle mechanics—to contemplate and to project a faster, more powerful, and less fatiguing form of personal transportation" (Hounshell, 190). One such mechanic, Hiram Percy Maxim, writing in 1937, related his epiphany concerning the coming of the horseless carriage:

I saw [transportation] emerging from a crude stage in which mankind was limited to the railroad, to the horse, or to shank's mare. The bicycle was just becoming popular and it represented a very significant advance, I felt. Here I was covering the distance between Salem and Lynn on a bicycle. Here was a revolutionary change in transportation. My bicycle was propelled at a respectable speed by a mechanism operated by my own muscles. It carried me over a lonely country road in the middle of the night, covering the distance in considerably less than an hour. A horse and carriage would require nearly two hours. A railroad train would require half an hour, and it would carry me only from station to station. And I must conform to its time-table, which was not always convenient. (cited in Hounshell, 214)

Maxim realized the importance of personal transportation independent of a railroad's timetable and hit upon the idea of a self-propelled vehicle. He maintained that with the increased usage of bicycles, Americans became more interested in fast, cheap personal transportation. This "created a new demand which it was beyond the ability of the railroad to supply. Then it came about that the bicycle could not satisfy the demand it had created. A mechanically propelled vehicle was wanted instead of a foot-propelled one, and we now know that the automobile was the answer" (cited in Hounshell, 214).

THE BIRTH OF THE AUTOMOBILE

Many technologies were important to nineteenth century life while also laying the foundation for advances in the twentieth century. As an ancient mode of transportation, the carriages and wagons did not represent a unique development in the nineteenth century; the carriage and wagon industry did, however, develop using advancing technologies and helped to lay the groundwork for the century of the automobile. In fact, one of the most successful carriage and wagon manufacturers in the United States, the Studebaker Company, would become an early leader in the American automobile industry.

By the middle of the nineteenth century, "the wagon and carriage trade in the United States was undergoing what contemporaries regarded as a revolution" (Hounshell, 146). These manufacturers found that the only way to profitably operate their companies was to adopt mass production techniques by assembling ready-made parts into the final product. The Studebaker company of South Bend, Indiana, adopted these practices, using them to mass-produce carriages and wagons utilizing their own machinery and at the same time cutting the cost of a typical wagon by half (Hounshell, 147).

In the last decades of the nineteenth century, the Studebaker Company adopted two manufacturing techniques that allowed it to become the largest wagon and carriage maker in the United States. These two technologies, resistance welding and sheet metal stamping, meant that Studebaker could mass-produce its products to the tune of 75,000 vehicles in 1895 alone (Hounshell, 149). The use of electric resistance welding allowed Studebaker, and other manufacturers who followed suit, to replace "large numbers of skilled blacksmiths with machines" (Hounshell, 149). Shortly after the turn of the century, the company began applying its know-how to the manufacture of automobiles.

The automobile appeared in the United States too late in the nineteenth century to have a serious impact on everyday life. However, its transformation of American life makes the development of the automobile during the nineteenth century an important bookend to a century of great advances in transportation.

The first problem in any discussion concerning the invention of the automobile comes in defining just what one considers an automobile. For instance, inventors tinkered with horseless carriages powered by steam throughout the nineteenth century. Unlike railroads, these steam carriages that did not require a rail, making them the first "auto" mobiles. However, the bulk of the engine and its fuel prevented these steam-powered carriages from finding practical usage. Therefore, we define (as others usually do) the automobile as a carriage powered by an internal combustion engine.

It is very difficult to assign the honor of inventor of the automobile. The last few decades of the nineteenth century found many would-be inventors in the United States and in Europe working on combustion engines and carriages driven by such engines. In Germany, for instance, Daimler and Benz were among those racing to perfect their inventions. In the United States, there were countless pioneers working in backyard workshops or industrial machine shops to build a working automobile. Three of these American visionaries were George Selden and the Duryea brothers, Charles and Frank.

Selden, a patent attorney, began designing a combustion engine for his "road engine" in the 1870s. Not being a mechanic himself, Selden did not actually build his automobile until decades later, putting off applying for a patent until 1895. Although Selden and his company never produced and marketed his invention, other automobile makers were required to pay Selden a licensing fee because of his early patent. Similarly, although not the first to build an automobile in the United States, the Duryea brothers perhaps influenced the industry more than anyone else until Henry Ford. The brothers built their first automobile in 1893, basing their design on extensive studies of mechanical engineering made primarily by the younger Duryea, Frank. The Duryeas' reputation as the first successful builders of automobiles in the United States was cemented when their entry won the highly publicized first American automobile race in Chicago in 1895. Although the Duryeas continued to manufacture and market automobiles into the first quarter of the next century, their lack of business success has left them as footnotes in history books.

The automobile is often treated as a single invention; but actually, it was a conglomeration of various inventions brought together by ingenious men to serve one purpose. Many of these individual inventions changed everyday life in America in more ways than just the automobile. Consider the discovery of vulcanized rubber by an American inventor who persisted like few other men. Charles Goodyear weathered decades of failure, poverty, and near starvation before finally inventing the process that made the Goodyear name famous. Interestingly, after years of failed experiments, Goodyear's inspiration came quite unexpectedly. He noticed, after accidentally dropping a piece of rubber on a hot stove, that the charred remains exhibited the properties of weather resistance for which he had been searching. After another series of experiments, Goodyear discovered just the right heating method to make the rubber that has since found so many uses. Instead of melting in the summer and freezing to a brittle state in the winter, Goodyear's rubber maintained its "rubbery" characteristics year-round, impervious to the weather.

In spite of his invention's immediately apparent usefulness, Goodyear was not an adept businessman and failed to capitalize completely on it. Although not as destitute as he was earlier in life, Goodyear died in debt, leaving a legacy of rubber that would allow such things as inflatable automobile tires to make their considerable mark on everyday life in America.

There is perhaps no other category in which science and technology has changed everyday life as much as transportation. At the beginning of the nineteenth century, people were limited to how fast, how far, and even what direction they could travel by the vagaries of the wind while at sea or the physical limitations of the horse on land. Today, people travel on a scale unimagined two centuries ago. The ability to move about easily altered traditional demographic patterns, and the concurrent ability to transport goods around the world led to the formation of a global economy. The initial stages of this revolution in transportation can be found in the technological advances of the nineteenth century.

3

Communications

Suppose it is 1800 and you have important information to send to a relative, friend, or business partner—maybe news of a birth or death, or a time-sensitive business matter. The problem is that you live in the Deep South and the prospective receiver of the information resides in New England. In turn-of-the-century America, it takes close to three weeks for a letter to be sent across the country, by which time the news is no longer "new."

Such was the state of communication in America, indeed the world, in the early nineteenth century. Communications were hand carried by messengers on horseback or by ship. Yet, as the United States expanded westward, the problem of communication grew exponentially. In Europe, where distances were less and roads were better, mail could be delivered relatively quickly and with some degree of reliability. In the ever-expanding United States, however, with its poor or nonexistent roads and its untamed wilderness, mail and other information could not be delivered quickly or reliably.

The development of improved systems of communications proved to be critical as the country experienced the growing pains of the nineteenth century. Improvements to transportation, discussed in Chapter 2, made significant contributions to faster, more efficient, and more reliable delivery of mail and other information. The benefits of the steamboat and the railroad as mail carriers were realized almost immediately after their arrival on the American scene. Yet these new technologies simply resulted in faster means of delivering age-old forms of communication. The real revolution in communications in the nineteenth century came with the development of new technologies that changed the message and the way the message was delivered. The typewriter began a revolution in *how* communications were written, and the telegraph and telephone changed forever the *type* of communication to be exchanged. Finally, Eastman's work in recording the visual and Edison's inventions for recording the oral laid the groundwork for a completely new idea of the *meaning* of communication.

Each of these advances in communication was based on technological and/or scientific breakthroughs. Since communication is an inherent component of human existence, these breakthroughs resulted in a complete transformation of everyday life in America.

WHAT HATH GOD WROUGHT?

With these words, a verse from the biblical book of Numbers, Samuel F.B. Morse ushered in the age of the telegraph in the United States. The importance of the telegraph to communication was incalculable. Its introduction changed the scale of communication by an order of magnitude. Before the telegraph, all messages were hand carried by messengers on foot or horseback, or by ships. The speed with which the message arrived at its destination was limited by the messenger's speed, a situation that had not changed in the history of mankind. (In fact, while traveling on business, a young Morse missed his wife's funeral, receiving word of her death too late to return—an event that later inspired his invention of the telegraph.) With Morse's invention, messages were sent and received over vast distances almost instantaneously, and the world would never be the same.

The experiments of another American, less famous than Morse today but well-known in nineteenth century America as one of the country's leading scientists, prepared the way for the telegraph. In 1830, Joseph Henry displayed the power of the newly discovered electromagnet. Henry sent an electric current over a mile-long wire that signaled a device to strike a bell. Henry's improvements to the electromagnet and his demonstration of a crude signaling device provided the impetus for the invention of a working telegraph. In fact, if Henry had been more interested in personal and commercial gain, he might have earned the title of "father of the telegraph." Instead, that honor goes to a fellow American greatly influenced by Henry's work.

Samuel Morse, a successful portrait painter, was on a ship bound for the United States from Europe in 1832 when he first heard of the capabilities of the electromagnet. Almost immediately, he realized the potential for using such a device for sending messages over long distances. Although various inventors had already built crude telegraphs, each invention involved the use of too many wires to be practical. Morse's first attempts to build a device also proved overly complicated and impractical. By 1835, however, Morse had successfully built a one-wire system and was working to perfect a new language for telegraphy, Morse Code. Although Morse

Samuel F. B. Morse. Library of Congress.

began demonstrating his invention in 1837, it was not until 1844 that the true potential of the telegraph was demonstrated. Using a grant from Congress of $30,000, Morse constructed a line between Washington and Baltimore and sent his now-famous quote from the Bible. (Actually, before the line was totally completed, news from the 1844 political convention in Baltimore was sent over the partially completed line to Washington— historically the first news sent by telegraph, but not as dramatic a story as "What hath God wrought?")

At first, messages sent by Morse's telegraph were recorded on paper with a series of dots and dashes, to be deciphered later. Soon, however, the telegraph inventor reorganized these same dots and dashes into today's Morse Code and operators were taught to "read" the message by the sounds the device produced.

The impact of the telegraph was almost immediate and its growth rate was astounding. Morse and his partners opened lines between major cities in the United States and were soon challenged by competitors in the new business of telegraphy. Only a decade after that first line between Washington and Baltimore was completed, there was already more than 20,000 miles of telegraph wire in operation in the United States.

Two American industries, both still in their infancy, began experiencing incredible growth thanks in part to the telegraph. When the Erie Railroad began dispatching its trains by telegraph in 1851, a long and profitable relationship between the two emerging technologies began. As other railroads began using the telegraph, train schedules became more reliable and the train/telegraph station assumed a central place in large cities and small whistle-stops alike. The railroad industry quickly became one of the largest employers of skilled telegraph operators.

Another industry highly suited to the capabilities of the new telegraph was the newspaper business. Before the telegraph, only local news was truly "new." National stories took days, perhaps weeks, to reach across the country, and international news might be months old before it became available to the typical American. With the advent of the telegraph, newspapers in New York could receive news from Philadelphia, Boston, and eventually from overseas in a timely manner. Even more important to rural Americans, the local newspaper, which had previously satisfied itself with printing local gossip and such, now had access to news from the world at large.

A new type of competition arose among newspapers to see which one could get the news out fastest to an insatiable public. The telegraph became an important tool in this contest and led directly to the establishment of cooperative news services such as the Associated Press (AP) and the United Press International (UPI). The AP engaged the telegraph to relay breaking news to newspapers across the country. In fact, the AP was founded by a group of rival New York City newspapers in part to share the cost of receiving news over the telegraph. The telegraph truly made the world, at least from an information standpoint, a very small place.

The telegraph changed the way American businesspeople went about their daily work. The pace of business picked up considerably as time became an important factor in business transactions. No longer did a businessperson in New York have to wait several days after sending a messaging to an associate in Philadelphia before receiving a reply—several weeks, or longer, if the associate happened to be in San Francisco. Those active in the stock market were especially affected as "tickers" made stock data almost instantaneously known throughout the country. They learned that they must react quickly to new information or possibly lose business to a faster-acting competitor.

As the new technology expanded into the far reaches of the United States, the telegraph and telegraph operator became the central feature of most towns. Railroad schedules, news, business and financial information, and even the official time were all sent along the telegraph lines.

This instantaneous communication led to a fundamental change in the pace of life for many Americans. In today's world of satellite communications, CNN, and the Internet, it is difficult to grasp the significance of the new invention. The telegraph meant "business that used to occur at a leisurely pace was telescoped into minutes or hours of time" (Spar, 70). In the twenty-first century, business and industry is truly international in scope. In the nineteenth century, however, the telegraph provided for the first time the opportunity for "merchants in Boston [to] place orders in Atlanta overnight; farmers in Ohio could check the daily price of hogs in Chicago" (Spar, 70). The pace of business, and of life in general, was changed forever.

By the later part of the nineteenth century, the telegraph became an important tool for various types of businesses. Shipping and financial concerns—as well as newspapers—found an outlet for time-sensitive information through the telegraph. By the 1880s, approximately 80 percent of the messages sent over Western Union telegraph lines were business related (Israel, 265).

In addition to official and business messages, the telegraph allowed people in everyday life to send and receive messages about deaths, births, holiday greetings, and all forms of social correspondence. Information that used to take days, weeks, or even months to arrive at its destination was now sent almost instantaneously. The telegraph operator became one of the most important citizens of a town, as his skill and knowledge connected the townsfolk to the rest of the world.

The telegraph also made life safer for ordinary citizens, both in the cities and in the countryside. In the West, the telegraph was instrumental in tracking down outlaws by sending descriptions around the country. In cities, telegraphs were used to summon doctors, firefighters, police, and other emergency personnel. In addition to using general-use telegraph lines for such emergencies, companies developed their own private lines for calling firefighters, police, and doctors—or just for calling a taxi (Israel, 265).

The telegraph giant, Western Union, built the first transcontinental telegraph in 1861, eight years before the completion of the transcontinental railroad. With the completion of the line, the fabled Pony Express was rendered obsolete. Instead of waiting weeks for messages to be carried across the country, the telegraph accomplished the feat almost instantaneously. Western Union came to dominate the American telegraph market. In 1873 alone, it sent more than 12 million telegraphs (Spar, 111), and by the early twentieth century the main office in New York City handled hundreds of thousands of messages per day. As Western Union grew in size and power, an uproar arose from politicians and citizens alike. With the telegraph becoming increasingly more important to life in America, the fear of monopolistic practices from the telegraph giant, exacerbated by its close ties to the news giant Associated Press, resulted in several attempts to regulate the telegraph industry. In spite of these fears, Western Union continued to expand its operations.

The first attempt to lay a trans-Atlantic telegraph cable was made in 1857, under the management of a successful American businessman, Cyrus Field. In 1858, a cable was successfully completed but worked for only a short time. After several more failures, Field's team established a cable connecting Ireland and Newfoundland in 1866, initiating a revolution in world communications. With the successful establishment of several more trans-Atlantic cables in the following years, communication between Europe and the United States changed forever. No longer dependent on ships to carry messages across the vast ocean, the cable changed politics and diplomacy, business and industry, war, and every aspect of trans-Atlantic news and communication. Many believed the telegraph signaled a new era of peaceful relations among all nations.

Contemporary observers who watched its use grow exponentially understood the importance of the telegraph. The commentary of a nineteenth-century British writer summarizes nicely the perception of the new technology:

[The telegraph] is employed in transmitting messages to and from bankers, merchants, members of Congress, officers of government, brokers, and police officers; parties who by agreement have to meet each other at the two stations, or have been sent for by one of the parties; items of news, election returns, announcements of deaths, inquiries respecting the health of families and individuals, daily proceedings of the Senate and the House of Representatives, orders for goods, inquiries respecting the sailing of vessels, proceedings of cases in various courts, summoning of witnesses, messages for express trains, invitations, the receipt of money at one station and its payment at another; for persons requesting the transmission of funds from debtors, consultation of physicians, and messages of every character usually sent by mail. (cited in Standage, 60–61)

As indicated by this description, telegraphy touched people from all walks of life.

As with many new technologies, ignorance of the technical details of the workings of the telegraph was widespread. When Western Union began wiring money across the nation, many people assumed the same could be done with other goods, from articles of clothing to family pets. If Western Union could squeeze money through the thin wires, it was thought, why not other material goods?

The technology of telegraphy was applied to countless other tasks in the United States. Several inventors adapted telegraphic technology to devise ingenious fire alarm systems in Boston, New York City, Philadelphia, and other major cities. Although superior to old systems requiring watchmen around the city, the new telegraphic fire alarms proved slow to catch on. Improvements to telegraphy increased the volume, speed, and accuracy of the new form of communication. Multiplexing, the ability to transmit multiple messages over one wire at the same time, was one such advance. Thomas Edison and others contributed innovations in this field.

Another adaptation made to the telegraphic technology was the stock ticker, a device that provided timely Wall Street stock prices to investors. In fact, a young Thomas Edison, already experienced as a telegraph operator and with several improvements to the telegraph under his belt, found his first commercial success with the development of an improved stock ticker. Another famous American inventor, Alexander Graham Bell, was investigating methods to carry multiple messages over a single wire when he accidentally made a discovery that changed the world—the telephone.

By the end of the century, the heyday of the telegraph was coming to an end. Although the telegraph held a place in communications well into the twentieth century, two inventions of the later part of the nineteenth century began to encroach on the telegraph's domain: The "wireless telegraph," or radio, made communication possible even where no lines existed, and the telephone enabled voice communications without the need for a skilled intermediary such as the telegraph operator. As long-distance communications became easier and more readily available to the common people, the prominence of the telegraph began to wane.

THE "SPEAKING TELEGRAPH"

Today, the telegraph is a distant memory. In the last quarter of the nineteenth century, however, the telegraph was one of the most prevalent technologies in America. So, when Bell announced the invention of his new device, it was first seen as simply an improvement to the telegraph— a speaking telegraph. Only later were its unique characteristics fully understood and exploited.

Alexander Graham Bell was uniquely situated to invent the telephone. His background and training in the teaching of the deaf gave him insight into the physical characteristics of speech and his natural curiosity led him to experiment with devices that might be made to transmit sounds and, later, speech. The only thing Bell lacked was mechanical aptitude, a shortcoming solved when he convinced Thomas Watson, an accomplished mechanic, to become his assistant. Together, Bell and Watson created a device that would, in the words of Bell's foremost biographer, Robert Bruce, result in the "conquest of solitude."

After immigrating to the United States from Scotland via Canada, Bell began teaching at a school for the deaf while conducting experiments in his spare time. At first his experiments consisted of attempts to perfect a "harmonic telegraph," a telegraph that would send multiple messages over a single wire using musical notes. His benefactor, Gardiner Hubbard (the father of Mabel, who would later become Bell's wife), pushed the young teacher and inventor to forgo dreams of transmitting speech across a wire and concentrate instead on improving the telegraph. Bell, however, continued his research on the telephone. Bell and Watson made several technological advances, including the use of diaphragms modeled after the human ear to transmit and receive the vibrations of speech. In 1876, Bell made the first telephone "call." While experimenting on a new device with Watson, Bell spilled acid in his lap and called, "Mr. Watson, come here. I want you." (Actually, several versions of Bell's words spoken over the first telephone are in circulation. Even though both Bell and Watson claimed that the event occurred essentially as reported, some historians doubt the authenticity of the story and suspect a less dramatic first transmission actually occurred.) Watson heard these words over the line strung to another room of the house and came running into Bell's room exclaiming that he had *heard* Bell's words transmitted through the machine.

At first, most observers treated the new invention as a toy—that is, if they believed it worked at all. This all began to change in one of the most dramatic stories in the history of technological innovation. It so happened that only a few months after Bell's first voice transmission, the inventor was given a small space to exhibit his device at the Centennial Exhibition in Philadelphia. Bell only appeared at the Exposition at the urging of his future wife, Mabel. Once there, Bell and his telephone were ignored. In fact, it was only after the visiting Emperor Pedro of Brazil recognized Bell from a previous encounter at his school for the deaf that anyone paid any attention to the inventor or the invention. The demonstration so impressed the Emperor and several other distinguished visitors that Bell's revolutionary machine was, for the first time, taken seriously; the telephone was on its way to revolutionizing communication.

As with most new inventions, there were rough times ahead for Bell and the telephone. Bell was not a businessman, but, fortunately for him, he had several backers who were. The Bell Telephone Association (later American Bell Telephone Company) battled opponents in court over copyright issues and raced competitors to establish telephone service to the country. Soon after establishing the first telephone connections in the United States, Bell Telephone offered to sell all of its assets and copyrights to the telegraph giant, Western Union, for $100,000. Western Union, later to become one of Bell's biggest competitors in the telephone business, turned down the offer, at the time believing the telephone to be nothing more than a fad.

The first telephones used existing lines borrowed from telegraphs, burglar alarm systems, and the like. Barely a year after Bell's debut with his invention, the first dedicated telephone line was constructed. These first telephones were much different than modern devices. There were no telephone "systems"; instead, customers would lease two telephones, string a wire between two locations with the telephones at either end, and proceed to talk through the static. The receiving and transmitting components of these first telephones were not separated into earpieces and mouthpieces, as future telephones would be. Instead, both components were located in the same place, requiring the users to speak into the device, and then put their ear to the same location to hear a response.

Because the first transmitters were crude, sound quality degraded quickly over longer wires; and because these wires were grounded to the earth, all sorts of static interfered with the conversation:

Such a jangle of meaningless noises had never been heard by human ears. There were spluttering and bubbling, jerking and rasping, whistling and screaming. There were the rustling of leaves, the croaking of frogs, the hissing of steam, the flapping of birds' wings. There were clicks from telegraph wires, scraps of talk from other telephones and curious little squeals that were unlike any known sound. The lines running east and west were noisier than the lines running north and south. The night was noisier than the day, and at the ghostly hour of midnight the babel was at its height. (Brooks, 85–86)

One by one ingenious engineers bringing a new technology to the American public overcame these technical difficulties.

Even after telephone exchanges were developed, complete with switch-board operators assisting subscribers with connecting their calls, telephones were far from easy to operate:

The typical telephone system of the 1880s was a cumbersome affair. The instrument itself was a set of three boxes. The top box held a magneto generator, a crank, and a bell. The middle box had a speaker tube protruding forward and a receiver tube hanging from the side. The third box contained a wet-cell battery that needed to be refilled periodically and occasionally leaked. A caller turned the crank to signal the switchboard operator; the signal mechanically released a shutter on the switchboard in the central office, showing the origin of the call. The operator plugged her head-set into the designated socket and asked the caller whom he or she was seeking. Then the operator rang the desired party and connected the two by wires and plugs in the switchboard. The two parties talked, usually loudly and with accompanying static, and then hung up. In some systems the caller cranked again to signal the end of the conversation. In others, the operator listened in periodically to find out when the conversation was over so that she could disconnect the plugs. (Fischer, 37)

From its conception in 1876, telephone usage grew to more than 60,000 units by 1880 and mushroomed to more than 1.4 million phones in the United States by 1900. The first exchange to use telephone numbers instead of residents' names was in Lowell, Massachusetts, in 1879. The first long-distance telephone service, between Boston and Providence, was inaugurated in 1881 (Brooks, 89). Service between New York and Chicago began in 1892, but it was not until 1915 that the telephone con-nected the East Coast to the West Coast. As fortune would have it, Bell and Watson themselves participated in the first transcontinental tele-phone demonstration. Bell on the East Coast told Watson on the West Coast, "Mr. Watson, please come here. I need you," to which Watson replied, "I can, but it would take two weeks now!" (cited in de Camp, 167).

In the first few years, the new industry rapidly seeded the continent with telephone exchanges, as the Bell Telephone Association and its pre-1880

View of the switchboard in the Mountain States Telephone and Telegraph Company in Pueblo, Colorado, 1897. Courtesy, Colorado Historical Society.

competitors rushed to claim territory. For example, between the third week of February and the third week of April 1878, first exchanges opened in California, New York, Delaware, and Massachusetts. The growth was so sudden that the U.S. Census Bureau confessed in 1880 that neither it "nor any statistical agency can deal in a wholly satisfactory manner with anything which is subject to rapid and violent changes" (Fischer, 87).

As the popularity of the telephone skyrocketed, the magical device began affecting everyday life in the city and in the country. At first, only a few people in each town had telephone access—the town doctor and maybe the local druggist. Of course, what good is a telephone to the doctor if other people in town, his patients, didn't have telephones? Thus, telephone access had a snowball effect, as those without desired to contact those with the new device.

In addition to medical and emergency personnel, a few businesses and some of a town's wealthier residents installed telephone service. The appearance and subsequent growth of telephone service in towns across America followed a familiar pattern:

The first few telephones in many nineteenth-century towns appeared at the railroad station, the druggist, a major landowner's home, or the sawmill, and were connected by copper wire to a switchboard in a larger town. When the regional Bell company decided that the town's growth justified a local exchange, it franchised a native businessman or, in a later era, posted a salaried agent to solicit subscribers and build the switching station. Residents often viewed such agents suspiciously, as representatives of a foreign "trust." After the expiration of the Bell monopoly in 1893, hundreds of local entrepreneurs tried to set up their own independent exchanges. Whether Bell or independent, a telephone enterprise required 15 to 25 subscribers to survive. Many towns lacked telephone service altogether, or had only a few telephones at the end of a toll line to a neighboring town. (Fischer, 123)

The sequence of events leading to permanent telephone service for American cities and towns is exemplified by the experiences of one California town:

In 1879 a Western Union subsidiary helped place the first telephone line in San Rafael, running between Thompson's Drug Store and doctors' offices. A longdistance line also ran from the construction site of Mt. Tamalpais Cemetery via underwater cable across the Golden Gate to San Francisco. In 1882 Iverson's Wood and Coal Yard advertised its telephone line to Gieske's Grocery, inviting customers to phone in their coal orders when shopping at Gieske's. Western Union built the first local switchboard in 1884, with about 30 subscribers wired to it. Other interests purchased the exchange from Western Union in 1885 and then sold it to Bell's Sunset Company five years later for $900. Sunset's first manager, H. B. Armstrong, was also the local Wells Fargo agent, and his daughter was the switchboard operator. E. E. Bogle, who later became a successful local businessman, took over the exchange management in 1894 and held it for 14 years. His tasks included setting up poles, stringing wire, billing, and being the relief operator. (Fischer, 134–135)

By the last decade of the nineteenth century, telephone companies found limited success "selling" their services to businesses, yet little progress in convincing individuals to subscribe in their homes:

Bell found some businessmen hesitant to replace the telegraph with the telephone because they valued a written record. Nevertheless, some manufacturers, lawyers, bankers, and the like—and later small shopkeepers—adopted the technology. In 1891 the New York and New Jersey Telephone Company served 937 physicians and hospitals, 401 drug stores, 363 liquor stores, 315 livery stables, 162 metalworking plants, 146 lawyers, 126 contractors, 100 printing shops—7322 commercial customers all told—but only 1442 residences. Residences with telephones were typically those of doctors or of business owners or managers. (Fischer, 41)

New York and New Jersey were not alone in sustaining growth in telephone usage. By 1893, there was approximately one telephone for every 250 people in the United States, a more than fourfold increase since 1880, although about two-thirds of those phones remained in businesses (Fischer, 40). Although telephone use grew steadily in the nineteenth century—especially in larger towns and cities—by 1900 only 3 percent of American households contained a telephone (Fischer, 144).

Rates for early telephone subscribers were very high. Bell's telephone affiliates "took every advantage of their monopoly to levy what the market could bear" (Fischer, 39). However, with improved technology and increased competition from other countries, subscription rates began to drop by the end of the century. As with most new technologies, there was a period of uncertainty in which the telephone companies experimented with their service and how to profit from it:

The common practice during this era and beyond was to charge customers a flat-rate for the telephone service, allowing unlimited calls. During the 1880s local Bell companies repeatedly debated and experimented with a message-rate formula, charging by the call. One argument in favor of this approach was that it would permit the basic rental fee to be lowered and thereby encourage small users, such as families, to subscribe. Edward J. Hall was a leading proponent, labeled by some the "father of the message-rate system." Another reason for a pricing change ... was that ending flat-rate service would discourage use, and thus "cut off all the superfluous business that tends to make the operation of the business so unremunerative." Existing customers, however, resisted the change by complaining, by petitioning the town officials who issued permits for telephone poles, or, as in Rochester, by boycotting the telephone service. Not until after the era of monopoly did message-rate service become common, although still not universal, in Bell's largest exchanges. (Fischer, 39)

Other factors affected the direction in which telephone service grew:

Public phones also spurred telephone use. Many were free to the users. Stores, particularly pharmacies that adopted telephones early to accommodate physicians, offered customers free use of their (flat-rate) telephones as a public service and a commercial inducement. Eventually, many druggists tired of the crowding around their telephones, and the telephone companies tired of nonsubscribers clogging their lines. By the turn of the century nickel-in-the-slot public telephones were common throughout major urban areas. (Fischer, 50)

At the same time that telephone companies were struggling with pricing schemes, telephone subscribers were trying to decide exactly what to do with the new device. Was the telephone a tool for emergency use only, was it a toy for the wealthy, or was it a serious business tool? Episodes across America bear witness to the unusual interpretations of the applications of the telephone. For instance, in 1893 citizens of Antioch, California, gathered together at the Methodist Episcopal Church and heard what a local journalist called "the most unique and novel entertainment ever given in Antioch": Nine musical numbers performed three blocks away and brought to them by telephone wire (Fischer, 122).

In the city, the telephone changed the way business was done. The telephone eliminated the need for face-to-face contact on all business transactions, helping to clear the streets of armies of messengers. Financial information could be had immediately, and not only by a select few

New Yorkers on hand at the financial markets. Bankers, financers, and speculators in Boston, Chicago, or anywhere else with telephone access could stay abreast with financial news. The telephone also proved to be a convenience for which most city dwellers wished.

As more subscribers had telephones installed, the need for more telephone employees rose. At first, telephone companies used primarily young men as operators of their new switchboards. Later, they found that young women were better suited (and more easily controlled) than the young men for switchboard operators. The telephone company became one of the first major industries to create employment specifically for women.

The telephone also changed the very landscape of the city. The tangle of wires strung from poles and rooftops quickly became a blight on the urban landscape. The telegraph companies, the telephone companies, the electric companies, and a vast array of public and private enterprises contributed to the mess. Several factors contributed to a virtual flood of overhead telephone wires: competing telephone companies, a lack of central switchboards, and the explosive growth of telephone usage all led to a canopy of wires strung across a jungle of telephone poles. Not only did this situation create an eyesore, regular maintenance of lines and the extra maintenance required after storms began taking a toll on telephone company profits. The vast array of electric wires also created static interference with the adjacent telephone lines, possibly slowing the spread of the telephone in the 1880s (Fischer, 38). In 1888 the New York City Board of Electrical Control reported that "the avenues and streets showed a forest of tall poles, many of them carrying several hundred wires"; furthermore, "as these poles necessarily differ in height the wires upon them form a complete network, rendering the efficient use of the hooks and ladders and life saving apparatus of the fire department almost impossible" (cited in Nye 1990, 47–48). Even in the 1890s, when New York passed laws requiring such wires to be buried, the various utility companies ignored the law. New York's mayor finally ordered the poles to be chopped down, wires and all, as "citizens stood at a prudent distance and applauded" (Nye 1990, 48). New advances in protecting buried lines finally allowed New York and other major cities to clean up the mess caused by overhead telephone lines.

Near the end of the nineteenth century, the telephone began making its appearance in rural America. Methods for delivering telephone service to rural subscribers, however, were different than those experienced by urban telephone users. In order to receive telephone service, rural residents usually formed cooperatives:

Typically, a leading farmer or a small-town merchant or doctor solicited members for a farm line or a telephone cooperative. Investing $15 to $50 and often labor and materials, 2 or 3 dozen families became shareholders. Annual rental fees for the telephone ran from $3 to $18 a year. If the system had a switchboard—and some did not, operating as one big party line—a farm wife or daughter served as a daytime operator. Typically, there was no night service. Some systems connected to larger companies' switchboards in towns, enabling contact with the wider world. Most of these operations remained small, had little cash, used inferior equipment, postponed needed maintenance, and suffered from poor sound and occasional breakdowns. In some places, rural lines were literally barbed-wire affairs, running their currents over farmers' metallic fences. Managers often underestimated costs, failed to depreciate materials, and relied on subscribers to maintain their own equipment. One elderly Indiana woman recalled, "When I was young, the farmers through here organized their own telephone company.... Then that disbanded, and for a long time we didn't have a telephone. Then Mr. Schonfeld in Butlerville, who had the exchange, came out through the country and asked if we would like to have a telephone line. So he put up a line, but as he became older and wasn't able to take care of it, the line went into disuse again." Eventually, many of these companies failed, consolidated, or joined a larger system. (Fischer, 94–95)

If the telephone had an enormous impact on city life, its effect on rural life was equal, if not greater. Connecting widely separated farmhouses had real and psychological affects on the occupants. The telephone allowed rural citizens to contact emergency personnel in the event of sickness, fire, or other disasters. Less obviously, the telephone connected people socially in a way that farmers had never known. The telephone became so important in rural areas that several families would take it upon themselves to build a homemade telephone system where the telephone companies had not yet ventured. These rural telephone cooperatives popularized the use of the "party" line, a single line over which several telephones were connected.

When the telephone first appeared in a rural area, people there, much like the people who used the first telephones in the city, were not sure what to make of the mysterious device. Reaction ranged from surprise to fear. The first time using a telephone, many users were so self-conscious about talking into a machine that many simply giggled uncontrollably. People yelled into the device—the farther the call the louder they yelled. There was even fear that one might catch a contagious disease by talking with someone over the telephone who was sick. Telephone subscribers would use the telephone to check the time, eavesdrop on party lines, or engage in an activity that continues today to be of prime importance for a telephone—gossip.

The telephone caused a whole new set of social issues to arise. Life was irrevocably changed when a telephone was installed, with its appearance leading to a "habit of tenseness and alertness, of demanding and expecting immediate results, whether in business, love, or other forms of social intercourse" (Brooks, 118). Even the etiquette of telephone usage had to be worked out. How should a telephone be answered? (Bell himself had an aversion to "Hello," preferring to answer "Hoy!") For what purposes should it be used? What are the appropriate uses of a party line? Other forms of communication began to change as the telephone became more common. For instance, people today lament the demise of the art of letter writing, a direct consequence of the telephone.

Another issue was the debate over government regulation of the telephone industry. Two components of this debate proved especially divisive. First, until Bell's original patents expired in the 1890s, telephone service was relatively expensive and therefore a luxury many Americans could not afford. Second, with the proliferation of competing companies and Bell's refusal to connect his systems with any other, the possession of a telephone did not guarantee access to other telephone users whose service was handled by a competitor. These issues were eventually addressed, and the telephone, by the middle of the next century, became one of the most ubiquitous elements of most American households.

The telephone affected everyday life in America in ways that other technological advances did not. Faster modes of travel, such as steamboats and trains, resulted in faster communication, but these were not instantaneous. The telegraph did provide instant communication; yet, the telephone had many distinct advantages other than the obvious one that it transmitted voices. The telephone was cheaper than telegraphs (eventually), and it required no special training (anyone could talk); therefore, it could be placed in every home. The telephone truly changed everyday life in the American home.

SEEING (AND HEARING) IS BELIEVING

Sight has always played a central role in human communications. To see an event it was necessary that a person be in the general proximity at the time it happened. The development of photography in the nineteenth century changed this, so that even someone across a continent might experience events, places, and people that they had never, and would never, come into direct contact.

Photography arose in the 1830s with the work of Frenchman Louis Daguerre. To produce this forerunner to the modern photograph— a daguerreotype—"a silver-coated copper plate [was] exposed to iodine vapors just prior to exposure to light though a camera. Once exposed, the plate was treated with mercury vapors to develop the latent image and then fixed in a bath of sodium thiosulfate" (Wajda, 496). Daguerre's method was an immediate success, although the bulky equipment and chemicals—not to mention the fact that, unlike modern photographs, the daguerreotype produced a positive image that could not be reproduced—limited who could participate and where. Soon, American inventors and entrepreneurs took up the new art of producing (and improving) daguerreotypes. Having one's portrait produced by the magical new device became quite a fad all over the country. At mid-century, most major U.S. cities had daguerreotype studios (more than 100 in New York City alone) and the profession supported several thousand daguerreotypists in America (Marcus and Segal, 92). In fact, by 1850 "a photographer was available for hire in almost every county of every state, as well as in the territories" (Stauffer, 530). Americans such as John Draper and Alexander Wolcott made important improvements to the process, reducing exposure time so that sittings for portraits became less time-consuming.

Why did the daguerreotype become such a fad in America through the middle part of the nineteenth century? First and foremost, the rising middle class was interested in obtaining portraits of themselves, as well as their families, but could not afford the sitting fees charged by most portrait painters. Beyond this, however, middle- and upper-class Americans were interested in more than just obtaining a nice picture; sitting for portraits was an idealized process that sought to capture an "appearance [that] seemed an outward manifestation of character; it revealed the inner self" (Marcus and Segal, 93). By comparing portraits from different periods of their life, the subject might actually track the development of their character and compare that development to that of "the distinctly American archetype" (Marcus and Segal, 93). With improvements to the photographic process, along with other innovations such as stereography—a process by which two lenses were used to produce a three-dimensional image—photography became an increasingly familiar part of life for many Americans in the nineteenth century.

A new boom in the growth of photography took place with the discovery of a new process in which multiple prints could be made from a negative. Using this new process, photographers could satisfy "American consumers' desires for multiple prints—not only of themselves but also of celebrities and of the politicians, generals, and statesmen whose newsworthiness warranted a trip to the photographer" (Wajda, 497). The *cartes de visite* (visiting card) was a forerunner to the modern snapshot. Its popularity was evidenced by the appearance of photo albums containing this type of photograph in many middle-class homes, and by the popularity of photographic cards containing the image of famous people; one such photograph of Abraham Lincoln, taken by the famous Civil War chronicler Matthew Brady, sold more than 100,000 copies (Stauffer, 530). The appearance of a photographic system that allowed multiple prints set the stage for the last nineteenth-century innovation in photography—one that would ultimately lead to the "democratization" of the art.

The invention of the dry plate method greatly reduced the need for specialized chemicals, and also reduced the time required to develop a picture; yet, the process remained a time-consuming and difficult task better left to professional photographers. The American inventor George Eastman, who patented a dry plate method of his own and began building a company based on this method, was the first to envision photography as an activity for the common person. After years of experimentation, Eastman invented the first rolled film, a process that allowed him to build small, handheld cameras intended for general public use. In 1888, Eastman began a company to market his new invention, and Kodak (a name Eastman made up for no particular reason) was born.

Eastman offered the first Kodak camera preloaded with the new rolled film. After completing exposure of the role, the consumer returned the entire camera to company headquarters, where Kodak technicians developed the film. The company reloaded the camera and returned it to the customer along with the photographic prints. "You Press the Button, We do the Rest" became the company's advertising slogan. Eastman and Kodak continued to improve the camera while reducing its costs, until by 1900 any would-be photographer could purchase a Kodak for only one dollar. By ignoring the concerns of professional photographers and focusing instead on the average person, Eastman "had democratized image-making for the world" (Jenkins 1982, 134). Photography "irrevocably changed the means by which Americans conceptualized their world. Once dependent on the spoken or written word, or on artists' conceptions rendered in paint or ink, Americans now could turn to 'writing with light' for authentic, truthful images of events, personages, and faraway scenes, seeing themselves in a photograph as if they were viewing the scene in person" (Wajda, 495).

A Kodak camera creates a sensation among children. Library of Congress.

Another technology that helped bring the visual to the masses was lithography. Around the turn of the nineteenth century, this innovative process—one that uses chemicals to affix a drawing on limestone to paper or other media—began in Europe. By the end of the first quarter of the nineteenth century, American entrepreneurs were doing a growing business in lithography. Artists found they could make drawings of a multitude of subjects, including portraits of actors and other famous people, views of disasters, sentimental scenes, landscape views, and depictions of buildings and cities (Barnhill, 224). Most importantly, the prints were inexpensive enough—only pennies each—that middle-class and even poorer Americans could own a piece of this new art form.

If viewing pictures of objects far removed from the viewer was revolutionary, hearing recordings of voices and sounds was just as shocking for the average person in the nineteenth century. The telephone carried voices across great distances in real time, but it was Thomas Edison's phonograph

Thomas Edison and his phonograph. Library of Congress.

that provided a record of voices and sounds to be heard anytime, anyplace. Edison was actually working on an improved telegraph when he stumbled upon the principles of the phonograph. His first machine utilized a stylus (needle) to make indentations on a cylinder, which, when played back with another needle, reproduced the original sounds. "Mary had a little lamb" became the first message ever recorded and played back, beginning Edison's meteoric rise to fame.

Edison founded a company to market his invention, producing phonographs to serve as office dictation machines and early forms of jukeboxes, and even to make talking dolls. Certain limitations of the cylinder phonograph, however, restricted the company's success. By the 1910s, new technology in the form of disc phonographs began to displace Edison's invention. By then, many of Edison's visions for the phonograph had come true: Dictation machines, music boxes, and recorded books were just a few of the novel technologies spawned by the phonograph. By the end of the nineteenth century, a typical American could listen to the recorded word on a home phonograph and produce a visual record of events and people using their own Kodak cameras. These innovations placed sophisticated machines in the hands of anyone interested in participating in a new technological world.

ADVANCES IN WRITING

The printing press holds a special place in the history of communications. Gutenberg's invention in the fifteenth century, as well as improvements made over subsequent centuries, made literacy a foundation of social, intellectual, and scientific advance. The most important improvement to the printing press in the nineteenth century—and perhaps since Gutenberg's invention itself—came from an American inventor, Richard M. Hoe. Hoe invented and patented the first useful rotary press in the 1840s. The Hoe rotary press greatly increased the speed and decreased the cost of printing, spawning a period of incredible growth for the American printing industry.

A few decades later another American, William A. Bullock, provided another boost to the printing industry with his invention of the web perfecting press. This press accomplished all of the printing process by using a roll of continuous-feed paper while printing on both sides at the same time, all at an incredible rate of speed. The new and improved printing presses had a particularly profound effect on everyday life in America. Resulting in an abundance of inexpensive books, magazines, newspapers, broadsides, and leaflets, the printing press played an expanding role in educating Americans in far-flung communities without access to traditional educational opportunities.

In addition to allowing Americans to keep up with the news and views from their own country, inexpensive printed materials gave citizens of this isolated country, for the first time, ready access to the culture of Europe and beyond. The explosion of the print industry and American literacy went hand-in-hand in the 1840s, as witnessed by a set of amazing statistics. From 1840 to 1850, the population of the United States increased approximately 35 percent, from 17 million to 23 million (all statistics quoted from Bode, 150). In the same decade, the value of books published in the country increased by over 107 percent—from $2,850,000 to $5,900,000—while the number of literate Americans increased almost 71 percent (6,440,000 to 11,000,000). The newspaper industry saw a similar explosion, with the number of dailies increasing from 138 to 254 and the number of weeklies from 1,266 to 2,048.

Advances in printing presses brought newspapers to the cities. The *New York Sun*, founded in 1833 by Benjamin H. Day, sold for a penny— a fraction of the cost of his competitors' papers. It printed eye-catching news stories aimed at the general public. Day used boys to hawk his papers in the streets, teaching them to shout the headlines to draw attention to the paper. He also pioneered the use of advertisers and advertising dollars to significantly increase the paper's income, so that the price could be kept down for the reading public. With the help of new printing technologies, the newspaper moved west with the settlers. By 1830, America had between 1,000 and 1,200 newspapers, three times as many as in France or England (Jamison, 421). Jamison describes the importance of the town's newspaper:

The role of the frontier and small-town press went beyond news and politics. In towns with no schools, newspapers might be the only voice of literacy. The press helped to educate the public, and the network of papers, linked by the postal exchange system, provided a mechanism for common dialogue in a nation of small and often scattered communities. (Jamison, 421)

What was the increasingly literate population reading, thanks to the printing press? Hand-in-hand with the explosion in newspapers, the American public developed an insatiable appetite for short stories. For many reasons, "the short story was a genre perfectly suited to the rising middle classes. Not only were short stories written in the language of the people; they could be read and absorbed in one sitting and then discarded" (Stauffer, 529). Entire novels were published in serial form in American newspapers and magazines. Other popular forms of literature included sermons, trial reports, and novels. The popularity of nineteenth-century American writers such as Herman Melville, Nathaniel Hawthorne, and James Fenimore Cooper can be at least partially attributed to the increasingly easy access to their works brought about by advances in the printing industry.

By the end of the century, newspapers were part of the everyday life of a majority of Americans. Not all newspaper readers, however, were necessarily interested in furthering their education or knowledge of world events; many read penny newspapers for "their lurid murder stories, half-toned photographs, and Sunday color supplements" (Kent, 25). Like the penny papers, dime magazines became popular with the reading public. Countless Americans read magazines "like *Munsey's* and *McClure's*, and the titillating *Police Gazette*, whose plump chorus girl covers and sports stories made it so popular in barbershops and saloons" (Kent, 25). The newspapers and magazines made performers famous across the country, where on "Saturday afternoons 'matinee girls,' fixated on celebrity actors and actresses such as Henry Montague and Maude Adams, filled the theatres" (Kent, 25). By 1900, inexpensive newspapers and magazines created and supported popular culture in much the same way television would in the second half of the twentieth century.

Several other inventions of the nineteenth century, although admittedly not comparable to the printing press in their influence, nonetheless contributed to the fundamental changes occurring in communication. One such device was the first commercially successful typewriter. Inventors had conceived of machines to mechanize the writing process almost since the appearance of the printing press. It was not until the 1870s, however, that such a machine was manufactured and offered to the public. One possible reason for this time lapse is simply the lack of a perceived need. Clerical labor was rather cheap and readily available and, at least until the industrial revolution, manufacturing a typewriter was not a priority ("The Virtual Typewriter Museum").

An American inventor, Christopher Sholes, is generally considered the father of the modern typewriter. Working with Samuel W. Soule and Carlos Glidden, Sholes patented his device in 1868. After Remington, the weapons manufacturer, began manufacturing the new typewriter in the 1870s, some of the public enthusiastically adopted the invention. Like most new inventions, the typewriter drew a mixed response from the public. Many stories tell of the first reactions of people who had never seen typewritten work, ranging from believing the writer had printed *very* neatly to assuming the letter was a printed circular or advertisement.

The first typewriters were rather awkward devices using a type bar system in which the keys operated individual bars associated with letters of the alphabet. The bars struck the paper from underneath, meaning the typist could not see what was being typed. Sholes' first experimental models jammed when the type bars were struck too close together. To alleviate this problem, Sholes arranged the keyboard so that letters commonly found close together in words, such as t and h, were placed far apart on the typewriter. This reduced the jamming problem and resulted in what we know today as the QWERTY keyboard.

Other improvements to the typewriter quickly increased its public appeal. The invention of the type wheel, first patented by American George Blickensderfer in 1889, provided several advantages to the type bar system. It was lighter and cheaper than the original typewriters, and its wheel was interchangeable so that different fonts or different languages could easily be used. Even Thomas Edison got in on the act. Sholes and his partners took their device to Edison's lab, where the renowned inventor made suggestions for improving the machine.

Schools for typists were founded within five years of the appearance of the first commercial typewriter, and contests to determine the "world's fastest typist" were commonplace. The schools and contests served to spread and popularize the "touch" method of typing. Soon businesses, courtrooms, newspaper offices, and writers of all sorts were using the new device. Always interested in technology, Mark Twain became the first author to submit a typewritten manuscript to a publisher.

Probably the most striking effect the typewriter had on society was its role in providing more opportunities for employment for women in business. Before the typewriter and the revolution it caused in the business office, those jobs that were traditionally reserved for women required an unskilled and uneducated worker (with a few exceptions, e.g., teaching and nursing). As the typewriter operator, or typist, found a niche in the American office, women trained to operate the new machine skillfully obtained more economic security than ever before. An early study on the history of the typewriter emphasizes the machine's influence on women in the workforce with a chapter titled "How Women Achieved Economic Emancipation Through the Writing Machine" (Vrooman). In fact, the author ascribes to the typewriter the beginnings of the feminist movement and, it seems, almost every advance made by women in the early twentieth century! Even if the typewriter's influence is exaggerated a bit, it is no exaggeration to say that the typewriter did revolutionize the place of women in the workforce. Even Sholes realized its value when he claimed, "I do feel that I have done something for the women who have always had to work so hard. This [the typewriter] will enable them more easily to earn a living" (cited in Vrooman, 142). Thanks in part to the typewriter and other office technologies, office clerical staff became one of the fastest growing occupational groups by the end of the nineteenth century, with 708,000 employees across the country in 1900 (Kent, 51).

The typewriter was by no means the only advance in writing technology that had profound effects on everyday life in nineteenth-century America. The first practical fountain pen changed the way Americans wrote in their homes almost as much as the typewriter changed the way they wrote in their offices. Inventions such as the linotype machine, the electric printing press, the rotary printing press, and the typeset machine revolutionized the print industry, making newspapers (and, to a lesser extent, magazines and books) inexpensive and readily available to the typical citizen. All of these technological wonders contributed to changes in the lives of businesspeople and farmers, city dwellers and rural residents, educated and uneducated, touching every facet of life in America.

By the end of the nineteenth century, advanced communications had made life in the United States very different than it had been at the beginning of the century:

New communications and media technologies gave national events a more instantaneous dimension. The advent of local and regional telephone systems joined midwestern farms and western ranches to the rest of the country and diminished the cruelty of rural isolation. In one of the innumerable small towns sprinkled across the hinterland, a speech by William Jennings Bryan or President McKinley evoked barbershop talk the following day. Locals lounging in town squares in upstate New York, or on Georgia courthouse porches, far from the ballparks where Ned Hanlon's National League champion Brooklyn Superbas, or the fire-eating John McGraw's Baltimore Orioles were playing, could get a play-by-play from the local newspaper ticker. Championship prize fights between the massively built ex-boilermaker Jim Jeffries and the stylish master boxer James Corbett evoked intense excitement and huge betting around the country. (Kent, 25)

Without the telegraph, newspapers, and telephones, political speeches and sporting events would have been old news, or not news at all, by the time the information reached most parts of the country.

Advances in communication would continue through the twentieth century, but none so revolutionary as those made in the nineteenth century. The nineteenth century saw the first mechanically recorded audio and visual images and the first instantaneous communication over vast distances. In this century of progress the speed of communication changed from that of a fast horse to that of a telephone or telegraph line, a revolution in communication indeed.

4

Out on the Farm

Like transportation and communication, agricultural practices around 1800 were not very different than the traditional practices many centuries old. Draft animals such as horses, mules, and oxen provided most of the power for farm work that humans could not provide themselves. Science and technology dramatically changed agricultural practices in nineteenth-century America. In 1800, 80 percent of all Americans were farmers (Pursell 1995, 109). By 1880, this number had dropped to just over 40 percent. (Pursell 1995, 114). Much of the reason for this decrease can be attributed to increased efficiency in agricultural practices. This increased efficiency can in turn be attributed to two things: an exponential rise in the use of machines and advanced tools on the farm and an ever-increasing application of scientific knowledge to farming practices.

Much of the impetus for automating agriculture came from certain emotions arising throughout the country in the nineteenth century. An increased sense of nationalism and the subsequent awakening of a spirit of enthusiasm for progress through technology and science influenced American thought. In the excitement for technological innovation, "agriculture played a particularly significant role ... for the individual landowning farmer had come to assume a pivotal role in the accepted structure of America's virtue-embodying social order" (Rosenberg 1997, 137). In other words, as the urbanization of America proceeded, the traditional view of agricultural as the backbone of the American Republic, so eloquently defended since Thomas Jefferson, continued to hold a special place in the American social milieu.

At the same time, farmers, like their urban counterparts, wanted improved lives, socially and economically. Later in the century, with the nightmare of the Civil War not long past, "agricultural newspapers and societies issued a recurring stream of complaints about farmers' isolation, the drudgery of farm work, and farmers' lack of financial awards and social standing" (Marcus and Segal, 187). The arrival of railroads, telegraphs, and telephones played a part in alleviating the feelings of isolation, and technology was already beginning to ease some of the burdens experienced by the farmer.

Statistics reveal the shifting demographics of the United States. Between 1820 and 1870, the rural population increased 2.9 times while the urban population increased 14.5 times (Pursell 1982, 72). In addition, from 1820 to 1900 the percentage of the American labor force involved in agriculture dropped from 72 percent to 38 percent (Ess, 36). Did mechanization and the subsequent rise in agricultural productivity lead to increased urbanization? Or did the population shift away from the farm drive the need to grow more food for people who, only a few generations before, had grown their own? Although the cause and effect is debatable, there is certainly no doubt that the population shift and the resulting farm labor shortage evolved hand in hand with the increased dependence on technology and scientific methods in agriculture.

The nineteenth century ushered in an era of inventiveness in agriculture unlike any other in history. From the cotton gin, actually invented just before the turn of the century; to the reaper, invented around mid-century; to the combustion engine tractor, which appeared near the end of the century, machines went from playing essentially no role in agriculture to being indispensable tools for the modern farm. In the process, the typical farm in America, and therefore the typical farmer, began a gradual evolution from the family sustenance farm to the large-scale operations associated with farming in the twentieth century.

THE SIMPLEST TOOL OF ALL

In a century that witnessed the invention of incredibly powerful and complicated machinery, an American improvement to an ancient implement led the way to settlement of virgin lands. Americans transformed the short, straight axe brought from Europe into a model with a long, curved handle made of hardwood, usually hickory. The new axe allowed settlers to clear forested land at a much faster pace. These new axes, originally handmade by blacksmiths, were soon manufactured in factories. The factories used machines that cut, heated, and tempered the blade, producing high-quality axes at low costs.

As Americans moved west from coastal areas, the first order of business wherever they settled was to clear land for farming. For this reason, the new and improved axe played a central role in the settlement of America.

As one chronicler of Western settlement queries, "I ask you to look at this splendid tool, the American axe, not more an implement of labor than an instrument of civilization. If you cannot use it, you are not American. If you do not understand it, you do not understand America" (cited in Nye 2003, 44). The axe led the way for farming, and thus for settlement. As historian David Nye so eloquently and succinctly describes:

A settler enters the vast primeval woods. Using a new technology, the American axe, he transforms the forest into field and meadow, allowing it to be farmed for the first time. Initial settlement draws others to the area. As the population increases, a community emerges. As the land is "improved," its value rises. The region prospers. (Nye 2003, 43)

Clearing the land for agriculture was not the only use for the handy tool. Log cabins—the traditional home of settlers, farmers, and woodsmen— were fashioned with the aid of an axe. In addition, the American axe hewed most of the furniture and other meager belongings inside the cabin.

The log cabin became a symbol of the American frontier; it was used symbolically to great political benefit by politicians from Andrew Jackson to Abraham Lincoln. A vivid description of a typical early nineteenth-century cabin, inhabited by a hunter and his family, comes from an English immigrant named Morris Birbeck:

The cabin, which may serve as a specimen of these rudiments of houses, was formed of round logs, with apertures of three of four inches between; no chimney, but large intervals before the "clapboards," for the escape of the smoke. The roof was, however, a more effectual covering than we have generally experienced, as it protected us very tolerably from a drenching night. Two bedsteads of unhewn logs, and cleft boards laid across;—two chairs, one of them without a bottom, and a low stool, were all the furniture required by this numerous family. A string of buffalo hide stretched across the hovel, was a wardrobe for their rags; and their utensils, consisting of a large iron pot, some baskets, the effective rifle and two that were superannuated, stood about in corners, and the fiddle, which was only silent when we were asleep, hung by them. (Nye 2003, 55).

This description of circumstances surrounding the lives of a frontier family in 1817 sheds light on just how little science and technology influenced everyday life at the beginning of the century. The entire cabin—from the walls to the roof (the floor probably being dirt)—could be attributed to the hunter's axe, as were the sparse furnishings. The iron pot was most likely fashioned by a local blacksmith, just as the baskets were probably made by local weavers, possibly even the settler's wife. The fiddle, the center of attention during nonworking hours, was almost certainly handmade. The only hints of technology in the cabin were the rifles, only one of which appeared to be in working order. The other two possibly awaited a time when a skilled gunsmith could fix them or make new parts to replace those that did not work. It would yet be many decades before Whitney, Colt, and others made it possible for a hunter to acquire interchangeable parts to repair a weapon.

THE COTTON GIN

The name Eli Whitney is familiar to almost all Americans. Renowned as the inventor of the cotton gin, Whitney's name is synonymous with the idea of American ingenuity. Interestingly, Whitney made his original fortune, not to mention achieved his original fame, as a pioneer in the mass production of firearms. Whitney championed the idea of interchangeability of parts and, in the process, became known for developing the American System of manufacturing. Although he had only partial success in creating muskets with truly interchangeable parts for the U.S. government, Whitney's plans, in his own words, to build tools "similar to an engraving on a copper plate from which may be taken a great number of impressions perceptibly alike" (Smith, 47) formed the basis for mass production techniques. Requirements for mass production in the arms industry spawned whole new industries to design and build tools and machines required for the production of weapons.

Eli Whitney did not create the first machine for removing seeds from cotton to prepare it for further processing. Long before the nineteenth century, a machine called a charka was used to separate the seeds from the long-staple cotton grown primarily in India. Unfortunately, this machine did not work on the short-staple cotton grown in the United States, making cotton an unprofitable crop in America. Meanwhile, Whitney and others realized the market for cotton was increasing with the growth of the textile industry in Britain. If only Southern cotton farmers could overcome the bottleneck caused by hand cleaning of cotton, they could capitalize on the burgeoning market. Whitney's machine, designed to work on the American type of cotton, produced a revolution in farming practices, especially in the South.

The first cotton gins were powered by a hand crank and could, in Whitney's own words, do the work of 10 men. Soon, bigger and more efficient gins powered by horses or water appeared. These machines replaced the work of 50 men! The southern United States soon became the world's major producer and exporter of cotton. American cotton exports grew from less than 10 million pounds in 1800 to more than 2 billion pounds in 1850 (Solbrig and Solbrig, 192)—an astounding increase of almost 20,000 percent. At the same time, land prices in the South rose as the profitability of growing cotton increased. "What would be the comparative value of the soil of our Southern and Southwestern States," asked Daniel Webster in 1836, "if the spinning of cotton by machinery, the power loom, and the cotton gin, were struck out of existence?" (cited in Nye 2003, 36). Perhaps no machine ever influenced a particular product, or geographic region, as much as the cotton gin influenced cotton and the American South.

THE FIRST COTTON-GIN.—Drawn by William L. Sheppard.—[See Page 814.]

The first cotton gin, an illustration by William L. Sheppard appearing in *Harper's Weekly* in 1869. Library of Congress.

Along with changes in farming practices, the cotton gin brought significant social changes. In his classic work *Yankee Science in the Making*, Dirk Struik points out that "rarely, if ever, was such a social revolution promoted by so simple a machine" (Struik, 183). The cotton gin and the resulting explosion of cotton production in the southern United States resulted in several negative social and agricultural phenomena. First, whereas ginning had previously presented the bottleneck to cotton production, picking the cotton became the new bottleneck. The need for labor boosted the practice of slavery in the South and led to larger plantations where cotton could be grown very profitably.

Second, cotton is a notoriously soil-depleting crop. With land rather plentiful and easy to come by and cotton production proving to be a lucrative business, Southern farmers tended to grow cotton in the same fields year after year until those fields were spent; then the cotton grower moved on to virgin lands. This type of farming practice contributed to the slow erosion and degradation of the fertile farmland of the South.

Finally, some historians place blame squarely on the shoulders of the cotton gin for the South's traditional agrarian lifestyle and its subsequent resistance to industrialization. Although this is certainly an oversimplified picture of the antebellum South, Whitney's invention did make possible the large cotton plantations that came to define the cotton-growing states.

Although the agrarian lifestyle dominated the southern United States in the nineteenth century, Southern farmers and growers were generally open to advanced farming practices. Contrary to the popular image of the South, plantation owners were among the first Americans to embrace new agricultural technologies:

When water, wind, and mule power proved inadequate, these men imported 16-horsepower Fawcett engines from Liverpool which cost $7,000 each. Bolted down to solid foundations and belted to line shafts, these engines furnished the power to drive the various plantation machines. Overseers and negro slaves both operated the engines. Thus the notion that all southern planters sat on the shaded porches of white mansions, reading Sir Walter Scott and drinking mint juleps, while all the slaves, in the image of *Uncle Tom's Cabin*, bent under the lash in the cotton fields needs revision. Planters made use of slave labor, it is true, but it should be remembered that they were also among the most mechanically and scientifically minded people in the nation. Eager to learn more about machinery, they introduced power farming to America, a move destined eventually to remove the backbreaking work for laborers in both North and South. (Wik, 92)

While the cotton gin was the most important farm machine to the plantation owners, other technologies emerged in other parts of the country—technologies that would prove just as critical to farming as the cotton gin was to growing cotton.

PLANTING, CULTIVATING, AND HARVESTING THE CROPS

The plow is nearly as old as farming itself. For centuries, farmers used plows made primarily of wood. With the appearance of iron plows, stronger, longer-lasting devices were available to farmers. In 1814, Jethro Wood patented a cast iron–tipped plow with interchangeable parts that proved very popular amongst American farmers. When one part broke, there was no need to replace the entire plow (Hurt, 101). Interchangeable parts, an innovation usually attributed to firearms manufacturers, actually began with Wood's plows. It was steel, however, that was destined to create a revolution in plow technology. Plows composed partially of steel, primarily in the share tip, were first built and sold in the United States in the early nineteenth century.

Although cast-iron plows were very successful in many areas of the United States, as the century wore on, one shortcoming continually came to light: The thick soil of the Western prairie habitually stuck to the moldboards, causing delays as the plower stopped to clean off the prairie soil. In response to this problem, in 1837 an Illinois blacksmith named John Deere built a wrought iron plow with a steel share. The story of Deere's invention, as told by historian Douglas Hurt, made the Deere name synonymous with American agriculture:

Sometime in 1837 Deere had an idea that would change farming in the Midwest and permanently etch his name in American agricultural history. In the sawmill of Leonard Andrus where he had gone to repair a pitman rod, he noticed a broken steel mill saw. Deere took the saw blade back to his blacksmith shop and cut off the teeth with a sledge hammer and chisel. Next, he cut a diamond-shaped moldboard from a piece of wrought iron that he then heated and bent over an anvil until it took the desired trapezoidal shape. To this moldboard Deere attached a steel share that he had cut from the saw blade. Last, he gave the moldboard a high polish. Deere's moldboard cut easily through prairie sod and allowed the soil to peel away without dulling the share or clogging the moldboard. His new plow was lighter than the prairie breakers, and it required only about half the draft for cast-iron plows. (Hurt, 137–38)

Unfortunately, Deere's first plows were prohibitively expensive. After years of perfecting his design and the process for manufacturing steel shares, sales began to increase, and Deere's new plow became the implement of choice among farmers throughout the country. By 1858, Deere's Moline, Illinois, factory was producing more than 13,000 steel plows per year (Ess, 33). The Deere plow, possibly more than any other machine or technological advance, made farming the endless prairie lands a practical venture.

"Plowing on the Prairies beyond the Mississippi," an illustration by Theodore Russell Davis appearing in *Harper's Weekly* in 1868. Denver Public Library, Western History Collection, Call No.: Z-3545.

American farmers and observers of American farming techniques were very proud of the advanced agricultural practices found in the United States. An essay titled "Plow Sentiment" appeared in 1885 extolling the virtues of American farm implements. The poetic lines began with a tribute to the advanced plows:

The young farmer, if possessed of any spirit, as he guides a well set, keen cutting American plow through the ground behind a spanking team, his well made implement answering promptly to his touch, shaving the roots, and covering all with the rushing furrow as it ripples from the polished mould-board, feels an exhilarating interest in his work, akin to that of the sailor who plows the waves with a light, trim vessel under a spanking breeze. (cited in Ardrey, 18)

When comparing American farming to that of foreign countries, the author is struck by "the marked superiority of American farmers," a superiority that "was largely due to the finish and capacity of the agricultural implements in this country." The author continues to proudly claim the superiority of American agriculture:

American inventors and manufacturers have done much by providing such superior tools, to educate and elevate our operating classes.... We labor with zest and a masterful spirit because our tools are in accord and give us perfect command over the work at hand. What a contrast between our plows and the thing so called in Russia, for instance, and what a contrast also between the respective operators. Like plow, like man.... It does seem as if the general diffusion of intelligence throughout the world, by paper, steam and electricity, would ere long awaken the foreign tiller of the soil, and penetrate even his stolid soul with an ambition for better things than what have come down to him scarcely improved for a thousand years and he ought to begin the new life with an American plow. (cited in Ardrey, 18–19)

The plow, such an overlooked and seemingly simple implement, was actually a great source of national pride. But preparing the ground for planting was only part of the process. Tools and machines for bringing in the harvest played a central role in the mechanization and resulting growth of American agriculture.

Grain harvesting during the first half of the nineteenth century was performed in much the same way as it had been for centuries—by hand. Although improved hand tools made the job marginally faster, reaping continued to be an arduous, time-consuming job. When an entire crop, ready for harvesting, might be wiped out due to inclement weather at any moment, time was of the essence. Harvesting by hand required the use of a scythe, or similar cutting instrument. An improved sort of scythe, the cradle, "was equipped with an arrangement of long tines or fingers to catch the grain as it was cut and enable the reaper deftly to lay it to one side in an even windrow ... it took a mighty biceps and an unbreakable back to make a good cradleman" (Langdon, 305). At best, a man with a cradle could cut four to six acres per day (Langdon, 306). On a small New England farm, four to six acres per day might have been sufficient; however, on the increasingly larger farms of the West, this harvest rate was a severe limitation to the number of acres of grain a farmer could realistically plant.

Simply cutting the grain was only the start of the process. Someone then had to follow behind the harvester to bind the grain into sheaves, another laborious task. The sheaves were piled together into shocks, a task that "required speed and skill so that the sheaves would stand upright and stay in place and protect the grain from the rain" (Langdon, 309). After the harvest was complete and the sheaves of grain had been stored in the barn, the threshing process began:

> To get the grain out of the heads and free from the husks or chaff the operation was the threshing. In the earlier days of the hand-tool period this was done on the barn floor with a flail. The sheaves were unbound and the gavel or unbounded sheaves were laid evenly on the floor in two rows with the heads overlapping. Then two men beat the grain heads with flails in alternate rhythmic blows.... When thoroughly threshed, the grain and chaff were scooped up into the large shallow winnowing basket or tray and tossed into the air so that the breeze would blow the chaff away while the grain would fall back into the basket or tray. (Langdon, 310–11)

From plowing to sowing to cultivating to reaping to threshing and winnowing, a wheat crop required an incredible amount of manual labor. Little wonder farms at the turn of the nineteenth century tended to be small.

The appearance of mechanical reapers in the United States dates to the early years of the nineteenth century. These reapers, however, were commercial failures, and American farmers continued to depend on the scythe or the sickle for harvesting grain. Change was imminent when Cyrus McCormick patented a much-improved device in 1834 that eventually became the most popular reaper on American farms. Even then, it was several decades before the McCormick reaper came into wide use, and even then only in certain areas of the country. Part of the reason for the delay in adopting the reaper was due to technical flaws that McCormick worked out over a number of years. But another reason for the slow acceptance of mechanical reapers was that for the machines to become economically feasible a whole new way of farming was required. Small farms, primarily operated for sustenance, could not justify the costs of reapers or other large machinery. The farmer's labor, supplemented by seasonal hired help, remained the most efficient way to operate a small farm. It so happens, however, that as McCormick began building improved reapers, labor costs began to rise and farm size was on the increase. Economic historian Paul A. David has calculated that it required a minimum farm size of 46.5 acres in order to make the reaper economically justified (cited in Basalla, 153).

American schoolchildren know Cyrus McCormick as the inventor of the mechanical reaper. As is usually the case in history, the truth is not quite so simple, as exhibited by David Hounshell's summary of the history of the reaper:

Almost from the beginning, participants in the reaper's history as well as those who chronicled its development fought vigorously over who really invented the reaper. As with the sewing machine, men had long dreamed of and tried to devise a mechanical means to reap grain, yet the basic element of such a machine eluded would-be inventors until the early 1830s. In the United States both Obed Hussey and Cyrus Hall McCormick, one from Ohio, the other from Virginia, hit upon the idea of using a vibrating knife or blade to cut the stalks of grain. Hussey made his reaper work effectively by vibrating the blade in slots cut in guide teeth or fingers. He patented this machine in 1833 and began to sell it in 1834. McCormick claimed that he had anticipated Hussey in the essentials of the reaper, but he did not patent his machine until mid-1834. McCormick's blade lacked the effective slotted finger bars of the Hussey machine. Yet, as is often the case in the history of American invention, McCormick moved through the courts to become eventually the famed hero who invented the reaper. (Hounshell, 154)

The McCormick reaper was extremely important to large-scale farming, but the early history of the machine was also fraught with difficulties for the farmer who purchased the machine. For instance, if a McCormick reaper required a replacement part, the farmer supplied the information to the McCormick dealer, including the part and the year his reaper was manufactured. The dealer might have the part in stock, or he might have to send for the part from the factory. Either way, once the part arrived the farmer still had to fit the part to his reaper, no simple task in a time when true interchangeability of parts had yet to arrive on the scene (Hounshell, 159).

Labor considerations, both at the factory and on the farm, greatly affected the design and production of McCormick reapers. A shortage in farm hands induced McCormick to introduce a self-raking reaper in the 1860s. This reaper "eliminated the need for a laborer to rake the cut grain off the reaper's platform" (Hounshell, 165). Interestingly, the McCormick factories were having difficulties in finding laborers to build their machines. McCormick's brothers, whom Cyrus had left in charge of the company while he traveled to Europe, wrote to the company's founder concerning the labor problems: "strikes have prevailed—men go off to escape [the] D[ra]ft ... Workmen such as we most needed are independent" (cited in Hounshell, 166). The labor shortage for McCormick's factories became an ongoing problem for decades to come.

By mid-century, McCormick's company was mass producing the new machines. McCormick's first reapers, like those invented by competitors such as Obed Hussey, simply cut the grain, leaving the rest of the process—raking, threshing, and binding—to laborers walking with or riding on the machine. In time, each of these processes was automated;

In this early advertisement, children happily play in a field recently harvested by a McCormick Harvesting Machine. Item #A0275. *Emergence of Advertising in America.* Rare Book, Manuscript and Special Collections, Duke University. Reprinted with permission.

eventually a "combine," a single machine that performed each task made harvesting a faster, more efficient process. Initially, horses, mules, or oxen powered these machines. The larger ones often required great teams of animals for propulsion. By 1860, approximately 70 percent of the West's wheat harvest was handled by mechanical reapers such as McCormick's (Hurt, 144). The sales of mechanical reapers—McCormick's and his competitors—continued to rise dramatically through the century. In 1880, they sold 60,000 of the machines; by 1880, the number had increased to 250,000 (Ess, 35). It became important, perhaps even a status symbol, for a "gentleman farmer" to own a McCormick reaper.

The power sources required for agricultural machines evolved with the machines themselves. The first devices usually required man- or horsepower.

In fact, the draft animal not only remained the primary source of farm power through the end of the century, but actually *increased* in numbers. From 1850 to 1900, the number of horses and mules employed to power farm machinery increased fourfold, to 25 million animals (Ess, 32). This dramatic increase goes hand in hand with the rising use of farm machinery, the number of tillable acres, and the increasing population in the United States during the half century. Complete automation, independent of animal power, came slowly to the American farm.

As the century progressed, however, experiments with steam power led to the expectation that the drudgery of farm work might soon be completely automated. A steam plow made its appearance in the United States before the beginning of the Civil War but was not commercially viable. Commercially successful steam traction engines appeared on the market by 1876; and by 1890, almost three thousand steam traction engines, and another three thousand steam threshers, were sold (Ess, 36). By the late nineteenth century, the steam engine provided power to many large-scale American farms. Steam engines applied to threshing machines, for example, allowed one California farmer to thresh 5,779 bushels of wheat in one day in 1874 (Wik, 92).

Although valuable in certain circumstances, steam-driven farm equipment was not the long-term solution the agricultural community sought. Steam engines were extremely heavy and unwieldy, not to mention expensive and difficult for the typical farmer to maintain. A reaper or other piece of farm equipment outfitted with a steam engine was just as likely to sink into the mud under its own weight as it was to complete the harvest. The combustion engine, developed near the end of the century, eventually made the tractor (and other machinery) indispensable to twentieth-century farming.

Large machinery such as reapers and combines had a tremendous impact on American agricultural productivity. The acreage of wheat grown in the United States doubled in only a dozen years, from 1866 to 1878 (Pursell 1982, 77). This incredible growth was due primarily to the explosion of farming in the prairie states and in California, where farmers were especially reliant on new plows to turn the tough virgin soil; large machines to harvest the vast, flat, and dry wheat fields; and the railroad to transport the grain to the growing urban population centers. By 1900, approximately two-thirds of the California wheat crop was harvested by mechanical reapers (Hurt, 200). The interesting paradox is that on an individual basis, technology failed to have an impact on the majority of farmers in the nation. Limited by the small-sized farms or by topography unfriendly to large machinery, the average farmer in the United States continued to depend on age-old farming techniques using handheld implements. Although new steel plows, hoes, and the like made many of the farmers' tasks somewhat easier, the use of new machinery was essentially limited to large farms or, in some cases, to traveling entrepreneurs who transported their equipment from farm to farm helping the small-time farmer bring in his harvest—for a fee of course.

In addition to machines for the harvest, countless other technical innovations increased productivity on the farm. During the first half of the century, most of the grain in the United States was planted by hand—a slow, inefficient process in which the grain seed was distributed by hand and then covered and worked into the soil by hand. By 1850, new and improved seed drills for efficient planting helped expedite the process. These drills encouraged uniform planting practice, which in turn made harvesting by mechanical means more practical. A large horse-drawn planter could drastically cut the time and manpower required to seed a field. After the grain was sown, mechanical cultivators, also drawn by horses or mules, relieved the farmer from tedious and backbreaking weeding chores while greatly reducing the time needed for cultivation.

Technological improvements in another centuries-old farming technique played an incalculable role in the agricultural development of the prairie and Western states. Irrigation is perhaps the oldest contribution of technology to farming practices. Yet, without new and improved irrigation methods, much of the land area of the United States would be essentially useless for agriculture. Massive and expensive irrigation canals and newly designed methods—particularly windmills—for accessing underground water reserves made the prairie states, and later California, agricultural powerhouses.

The Mormons who settled in Utah around the Great Salt Lake formed one of the first successful agricultural communities in the West using canals for irrigation. By 1866, these industrious farmers had built more than 1000 miles of canals watering 150,000 acres of farmland (Nye 2003, 211). Other irrigation projects in states like Kansas, Arizona, and especially California opened up immense semi-arid lands for agriculture. California settlers built canals from the Santa Anna River and the San Joaquin River, the first steps in a process that would turn Southern California into an agricultural powerhouse. By 1889, California was second only to Colorado in the number of acres of irrigated farmland (Nye 2003, 222).

As settlers discovered subsurface water under the vast prairies, efforts to access this untapped source for irrigation intensified. Improvements in windmill technology made it possible to irrigate vast areas previously considered useless for agriculture. In 1854, an American by the name of Daniel Halladay designed a new kind of windmill suited to the extreme wind conditions found in the West. Halladay's design allowed the windmill to control its speed and to orient itself in response to varying wind directions and speeds. By the 1860s, the Halladay windmill was the standard device for those farmers who could afford the factory-made machine.

Throughout the nineteenth century, windmills varied from handmade to relatively expensive and sophisticated factory-made devices. In fact, by 1880 there were 69 factories in the United States producing ready-to-assemble kits (Nye 2003, 212). By this time, windmills made entirely of metal were available. By the end of the century, these metal windmills had replaced the wooden type as the most popular choice among Western farmers. Farmers often cooperated to build reservoirs fed by dozens, or even hundreds, of windmills.

As irrigation became common in western lands, the federal government became more involved in actively encouraging settlers to come. The Desert Land Act of 1877 gave title to 640 acres to any settler who irrigated at least 80 acres within three years and paid $1.25 per acre. Unfortunately, both of these requirements were beyond the capabilities of many settlers, so the Act did not have as much impact on settlement as Congress had hoped (Nye 2003, 211). In spite of the occasional failure of settlers (and government policies), irrigation of semi-arid prairie lands made farmers less dependent on the weather and gave the United States an extremely consistent food production infrastructure.

FOOD PRESERVATION

Preserving the products of farming and ranching was an important prerequisite for increased productivity. It didn't matter how much food a farmer could produce if it spoiled before it arrived in the consumer's hands. Several technologies arose in the nineteenth century that benefited both farmers and consumers by making food products easier to obtain and safer to eat. One of these technologies, the canning process, became an important part in the everyday life of many Americans—when they were able to get the food out of the can!

Which came first, the chicken or the egg? Or, put another way, which came first, the can or the can opener? If you said the can, you were correct by almost half a century! Tin cans became relatively common for storing and preserving food early in the nineteenth century, but opening such cans required chisels or other forceful methods. Canned foods became particularly popular with soldiers, although they had "to attack their canned rations with knives, bayonets, and even rifle fire" (Petroski 1994, 186). Various can openers appeared beginning in the 1850s, although the device used in households today did not make it into American kitchens for some time to come. One early can opener was patented by an American, Ezra Warner, in 1858. Warner's invention was an improvement, although it still required a considerable amount of force to use. Warner defended his device against detractors:

The advantages of my improvement over all other instruments for this purpose consist in the smoothness and rapidity of the cut, as well as the ease with which it is worked, as a child may use it without difficulty, or risk, and in making the curved cutter susceptible of being removed, so that if one should be injured it may be replaced by another, thus saving all the other portions of the instrument, and consequently much expense, and in that the piercer will perforate the tin without causing the liquid to fly out, as it does in all those which make the perforation by percussion of any kind. (Petroski 1994, 188)

Obviously, preserving all of the food instead of losing some by "percussion" was important. Notice also that Warner included interchangeability of parts as an important aspect of his design. The modern can opener was not invented until the twentieth century, although another American, William Lyman, did patent a model that used the familiar wheel design in 1870. In spite of the absence of a workable can opener, the canning process was fairly widespread in the nineteenth century. Although not as consistently safe as the canned foods of today—sickness caused by improperly canned food was a common occurrence—canning brought a wide variety of foods to the American table for the first time.

Another innovation to preserve food to be delivered to the consumer's table came via the railroad. With the appearance of the refrigerated railcar late in the nineteenth century, farmers could raise vegetables and other highly perishable food items as cash crops, opening the way for various sections of the country, particularly California, to become agricultural centers. Farmers found that they could transport fresh fruits and vegetables to population centers in the refrigerated cars and make a very nice profit doing so. In addition, cattle ranchers reaped the benefits of refrigerated railcars as meatpackers began taking advantage of the new technology. By the end of the 1860s, "dressed" meat (meat prepared for the market) was shipped across the United States in the refrigerated cars. Meatpackers began developing distribution systems that included cold-storage warehouses in major cities, meaning that residents of those cities would have easier (and safer) access to meat year round. In smaller towns, where the customer base did not warrant a cold-storage facility, "peddler cars" sold to small retailers or directly to the public (Saffell, 276). In this way, more and more Americans gained access to beef, pork, lamb, and other meats they had seldom been able to buy before.

With the increased popularity of dressed beef, made ready to travel in refrigerated cars to distant venues, the meatpacking plants began implementing new technologies in their production lines. New and improved refrigeration equipment, electric lighting, specialized machinery, and trolley systems to transport the carcasses within the plant were all devices designed to improve the efficiency of a meatpacking plant (Saffell, 277). In spite of the improved technology, working conditions for meatpacker employees were abysmal, to say the least. The working conditions included lack of ventilation in chill rooms and other health hazards that led to widespread pneumonia and tuberculosis among workers (Saffell, 277). These same working conditions—added to poor sanitary conditions in the plants—also led to a public outcry concerning the safety of the workers and of the meat that left the plants. Unfortunately, it was not until early in the next century that laws regulating the meatpacking industry began to make the process safer for both the worker and consumer.

TECHNOLOGY ON THE CATTLE RANCH

In the 1870s, three technologies converged on the Great Plains that had long-lasting affects on the cattle ranching industry: barbed wire, railroads, and windmills. When ranchers discovered how to use these technologies to their advantage, coupled with the ever-increasing demand for beef from the northern and eastern sections of the country, life on the plains from Texas to Montana changed forever.

When compared to such complicated machines as the cotton gin or the tractor, the simple barbed wire seems an innocuous invention. Yet this simple idea, patented in the United States as early as 1868 but popularized by Joseph Glidden's design in 1874, transformed life in the West as perhaps no other device of the nineteenth century. The western United States was a wide-open country where cowboys herded and drove cattle over miles and miles of unfenced land. One reason the land was unfenced, unlike land in the more settled areas of the country, was the scarcity of wood or other fence-building materials. Simple wire was not adequate because herds of cattle would simply push through the fence. Barbed wire was cheap, easy to install, and effectively stopped cattle from pushing through.

With the appearance of the barbed wire fence, the days of free-range grazing and long cattle drives were numbered. Replacing these practices were organized farms and ranches, fenced to keep their livestock in and others' out. Disputes arose between farmers and ranchers, as well as with settlers who were looking for land to farm, but the value of barbed wire was obvious; it was here to stay.

The use of barbed wire served several purposes. First, as settlers brought more expensive breeds of cattle in to the western plains, ranchers needed the security of barbed wire to keep their investments in and to keep other, less desirable breeds out. No rancher wanted a tough, rangy Longhorn breeding with their new Herefords or Angus cattle. Second, by cross-fencing their pastures, ranchers gained more control of their breeding of various stock. Finally, barbed wire allowed ranchers to confine their stock to pastures with access to good grass for grazing and to water.

As mentioned previously, the railroad had a tremendous impact on farming in the United States. The railroad also had a profound impact on cattle ranching. Until the last quarter of the nineteenth century, cattle were taken to markets on long, arduous cattle drives sometimes covering hundreds of miles. These drives, although excellent fodder for the romanticized depictions by twentieth century films, were hard on the cattle and the cowboys alike. Certain breeds of cattle, such as the famed Texas Longhorn, were popular for their sturdiness and ability to live, and even thrive, through the difficult journey. Unfortunately, neither the breed nor the conditions on the drive lent themselves to producing the best quality beef. Sometimes cattle ranchers in Texas, for instance, might drive their herd north to a railhead in Kansas, where they would breed their tough Longhorns with another breed known for the quality of its meat, thus attaining the best of both worlds—and making a nice profit. As the railroads reached further into the prairie, the need for these long drives disappeared; therefore, the advantages to raising Longhorns and other inferior beef-producing breeds vanished.

The last of the trilogy of technologies responsible for the rise of cattle ranching on the Western plains is the windmill. Just as many farmers had already discovered, the use of windmills to raise underground water to the surface provided cattle ranchers access to a seemingly scarce resource across vast sections of the middle of the country. Whereas direct access to rivers had previously been of utmost importance, with windmills a rancher could obtain enough water to maintain his herd anywhere the water table was high enough and the wind was strong enough; fortunately, this described large areas of the plains.

SCIENTIFIC FARMING

Technological advances were not the only factors contributing to the giant steps made in agriculture in nineteenth-century America. The realization, dawning more slowly on some than on others, that science might be profitably applied to agricultural methods, led to large gains in agriculture efficiency and output. Farming and farmers were generally held in the same high esteem established by Thomas Jefferson around the turn of the century. Jefferson held that the self- sufficient farmer formed the backbone of American democracy. His interest in advancing agricultural practices by applying modern scientific techniques laid the foundation for just such a belief throughout the whole country. To use a technological metaphor, farming "may be considered the great wheel which moves all the machinery of society" (Buel, 4). Although many Americans—especially the poor, uneducated farmer of the South and West—may not have subscribed to such philosophical views, they were pervasive enough to constitute a major force in American society.

Many of the ideas concerning the role of progress in agriculture were written, circulated, and published in farmers' almanacs, journals, and handbooks. Farming periodicals dedicated much of their space to scientific farming and the application of technology to agriculture. One of these early periodicals, the *Farmer's Register,* emphasized agricultural machinery, and another, the *Prairie Farmer,* concentrated on common school education for farmers and on farm machinery (Wik, 84). A typical example comes from Jesse Buel's *The Farmer's Companion; or, Essays on the Principles and Practice of American Husbandry,* published in 1840. Buel was a successful printer and editor who left his career to immerse himself in a quest to create a model farm outside of Albany, New York (Bode, 4). He spent the rest of his life creating his ideal farm and working as a spokesman for enlightened farming in America. Buel firmly believed that "the more it [agriculture] is enlightened by science, the more abundant will be its products" (Buel, 7). With a working knowledge of the scientific practices in agriculture, the farmer would find that:

The elements are subservient to his use; the vegetable and animal kingdoms are subject to his control! And the natural laws which govern them all, and which exert a controlling influence upon his prosperity and happiness, are constantly developing to his mind the new harmonies, new beauties, perfect order, and profound wisdom, in the works of Nature which surround him (Buel, 11–12).

Although Buel seems to wax poetic, the notion of the gentleman farmer subjugating nature with his knowledge of science had a powerful influence in America.

Of course, small farmers trying to scratch out a living for themselves and their families might scoff at Buel's notions, certain that they had neither the time nor the inclination to engage in such affairs. Buel, however, maintained that the farmer actually possessed more time to pursue scientific studies than those in other professions. Whereas those in industry or mercantilism might work day and night in their chosen professions, Buel claimed that the farmer had the night time hours to spend in study and contemplation, "to the improvement of his mind—to the acquisition of useful knowledge" (Buel, 12). In fact, Buel even listed the various studies a farmer might undertake, from the properties of soils and usefulness of different fertilizers, to methods of irrigation and crop rotation, to scientific methods in animal husbandry. All of these intellectual pursuits would lead not only to improved agricultural techniques and outputs, but a more general benefit to society as a whole; for "whatever tends to improve the intellectual condition of the farmer ... essentially contributes to the good order of society at large and to the perpetuity of our country's freedom" (Buel, 7).

Granted that the typical farmer did not adhere to, and probably was not interested in, the extremes to which Buel went in maintaining a model farm; however, the idea that agricultural practices could be improved with knowledge and applications of science found its way into the very fabric of American agriculture in the nineteenth century. Another growing branch of science—chemistry—met with a similar fate, as proponents of progressive agriculture often clashed with skeptical farmers intent on maintaining traditional farming practices.

American industries in the second half of the nineteenth century found an ever-increasing need for chemistry and trained chemists in their businesses. Chemists helped produce products as wide-ranging as fertilizers, explosives, industrial dyes, and plastics, as well as chemicals for the photographic and petroleum industries. The process of integrating chemistry into industry was slow, but inevitable, as "chemists slowly worked their way into industry, and the United States moved toward parity with the more advanced chemical industry of Germany" (Birr, 62). In the early part of the century, "trained chemists served as consultants or were hired by firms to analyze raw materials and help control processes." As American industry grew in the second half of the century, chemists "were beginning to exercise some technical independence and initiative, and by the end of the century, most chemical plants had a chemist or two and a laboratory or sorts on the premises" (Birr, 62). Without contributions from chemists and the science of chemistry, many of the products Americans came to use daily would not have been possible.

Chemistry—and science in general—played an ambiguous role in American agriculture during the nineteenth century. The American scientific community realized the importance of basic chemical research for the growth and advance of agricultural and industrial concerns. Scientists insisted that agriculture "must be made rational and scientific" (Rosenberg, 144). As the century progressed, these views were adopted by an increasing number of politicians who lent their support for the funding and organization of chemical research, and by farmers whose support was crucial to "selling" the importance of science to agriculture. During the 1850s, Congress overcame its aversion to funding agricultural research by, in rapid succession, granting "$35,000 for agricultural experimental work on a two-acre plot near Missouri Avenue in Washington, D.C."; hiring an entomologist to join the Patent Office, as well as hiring a chemist and a botanist for research positions; and arranging with the Smithsonian Institution to publish meteorological statistics (Wik, 90). Government support of scientific research aimed at improving agriculture in America became more pronounced as the century wore on.

A specific instance in which the government saw a problem affecting American farmers and acted to successfully provide a solution involved the control of tick fever in Western cattle. Theobald Smith, a pathologist for the Bureau of Animal Husbandry—established by Congress in 1884—discovered the nature of the disease, and more importantly, that it was transmitted by ticks. The Bureau instigated a long-term program to eradicate the disease, saving cattle ranchers millions of dollars in lost livestock (Wik, 97). A fortunate ancillary to Smith's success was that his was "the first demonstration that disease-producing microorganisms could be transmitted by an insect carrier ... thus paving the way for the understanding and control of such serious maladies as malaria, typhus, bubonic plague, and Rocky Mountain spotted fever" (Wik, 97). Here we find an instance in which scientific research aimed at a specific problem paid dividends in unsuspecting (and seemingly unrelated) ways.

There remained, however, a large gap between the producer of science and the consumer. The desire of the scientist to engage in basic research often conflicted with the insistence of the public to realize immediate practical results. Some science popularizers maintained that "every farm should be considered a chemical laboratory and every farmer a practical chemist and philosopher" (Rosenberg, 147). In contrast, some farmers disdained "book farming" just as artisans and others without scientific training often questioned the utility of basic science.

Around the middle of the nineteenth century, American chemistry, like many other American sciences, began to take on a decidedly German flair. Seeking graduate training in chemistry in Germany, many of these young scholars were greatly influenced by Justus von Liebig's classic work, *Organic Chemistry in its Application to Agriculture and Physiology*. By bringing advanced notions of chemistry and its applications back to their own country, agricultural chemists were at the forefront of scientific research and education in the United States. In fact, the first chair at the first scientific school (established at Yale in 1847) belonged to the field of agricultural chemistry. Thanks to its immediate and obvious applications to agriculture and industry, chemistry became one of the first sciences institutionalized in universities and government agencies. (Chapter 9 discusses some of these institutions further.)

One of the earliest contributions made by chemists to American agriculture was soil analysis. Originally believed to be a panacea for the depleted soils of eastern lands, chemists slowly began to realize that the simplistic approach of analyzing a soil sample to determine the chemicals needed for replenishment was not a magic wand. Commercial chemical fertilizers made their way into the market by mid-century. By the turn of the twentieth century, American farmers used almost 2 million tons of commercial fertilizer annually. Although chemists made advances in the area of soil analysis and fertilization throughout the century, these advances were made at a pace that did not satisfy the farmer who wanted fertile fields *this* season.

The list of scientific contributions to nineteenth-century agriculture is long. Stephen Babcock developed a simple, accurate, yet inexpensive test to determine the amount of butterfat in milk. This solved an ongoing problem of compensating dairy farmers fairly based on the butterfat content of their milk. Luther Burbank developed hundreds of strains of plants from plums to lilies to the Burbank, or Idaho, potato. Norbert Rillieux, the son of a plantation owner and a New Orleans slave, developed a much-improved process for refining sugar from sugar cane. Rillieux, who received a first-class education in France, invented a new type of evaporator that revolutionized the sugar industry by making sugar cheaper for the consumer and sugar production safer for workers involved in the process. Countless other Americans contributed their own discoveries and inventions to the ongoing quest to feed a growing population.

As this chapter indicates, scientific and technological advances had a tremendous impact on agriculture and the typical farmer in America during the nineteenth century. Farm statistics support this. In 1820, the average farm worker could raise enough food for 4.1 people; by 1900 this figure had risen to 7 people (Pursell 1995, 119). Also in 1800, to produce an acre of wheat required 56 worker-hours; by 1900 this number had fallen to 15 worker-hours (Pursell 1995, 119). Did the decreased number of worker-hours to produce an increased amount of food lead to the urbanization of America, or was it the other way around? Did increased urbanization lead to a need to increase farm production through science and technology? This is a classic chicken-and-egg dilemma that can probably never be authoritatively answered. One can conclude, however, that urbanization and agricultural production went hand in hand in nineteenth-century America.

Finally, it should be noted that the relationship between farmers and technological advances was not always friendly and fruitful. The nineteenth century witnessed the first hint of backlash against the scientific and technological changes that many Americans accepted and embraced. It is true that improved modes of transportation helped to speed along technological developments in agriculture. With canals, steamships, and railroads, farmers were able to move more of their products to market in a shorter period of time; the Erie Canal, in particular, played an important role in the development of the Midwest as a major grain-producing region. It is also true, however, that farmers and railroads often had unstable relationships. The importance of the railroads to agriculture, especially commercial agriculture, was obvious. The farmers of the prairie states certainly realized their dependency on the railroads for transporting their crops to urban markets. However, farmers often accused the railroads of unfair business practices such as price gouging. In fact, by the last third of the century, negative reactions against the railroads from all directions were commonplace. Partly in response to the railroads' unfair pricing practices, farmers in the prairie states formed the Grange, a fraternal group whose organizers envisioned it could fight the railroads and other commercial interests who were taking advantage of the farming community. Congress passed the Interstate Commerce Act in 1887 in an attempt to control the seemingly out-of-control railroad industry. The Act was an attempt, with limited success, to end price fixing and price gouging practices and to ensure equal treatment of the railroads' customers.

Dependence on the railroads was not the only negative aspect of mechanization. With commercialization came larger farms employing fewer workers and forcing the small farmer to the fringes of agriculture. The gradual swing away from sustenance farming to commercial farming also brought about a dependency on bankers and intermediaries that the small farmer had rarely experienced. The agricultural historian Douglas Hurt maintains, "Efficient production placed agriculturists at the mercy of others. Once they became commercial farmers, they were no longer masters of their destinies" (Hurt, 172). Science and technology were largely to blame for this shift in the everyday approach to farming.

The new reality in farming was that advances brought about by technology and science led to a gradual loss of autonomy for individual farmers. They became dependent on the railroad to transport their crops out and supplies in, on the banks to finance the ever-increasing amount of equipment needed on a modern farm, and unpredictable markets for their products. Nineteenth-century science and technology was certainly a two-edged sword for the American farmer.

5

It's Off to Work We Go

Industrialization had a tremendous impact on the common American in the nineteenth century. In 1800, the vast majority of Americans led a life dominated by locality. Farms were small and provided most, if not all, of the necessities of life. Artisans and craftsmen operated from small locales—most often from the home itself—and seldom participated in trade outside of their local area. Of course, all of these factors meant that the typical American lived and worked in a rural, rather than urban setting.

By 1900, the "typical" American had changed dramatically. The United States was an increasingly urban nation, and many more people worked in factories and lived in cities than lived and worked on farms. The spectacular growth of the manufacturing segment of American culture was due to many factors, with innovations in technology and science leading the way.

Industrialization did not happen all at once, nor did it spread smoothly and continuously once it had begun. Rather, small components of the workplace were automated, piece by piece, over a period of time. At the beginning of the century, "the production of consumer goods, from shoes and house wares to luxury coaches, remained located in artisan workshops" (Greenberg, 421). As the century progressed, these small, individually owned workshops faced more and more competition from factories mass-producing similar goods. Generally, the workshops either adapted or closed. The owner of the shop, or "master craftsman," was forced to expand from the traditional few journeymen under his tutelage to a larger number of workers. In order to cut costs, the location of the shop might be moved from the building in which the craftsman lived into "lower-rent manufacturing districts or wherever inexpensive space could be found" (Greenberg, 421). By the middle of the century, small-scale factories operating in less than ideal conditions replaced many of the small artisan workshops—the sweatshop was born in the United States. As a result, "in the push to increase production, keep costs low, and maintain workshop survival, craft skills that had been passed from master to journeyman and apprentice for centuries were divided and lost" (Greenberg, 422).

Acerbating the situation was an increasing reliance on immigrant labor in the workshop. With competition for jobs with Irish and Italian immigrants in the East, Chinese immigrants on the West Coast, and black laborers—including slaves hired out by their owners—in the South, white artisans and craftsmen came under more pressure to find jobs. To make matters worse, ownership did not consider laborers to be any more or less important than natural resources or machinery and equipment. In fact,

workers continued to be viewed as both necessary cogs in the industrial machine and, on occasion, as potential threats to elite power and privileges, but rarely, if ever, as partners in a great ongoing experiment. In those mining and manufacturing industries populated by foreign-born workers, Anglo-Saxon managers tended to look upon them as predestined to be toilers. Indeed, it was the rare industrialist, like one Bridgeport, Connecticut, factory owner, who would acknowledge that his employees "have had a large share in enabling me to make my money and I feel I owe them some recognition of that fact." Labor participation in decision-making was regarded as an abdication of management responsibility. (Kent, 59)

This sort of management theory sometimes ended in conflict. Workplace boycotts and even violence often resulted.

In 1810, only about 75,000 Americans worked in industry. By 1860, this number had risen to 1.3 million (Wahl, 422). Conditions in factories and sweatshops were often atrocious, but workers did make gains in the number of hours worked and increased wages through the century. In 1840, the typical factory worker worked 11 1/2 hours a day, six days per week. By the 1880s, federal legislation reduced the workday to 10 hours (Wahl, 423). Wages generally rose through the century, with a growing gap between skilled and unskilled workers as mechanization increased (Wahl, 423).

As the manufacturing industry grew in the United States, factories took on a distinctive American flavor. Traditionally located next to rivers (required as a power source), factories began to spread to the cities where they could take advantage of a ready workforce and access to transportation for importing raw materials and exporting finished products. A typical American factory was powered by steam engines, with intricate systems of belts, pulleys, and drive shafts to translate the power to the various machines located throughout the factory.

Endemic to these new kinds of factories was a new kind of worker. The nineteenth century witnessed the birth of the archetypal American factory worker: hard-working, dependable, moral, and upstanding—all traits expected from workers involved in the great democratic experiment that was the United States. Of course, with America's rejection of class systems, workers who displayed such traits were regularly promoted and given more responsibility, as well as the requisite salary and social standing that went along with it. The American dream was born.

In one sense, people powered this dream; however, in another very real sense, power came from nature and from advances in technology. Water power dominated in the early nineteenth century in the United States because so much of it was available in the East and because it was cheap. In fact, in 1803 there were only five steam engines in use in the United States (de la Pedraja, 224); by 1838, this number had grown to about 2,000 stationary steam engines (de la Pedraja, 225). Steam engines had several advantages over water power, including better reliability (sometimes streams ran swiftly, sometimes not at all), and more horsepower. "Thanks to the stationary steam engine, shops could produce more goods at lower prices than before, while riverboats carried the merchandise to markets throughout most of the country" (de la Pedraja, 225). Several American inventors contributed to the steam power revolution; two of the most important were Oliver Evans and George Corliss.

Oliver Evans is a neglected figure in American history, perhaps primarily because his ideas and inventions were ahead of his time, and it would be several decades after his death before many of them came into common use. Evans' innovations included a fully automated flour mill, including several new kinds of milling tools and machines. But Evans' most important contribution was his design for a new kind of steam engine, one operating under high pressure rather than the low-pressure steam engines then in general use. Evans envisioned many uses for his steam engine. He built steam-powered vehicles for use on land and water, and applied steam engines to various industrial purposes for mills and waterworks. The high-pressure steam engine of Evans' design became a staple in the industrial revolution yet to come in the United States.

American George H. Corliss patented an improved stationary steam engine in 1849. The Corliss engine was self-adjusting, meaning the engine could automatically increase or decrease the amount of steam going to the cylinder based on changing work requirements. Corliss and his new steam engine gained international fame when a single Corliss engine supplied power for the large array of machines on display at the Centennial Exhibition in Philadelphia in 1876. Other American inventors, most notably Charles T. Porter and John F. Allen, contributed important improvements to the steam engine. As steam engines improved, their use in various manufacturing industries increased. One of these, the textile mill, is representative of the industrial growth of nineteenth-century America.

MILLS

The rise of large-scale textile mills in the nineteenth century caused a profound change in the lives of multitudes of Americans, especially children and young, unmarried women. American textile production was primarily a home-based industry before the nineteenth century. Farm wives performed the labor themselves—from cleaning the raw material, generally wool or cotton, to spinning and weaving—until a finished clothing product resulted. This process was long and tedious, but necessary if the farmer's family were to be clothed. Around the turn of the nineteenth century, small mills began dotting the landscape wherever running water could be found to power the equipment. These small mills generally performed only part of the process, leaving the individual farm wife to finish the weaving. Early in the nineteenth century, larger mills made their appearance in the United States. These mills were significant for several reasons. They generally performed all of the operations of finishing textiles, leaving nothing to be done by the individual except purchase the final product. These large mills also required new machinery and new power sources as demand for their product rose. Finally, as the mills grew in size, the need for increasing numbers of employees initiated an irreversible change in the very fabric of American life. By the end of the century, industrialization meant that more Americans worked in factories and industrial settings than in agriculture. As other large industries grew, they often patterned their organization after the textile mills.

Surprisingly, the mechanization of the textile industry did not spell doom for small, independent craftswomen as it had for so many other artisans. One commentator on the state of the weaving industry in post-bellum America remarks:

notwithstanding the rapid substitution of power for the production of textile fabrics and the growth of large establishments from the results of accumulated capital, there is no actual decline in the number of hand looms in operation. There are fewer looms devoted to certain classes of goods, and in certain localities, than formerly; but the aggregate of such looms now in operation is probably fully equal to that in any former period. Philadelphia is now [1867] the great seat of hand-loom manufacturing and weaving in America. There are now within our knowledge 4700 hand looms in operation ... and it is probable that the true number approximates 6000. (cited in Ware, 61)

Despite the growth of textile mills in the United States, individual textile production continued to play an important role in the overall industry.

English immigrant Samuel Slater established the first large-scale textile mills in the United States. Slater worked in the textile mills of his home country from a young age and learned how to operate and build the machinery invented by Richard Arkwright. After secretly immigrating to the United States—the British attempted to keep their industrial secrets from the rest of the world—Slater established his first mill on a small Rhode Island river in 1893. Slater set a precedent for early milling operations by building onsite housing for his employees, as well as company stores, schools, and churches. His mills sometimes employed entire families, but primarily children worked Slater's mills. (The treatment of the child workers, along with the treatment received by workers in other mills, is discussed at length subsequently in this section.) Although Slater was the first successful mill owner in the United States, his mills were relatively small when compared to those build later in the century. A native-born American in neighboring Massachusetts, Francis Cabot Lowell established larger mills and built upon the system initiated by Slater.

Lowell played a central role in the development of manufacturing in the United States with his development of a new kind of process for producing textiles. During a visit to the great manufacturing centers of England, Lowell was impressed with the power looms and other machinery used in Britain's textile industry. Upon his return to the United States, he worked with a skilled mechanic, Paul Moody, to recreate and improve many of these machines. The result was the first self-contained factory for mass-producing cotton cloth. Whereas Slater's mills were limited to only the carding and spinning processes, Lowell developed the first practical power loom, making his factories the first to take the cotton from raw fiber to finished cloth.

Lowell and his partners located their venture in Waltham, Massachusetts, on the banks of the Charles River to take advantage of the water power for operating the new machinery. Later, Lowell established another mill on the Merrimack River at the site that would become Lowell, Massachusetts. Water power was central to the American manufacturing system; the number of watermills in America rose from less than 10,000 in 1800 to more than 50,000 just three decades later (Marcus and Segal, 53). Lowell and his associates continually made improvements to the machines until American mills were soon the most productive in the world. By mid-century, the mills in and around Lowell employed more than 8,000 people and produced more than fifty million yards of cloth every year.

Whereas Samuel Slater employed primarily children in his mills, the laborers used by Lowell were usually women who lived in company-built and maintained towns. Women composed 80–90 percent of the workforce in the American textile industry, most between the ages of 15 and 30 years old [Zinn, 115]. The working conditions were generally better than most factory workers in England experienced, but the lives of the young women, both on the job and off, were tightly controlled. Lowell envisioned a town in which these young women, gathered from surrounding farms, would live in "company-owned boarding houses" where the company would "take on responsibility for the moral lives of these workers" (Billington, 73). Furthermore, it was expected that the young women would "leave after earning enough money either for their own dowry or for help in their family's finances" (Billington, 73). Many times this dowry went toward marriage between one of the "mill girls" and overseers or supervisors at the factories. Lowell preferred hiring farm girls for their work capacity, and because if layoffs were necessary these girls could return to their homes without great despair.

The treatment of workers in the company-owned mill towns varied widely. Some who followed the Lowell system provided for the physical, moral, and intellectual well-being of the young female workers, as witnessed by a visitor to Waltham:

The factory people built the church which stands conspicuous on the green in the midst of the place. The minister's salary, eight hundred dollars last year, is raised by a tax on the pews. The corporation gave them the building for a Lyceum which they have furnished with a good library and where they have lectures every winter, the best that money can procure. The girls have, in many instances, private libraries of some value. (cited in Ware, 73)

This was certainly not the norm at all textile factories. Contrast the above benefits with the insensitive attitude exhibited by an agent for another factory:

I inquired of the agent of a principal factory whether it was the custom of the manufacturers to do anything for the physical, intellectual, and moral welfare of their working-people.... "We never do," he said. "As for myself, I regard my work-people just as I regard my machinery. So long as they can do my work for what I choose to pay them, I keep them, getting out of them all I can. What they do or how they fare outside my walls I don't know, nor do I consider it my business to know. They must look out for themselves as I do for myself. When my machines get old and useless, I reject them and get new, and these people are part of my machinery." (cited in Ware, 77)

Although the agent for the second factory sounds crass and uncaring, especially when compared to the seemingly utopian description of the first factory, many workers rebelled against the Waltham model as the century wore on. Although the Waltham system provided moral and intellectual stimulation for its workers, adherence to a strict code of conduct and a rigid system of controls on their personal lives often made workers feel little more than well-treated slaves. The freedom of working for employers who did not consider it their business to know what their employees chose to do on their own time appealed to a growing number of American factory workers.

The actual working and living conditions of the young women who were employed in Lowell's factory closely mirrored his utopian vision.

The hours, though long, were no longer than those of other factory workers and certainly no longer than farm labor required:

We go in at five o'clock; at seven we come out to breakfast; at half-past seven we return to our work, and stay until half-past twelve. At one, or quarter-past one four months in the year, we return to our work, and stay until seven at night. Then the evening is all our own. ("Susan," 32)

Primarily coming from small farms, the young women employed at Lowell's mills were accustomed to long hours of labor. Susan, the young letter-writer quoted here, points out she goes to work everyday—"not earlier than I should at home, nor do I work later" ("Susan," 35).

In Lowell's factory, there were different jobs of varying degrees of importance and difficulty, but all workers were treated well when compared to the norm of the day. There were specific areas where the cotton was cleaned, other rooms for spinning, and yet others for weaving. Although working conditions varied somewhat, there was a certain degree of uniformity. In a letter from one of these young female employees to a friend, the rooms where she and her coworkers spent their days are described as "very neat" with machinery that moved "with a gentle undulating motion" that the writer described as "really graceful" ("Susan," 30).

As with most jobs, there were hazards, even if they were mild by the standards of the time. The continuous loud noises of the mill followed the workers even while they were away from the job, but the young women adjusted, just as "people learn to sleep with the thunder of Niagara [Falls] in their ears, and a cotton mill is no worse" ("Susan," 31). The long hours of standing and repetitive work also led to aching, swelling feet as well as other repetitive use injuries—all in all, however, the work did "not require very violent exertion, as much of our farm work does ("Susan," 33), and factory workers were in better health than the general public.

Lowell was determined to look after the spiritual and moral well-being of his employees, as well as taking care of their physical needs. The surroundings were maintained in such a way as to make conditions as pleasant as possible, the buildings being "high spacious well-built edifices, with neat paths around them, and beautiful plots of greensward ...some of the corporations have beautiful flower gardens connected with the factories" ("Susan," 36). The inside of the buildings were equally well maintained and decorated:

The rooms are high, very light, kept nicely whitewashed, and extremely neat; with many plants in the window seats, and white cotton curtains to the windows. The machinery is very handsomely made and painted, and is placed in regular rows; thus, in a large mill, presenting a beautiful and uniform appearance. I have sometimes stood at one end of a row of green looms, when the girls were gone from between them, and seen the lathes moving back and forth, the harnesses up and down, the white cloth winding over the rollers, through the long perspective; and I have thought it beautiful ("Susan," 36).

The boardinghouses built to house the girls were designed to ensure that a boardinghouse "keeper" could keep watch over their charges. At first made of wood, later boardinghouses were large brick structures, with kitchens, common areas, and bedrooms shared by 4 to 8 girls. A typical boardinghouse might house 30 to 40 girls altogether (Lowell National Historical Park Handbook).

The pleasant surroundings and the fair treatment, as well as other perks such as concerts, lectures (including visits from Ralph Waldo Emerson and Charles Dickens), and holiday celebrations, meant the workers were generally cheerful; Susan maintains that she "never saw a happier set of beings" than her coworkers ("Susan," 32). These same girls dressed neatly and were "the prettiest in the city" ("Susan," 37). In fact, the only complaints from this intrepid letter-writer concerned the quality of the food (sounding much like a twentieth-century college student complaining about dormitory food) and the stifling heat of summer work—a discomfort many of the girls avoided by returning home for the summer months.

Visitors to Lowell's mills echoed this cheerful picture painted by a girl who experienced the factory life. The interest the girls took in their lectures struck such luminaries as Ralph Waldo Emerson and Charles Dickens, as did the cleanliness and general deportment they found in the mill girls (Nye 1994, 112). At least in the early decades of the mills, all seemed well for the factory employees. With tributes from young women such as Susan regularly published in the mill-owned magazine, the *Lowell Offering*, it would seem that factory work in America was much different than that of the dirty, dangerous, and exploitive British factory system.

Not all was good, however, for the young American women working in the textile factories. Women earned an average of less than 37 1/2 cents per day in 1836, working 12–16 hours per day. Strikes were not uncommon, with both men and women participating (Zinn, 115). Reformers published tracts lamenting the plight of factory workers and demanding changes, calling the workers "nothing more nor less than slaves in every sense of the word!" (Zinn, 117) Respiratory problems from particulates in the stale air, the constant presence of deafening noise, oppressive heat in the summer and dangerous cold in the winter, and varicose veins from long hours of standing in one place were just a few of the health problems confronting the women at Lowell's mills and others like them (Nye 1994, 116–17). These problems were ignored in the writings published in the *Lowell Offering*, a publication that was, after all, controlled by the mill owners.

Lowell—Portuguese mill girls. The girls are formally dressed, probably for church or a lecture sponsored by the mill. Library of Congress.

An 1849 visit to one of the Lowell mills by Dr. Josiah Curtis provides more evidence that life in the mills was often hazardous. Curtis, who presented his findings to the American Medical Association, addressed the lack of fresh air in the factory. He found that there was

[an average of] 55 [workers] for each room containing 64,670 cubic feet, inclusive of the space occupied by machinery.... Here then we find a certain number for a definite time in a limited space without any ventilation whatever, except that of an accidental nature at the doors of entrance in winter and the same with open windows in summer, and this, too, with the thermometer ranging from sixty-five to eighty-five degrees throughout the winter months.... In winter, moreover, for four months when the windows are closed and generally double, each room has fifty solar lamps burning morning and evening, which assist not only in impuring [sic] the confined air, but also in raising the temperature frequently to ninety degrees before closing work at night. In all kinds of weather, the operatives, with hastily adjusted dress, emerge from this atmosphere, to their boarding-places, partake of a plain but substantial dinner, and return to resume their labor in the space of forty-five minutes.

The air in these rooms, which ought to undergo an entire change hourly, remains day after day and even month after month with only the precarious change which open doors occasionally give! There being no ventilation at night, the imprisoned condition of many of the rooms in the morning is stifling, and almost intolerable to unaccustomed lungs. After the day's work is ended, two hours' release is enjoyed, a part of which is frequently spent in a crowded lecture room, and then they retire to dormitories scarcely better ventilated than the mills. From four to six, and sometimes even eight, are confined during the night in a single room of moderate dimensions. (cited in Ware, 98–99)

Catherine Beecher, a noted reformer working for women's rights, wrote about everyday life at the mill:

I was there in mid-winter, and every morning I was awakened at five, by the bells calling to labor. The time allowed for dressing and breakfast was so short, as many told me, that both were performed hurriedly, and then the work at the mill was begun by lamplight, and prosecuted without remission until twelve, and chiefly in a standing position. Then half an hour only allowed for dinner, from which the time for going and returning was deducted. Then back to the mills, to work till seven o'clock ... it must be remembered that all the hours of labor are spent in rooms where oil lamps, together with from 40 to 80 persons, are exhausting the healthful principle of the air ... and where the air is loaded with particles of cotton thrown from thousands of cards, spindles and looms. (cited in Zinn, 116)

Although the details of everyday life in the mill are essentially the same as those provided by "Susan," the perspectives offered by Dr. Curtis and Catherine Beecher shed a different light on the plight of the mill worker.

The lives of the young women who worked in Lowell's factory (and others founded on similar principles) paint an interesting picture of how at least one class of Americans was affected by the Industrial Revolution. In many places throughout Europe, but most particularly the industrialized towns of England, slums had arisen where the living conditions of factory employees were barely tolerable. Disease was rampant, there was insufficient food and rarely clean water, and crime was on the rise as people poured into the cities searching for work. Of course, these same conditions began appearing in major American cities; however, some industrialists like Lowell were very anxious that this would not be the norm for factory workers. Supervisors generally treated the young women employees with respect, not being "the overbearing tyrants which many suppose them to be" ("Susan," 34) and certainly not given to physically abusing the girls; exclaims Susan "and as for corporal punishment—mercy on me! To strike a female would cost any overseer his place" ("Susan," 38). In Lowell's factory, it was clear that a "profitable business came first but it went together with a labor force that was to be healthy and content" (Billington, 74). Altruistic as it may seem (and Lowell *was* concerned with his workers well-being), Lowell also understood that if he could keep the workforce happy, his factories would not experience the labor unrest already occurring in Great Britain.

In spite of Lowell's attempts to make his factories a worker's utopia, manufacturing in nineteenth-century America was often saddled with the same sort of social problems as those experienced in England and other European countries. Mechanization led to loss of jobs that in turn led to unions, worker protests, and general labor unrest. Lowell's ideas about molding the morality of young female workers notwithstanding, American manufacturers often employed children in unsafe and unhealthy conditions for long working days. An 1837 observer summarized a mill employee's remarks concerning the abuses met by the young laborers:

The children are tired when they leave the factory; [he] has known them to sleep in corners and other places, before leaving much fatigued, particularly those under twelve years of age.... [He] Has known the children to go to sleep on arriving home, before taking supper; [he] has known difficulty in keeping children awake at their work; [he] has known them to be struck to keep them awake. (cited in Nye 1994, 117)

The mechanization of the textile industry "changed the nature of work" for mill employees by "requiring that people work at a pace set by machines rather than allowing the workers to set the pace" (Endersby, 278). Especially for the first generation of mill workers, many of whom may never have seen a single machine much less a factory full of them, this was a drastic change in their world. And the pace kept increasing: "As workers became more skilled, management raised the number of machines per employee ... or they increase the machines' operating speeds" (Endersby, 278). As workers feared then, and feared throughout the Industrial Age, the mill owners began adding machinery rather than increasing labor or wages in order to increase productivity (Endersby, 278).

Throughout the nineteenth century, factories of various types emulated the system developed by Lowell and others. Some even attempted to improve working and living conditions for their employees—this before federal laws and regulations began requiring such improved conditions. The Westinghouse Air Brake Company, for example, voluntarily reduced its employees' work schedule to nine hours per day and 55 hours per week while giving them a half-day off on Saturday to go along with the traditional Sunday holiday.

As the century progressed, the exploitation of workers—especially women and children—that Lowell had so valiantly tried to stem became the norm for the American factory. By mid-century, the typical factory employed entire families whose children, through a lack of education, were generally relegated to low-paying factory jobs for their entire lives (Nye 2003, 126). Many of these employees were immigrants, and the day of self-contained company towns where the mill owners provided physical and moral oversight for the employees began to wane. Although the length of the workweek fell—from more than 70 hours per week in the 1830s to about 60 hours in the 1870s—working conditions and wages remained poor. Organization of workers against factory abuses began in antebellum America. A worker's newspaper, the *Voice of Industry*, was founded to decry the working conditions in Boston-area factories.

Later in the century, further reactions against science and technology occurred. As the negative repercussions of industrialization became evident, some Americans fought what they perceived as a materialistic threat to their way of life, and others took notice of the environmental consequences of industrialization. Dams interfered with fish migration and disrupted fishing while flooding farmland, often despite protests by the displaced farmer. Logging enterprises often moved into a region, cleared a large area of trees, then moved on without any concern for the environmental disaster they behind. Although environmentalism is usually considered a twentieth-century phenomenon, in the nineteenth century diverse groups of people had already begun to take notice of the environmental degradation that the Industrial Revolution spawned in the United States.

Thanks to Lowell and later industrialists, the production of textiles in the United States became the largest and most important industry in the country during the first half of the nineteenth century. After Lowell's death, his textile operations were moved to a spot that provided more water power for the increasing number of machines needed to meet the higher demand for manufactured textiles. With improvements to the machinery and the processes required to make the finished products, the textile industry became an important example of the manufacturing possibilities in the growing nation.

Textile mills were not the only industrial sites in antebellum America. Paper, flour, and saw mills also dotted the landscape anywhere swiftly flowing rivers could be harnessed to supply power for the machinery. In 1840, more than twice as many people worked in mills as in the iron industry, and three times as many as in machinery, hardware, cutlery, and firearms manufacturers combined (Nye 2003, 98). Usually, towns sprang up where the mills appeared. An observer in 1808 narrates the birth of a town:

To this mill, the surrounding lumberers, or fellers of timber bring their logs, and either sell them, or procure them to be sawed into boards or into plank, paying for the work in logs. The owner of the saw-mill becomes a rich man; builds a large wooden house, opens a shop, denominated a store, erects a still, and exchanges rum, molasses, flower [sic], and port, for logs. As the country has by this time begun to be cleared, a flower-mill is erected near the saw-mill. Sheep being brought upon the farms, a carding machine and fulling-mill follow. (cited in Nye 2003, 91–92)

So, according to this observer, technology begot technology. What was once sparsely inhabited woodland becomes farmland as the forest is cut and the lumber is milled. As the area becomes more settled, a flour mill becomes a necessity to process the grain grown on the surrounding farms. And, of course, a small textile mill follows, as demand for manufactured products increase. All the while, a town is appearing in the former wilderness:

For some years, as we may imagine, the store answers all the purposes of a public-house. The neighbours meet there, and spend half the day, in drinking and debating. But the mills becoming everyday more and more a point of attraction, a blacksmith, a shoemaker, a taylor, [*sic*] and various other artisans and artificers, successively assemble. The village, however, has scarcely advanced thus far, before half its inhabitants are in debt at the store, and before the other half are in debt all round. What therefore, is next wanted is a collecting attorney.... The attorney is also employed by the neighbours. (Nye 2003, 92)

As seen by this passage, progress brought on by technology is a mixed bag. Along with blacksmiths, shoemakers, and tailors, the members of the new community must deal with debt and "collecting attorneys." The last thing to make its way into town, according to our narrator, is a church—making the village complete. Sometimes the village remained a village, or eventually disappeared altogether. At other times, the village grew into a thriving city. In addition to Lowell, Massachusetts, other milling "villages" included Minneapolis, Rochester, Louisville, and Richmond, to name a few (Nye 2003, 104).

Interestingly, according to historian David Nye, the preceding narrative can be retold later in the century by replacing the mill with a canal, a railroad, or an irrigation dam as the central stimulus around which a new settlement grows. The pattern remains the same: A new technology appears in the wilderness—whether that wilderness is a forest or the central plains—and around that new technology all of the trappings of civilization spring up. This view of American history maintains that everyday life is not simply *affected* by science and technology, but *shaped* by it.

The location of villages, towns, and cities was often directly dependent on the location of industry such as mills; and, in turn, the location of the mills was predicated on several geographical factors. As mentioned previously, waterpower was of primary importance, at least until later in the century. In 1840, for instance, more than 66,000 mills in the United States were powered by water, whereas fewer than 1,000 were steam powered (Nye 2003, 98). A closely related need was a navigable waterway to float logs downstream to the sawmill, to export products of the mills and surrounding area, and to import those goods not produced locally. In addition, the flour mills, and therefore the towns, had to be centrally located so the farmer could conveniently bring his grain to be processed. Since, for instance, ground corn molded much faster than the unmilled kernels, the central location was also a must for frequent trips to the mill (Nye 2003, 94).

Technological advances added greatly to the proliferation of mills in the United States. Sawmills sprung up anywhere vast virgin forests offered lumber for the taking and nearby transportation systems—natural waterways, canals, or railroads—provided a means for moving the finished product to a market. Simple innovations such as improved axes and cross-cut saws contributed to increased logging, but with the advent of steam power, the logging industry took off. Water-powered sawmills made it possible to cut logs into lumber at an unprecedented rate. Inevitably, steam-powered sawmills slowly eclipsed them in number and importance.

THE IRON AND STEEL INDUSTRY

Processes for refining ores into useful metals have long been a part of man's history. Iron and steel played an important role in the Industrial Revolution, and several nineteenth-century innovations led to increased production. Most notably, when Englishman Henry Bessemer developed, through a fortuitous series of accidents and engineering insights, a new process for making steel (the now-famous Bessemer Process), demand for the product grew exponentially. From stronger rails and bridges to better machines for all purposes, steel put the exclamation point on the Industrial Revolution.

The growth of the U.S. iron and steel industry mirrored closely the development of other technologies in the country. The railroads depended on first iron, and later steel, for rails, railcars, and bridges. The steamship builders likewise used large quantities of iron and steel to build their vessels. The telegraph—and late in the century, telephone—industries needed high-quality products for the never-ending reels of wire required to connect America. Iron and steel were needed for farm and home equipment, building materials, and countless other manufacturing and industrial applications.

Antebellum America lagged far behind England in iron production, producing far less than was needed by burgeoning industrial concerns. With a seemingly never-ending supply of firewood from the great Eastern forests, America's iron industry depended on charcoal for processing the ore. Eventually, however, the changeover to coal smelting provided American iron producers with the competitive edge required to produce more, and higher quality, iron (Marcus and Segal, 103). Before 1840, nearly all of the American iron production was dependent on charcoal. By 1860, anthracite coal accounted for more than 56 percent of the iron production (S. P. Adams, 133), much of it taken from deposits in coal-rich Pennsylvania.

Although iron dominated the landscape of American industry through the middle decades of the nineteenth century, steel held out a promise for better, stronger, and longer-lasting bridges, rails, and other products. While Bessemer is rightly credited with developing a practical and efficient process for producing steel, an American, William Kelley, actually developed a similar process before Bessemer. Although Bessemer owned the first American patent on the process, the American Patent Office declared that it was Kelley who deserved priority for the basic idea. Alas, this was not to prove sufficient for Kelley's fortunes, as the rights to the actual equipment for efficiently carrying out the process remained with Bessemer. When Andrew Carnegie and his partners brought the Bessemer Process to the United States, steel production skyrocketed. By 1876, total U.S. production topped half a million tons of steel per year (Billington, 175). By far, the biggest consumer of American steel was the railroad industry. Steel rails were stronger and more flexible, and by the 1870s inexpensive enough to warrant widespread use. By 1877, steel used for rails exceeded iron rails by 100,000 tons (S. P. Adams, 135).

Steel was a critical component of another American technological icon— the skyscraper. Strong, relatively light, and by the later part of the nineteenth century relatively inexpensive, steel allowed cities to build higher and higher. American architects such as Louis Sullivan and William Jenney began designing and constructing buildings with steel frames, beginning in Chicago and New York. These new construction technologies, appearing late in the nineteenth century, initiated a trend in urban planning that would define large cities in twentieth-century America.

Concrete did not make a significant impact on American construction projects until late in the nineteenth century. The primary reason for the late appearance of such a vital construction material (at least as viewed from our modern era) was the low quality of various concretes produced in the country. When Americans finally began producing quality Portland cement in the 1870s, concrete usage began to rise. But it would be a decade later before the introduction of reinforced concrete began to make possible the use of concrete in such things as skyscrapers.

Skyscrapers were not only practical ways to utilize space in downtown areas; they also became symbols of power and progress. Companies competed to build taller buildings than their competitors as a means of drawing attention to themselves. Rival newspapers were particularly caught up in this competition. By the 1880s, rival New York newspapers—the *Tribune,* the *Observer,* and the *Herald*—had all completed multistory buildings in an attempt to top the others. In 1889, the *World* topped them all by building a 16-story office building, six stories more than any other building in New York (Nye 1994, 89). Soon insurance companies, telegraph companies, and banks joined the race upward. By the mid-1890s, people spoke regularly of the New York skyline (Nye 1994, 91).

Although work in the iron and steel industry was hot and physically demanding, the need for skilled workers also meant that the wages were considerably better than for other industries. However, later in the century, workers' unions formed across the country demanding better working conditions and better pay in the steel and iron factories. The formation of the Amalgamated Association of Iron and Steel Workers in 1876, with a membership of more than 24,000 workers by 1891 (S. P. Adams, 136), marked a high point for labor unions in the nineteenth century. As the steel industry became increasingly mechanized, two things happened to the makeup of the industry workforce: First, fewer skilled workers were required as machines automated the complicated processes previously performed by hand; and second, more unskilled workers were needed, a role generally filled by various immigrant groups (Keller, 231). In addition to providing a steady source of cheap labor, immigrants were more easily intimidated and discouraged from joining unions. This reduced the influence of unions such as the Amalgamated Association.

This led to one of the most important events in United States labor history. One of the few steel mills that remained unionized in 1892 was an Andrew Carnegie—held mill in Homestead, Pennsylvania. Instead of renewing the union contract, Carnegie decided to simply shut down the plant. Carnegie guards clashed violently with plant employees, resulting in intervention from the state militia. The episode ended with victory for Carnegie and an effective end to the influence of the Amalgamated Association (Keller, 231–32).

MINING

America has always been fortunate to be rich in ores, minerals, and other natural resources. Mining these resources was extremely important for industries of the United States during the nineteenth century. Advances in science and technology led the way as a small, agrarian country became, by the end of the nineteenth century, an industrial giant.

One of the earliest mineral resources mined extensively in the United States was coal. Coal mining used technologies that were generally primitive, although some advances were made in the nineteenth century. Fans used to circulate fresh air, a compressed-air jackhammer, and the safety lamp all made coal mining safer and more efficient (Mulcahy, 336–37). The real imprint of technology on coal mining, however, was left by the increased demand for coal from railroads, the iron and steel industries, and other American manufacturing and business concerns.

The successful miner became an expert geologist by necessity. They "learned to interpret the geological structures near their work areas and, drawing on their general knowledge, adapt their mining methods to them" (R.B. Gordon, 267). Although not formally educated, the miner developed these skills over many years of on-the-job training. In his report on the First Geological Survey of Pennsylvania, Henry Darwin Rogers maintained:

It is of the greatest importance in mining that the collier should make himself familiar with the derangements of the strata in his particular neighborhood, so as to determine for himself, if possible, the prevailing character and direction of the displacements. An intimate acquaintance with the underground workings of the adjoining mines, will very frequently show him that these follow a certain rule or law, and it will teach him to infer, from the presence of peculiar signs of irregularity, not only the nature of any fault or derangement which he may be approaching, but the readiest means for either avoiding or passing through it. (cited in R. B. Gordon, 267–68)

This informal education in the science of geology was an important tool for the coal miner.

What was it like to be a coal miner in nineteenth-century America? Coal mining was a dirty, dangerous, and cramped job requiring no small amount of skill, knowledge, and vigilance. The typical coal mine ran under the coal vein, where the miner drilled holes and used black powder to blow large areas of the trapped coal to pieces—a very dangerous procedure. The pieces were then loaded into a cart and taken to the surface. The miner was usually paid by the ton, so any impurities in the cart were not counted (Mulcahy, 334–36).

In a mining process such as this cave-ins were always a fear, as were flash floods and other natural disasters. Long-term exposure to the coal dust caused a high incidence of respiratory conditions, such as black-lung disease and silicosis. In addition to the dust, gases accumulating in the mines presented a constant threat. Methane, carbon monoxide, and carbon dioxide were all odorless, colorless gases that could overcome a miner before he was aware of a problem. Miners developed various methods for testing for these gases, all of which were uncertain. To test for methane, the miners could apply a "flame to a suspected pocket [of methane gas], which was very risky" (Mulcahy, 335). To test for carbon monoxide, the miners carried a caged canary into the mine—if the canary was overcome, the miners quickly left the area.

Although coal miners worked somewhat independently once they entered the mine, their success—and even their lives—often depended on the skill and watchfulness of others. While deep in a mineshaft, the miner

could be endangered by bad judgment on the part of the mine operator, by the aboveground staff handling the pumps, hoists, and ventilating equipment, or by almost anyone working underground in the mine. Other miners might, for example, block the ventilation system, cause an explosion by using candles when safety lamps were called for, or cause a crush by robbing too much coal from the pillars [that supported the ceilings of the mine shaft]. Each miner relied on the managers and owners of the mine for adequate ventilation and drainage systems and for the overall plan of mine developments. He could be endangered by the failure of past mine operators to keep adequate records of their work, thereby creating the possibility of inadvertently breaking into old, unmapped workings filled with gas or water, or by the operators of adjacent mines who, through greed or incompetent surveying, extended their underground workings beyond their property lines. (R. B. Gordon, 266)

Miners around the turn of the century posing with a pneumatic drill. Denver Public Library, Western History Collection, Call No.: Z-6330.

With all of these risks, it is little wonder that mining was (and still is) considered one of the most dangerous occupations a man could choose.

As technology spurred on the coal production, miners began to clash with mine owners and management over working conditions and wages. Among the most famous (or infamous) of these early labor movements were the Molly Maguires. Composed primarily of Irish Catholic immigrants working the coal mines of Pennsylvania, the Molly Maguires were part labor movement, part fraternal society, and part terrorist group. In the 1860s and 1870s the Molly Maguires reacted to mistreatment of labor by the large mining concerns with violence—from beatings to murder—against mining officials and police. By the late 1870s, the group had effectively collapsed, thanks primarily to the undercover work of a Pinkerton detective who collected enough evidence to convict and hang twenty leaders of the Molly Maguires for murder.

Other mining unions arose in the closing decades of the nineteenth century. The most important of, the United Mine Workers of America (UMWA), was formed by a merger between existing unions in 1890. The UMWA gained enough strength in the ensuing years to seriously challenge

Striking Polish mine workers clash with the "iron and coal police" in Pennsylvania. From an illustration in Frank Leslie's illustrated newspaper, 1888. Library of Congress.

mining companies on important workers' rights, such as working conditions and pay.

As the century wore on, periodic discoveries of precious ores and minerals precipitated "rushes" to various parts of the United States. Each of these flurries of mining activity brought about new technologies and new applications of science for bringing the ore to the surface. At the surface, the rush to mine precious ores resulted in boomtowns springing up all over the country. Many of the mineral discoveries are well-known to all Americans today: the California and Alaska gold rushes, in particular, are familiar to all schoolchildren. Other, lesser-known discoveries played equally important roles in their regions and in the country at large.

Copper brought thousands of fortune seekers to Michigan on the shores of Lake Superior in the 1840s. Boomtowns sprung up in the Copper Harbor region and copper mining continued in the area through the remainder of the century. Miners dug deep shafts searching for the mineral, and innovative machines were designed and built to lift the huge deposits of ore and then crush the rock in order to separate the usable mineral. Copper mining on the shore of Lake Superior led directly to settlement and development of that part of Michigan.

Copper was to play an important role in the application of technology to everyday life. Its use in weapons, building materials, and household kitchen utensils was evident. Later in the century, a new demand for copper erupted when it was discovered that its conductive properties made copper an ideal material for the thousands and thousands of miles of wire needed to transmit telegraphs, telephones, and electricity.

Perhaps in no other place in the nineteenth century were the detrimental environmental effects of technology exhibited more than in the California gold mining regions. Immigrants hailing from the mining-rich English region of Cornwall were recruited to operate many of these mines (Mulcahy, 338). From small-scale damming of rivers to the advent of hydraulic mining techniques, the California countryside was scarred in the name of financial gain. Mining companies used powerful jets of water to scour away massive hills and riverbanks to reach the gold buried below. What was left after all the gold was extracted was an irreparably damaged California landscape.

Science and technology contributed to fundamental changes in the workplace during the nineteenth century. Some of these changes are generally perceived as positive for the American worker: Mechanization led to less reliance on manual labor, industrialization resulted in the emergence of a consumer society in which more goods were available to a larger population, and the American economy grew to a size that would soon be unmatched by any other country in the world. However, many Americans were concerned (and still are) about the loss of autonomy and the resulting abuses that occur when an employer holds an employee's livelihood in his hands. Work in factories, mines, and other sites of industrial America was often difficult and dangerous. Only with the coming of workers' unions late in the century were many of these concerns addressed. Whether the perception is positive or negative, there is no denying that the life of the worker in industrial America was fundamentally different than anyone had ever previously experienced, or imagined.

6

Around the Home

At the turn of the nineteenth century, American families generally produced most of the everyday goods needed to run a household. From clothing to food, tools to soap—all were usually handcrafted at home. Technology and science, and the resulting industrialization, caused a fundamental change in American life. At the beginning of the century, when women made their own clothing, preserved their own food, and generally made do with the resources at hand, the home was the center of industry in a very real way. By the end of the century, the

connection of these industries with everyday life now consisted only in the people going downtown to the general store—or successively, to the retail store, the dry goods store, and the tailor's or the dressmaker's—selecting the material which pleased their individual tastes, buying it, and having it made up into a suit or dress—or buying the ready-made clothes. (Langdon, 264)

The same could be said for buying food at the grocer or the butcher and for many more of the everyday items to run a household.

As the cities grew and manufacturing increased, working-class people became "consumers" in the modern sense for the first time. The income from industrial jobs, along with the rise in corporate advertising, resulted in demand for

Swift's premium hams and bacon, "Schlitz, the beer that made Milwaukee famous," Wrigley chewing gum, and Bull Durham smoking tobacco. The families of bank clerks and machinists might breakfast on Grape Nuts ("Healthy Brains Move the World; Keep Them Healthy"), use packaged gelatin desserts, brush with Hood's tooth powder, and perhaps wash up with Sapollo soap.... "Ready to eat" foods and canned peas were appearing in grocery store windows. (Kent, 24)

The very definition of successful men (and women) changed with this newfound buying power. Instead of valuing the traditional abilities involved in farming and a self-sufficient lifestyle,

the identity of male skilled workers was increasingly tied to their ability as breadwinners. Their wives prized the heavy-laced curtains, overstuffed furniture, and bric-a-brac ornaments that were proof of respectability. Skilled Carolina mill town workmen prided themselves on the gilt clock cabinets in their parlors with gospel hymns and "God Bless Our Home" etched on the face, and rag carpets on the floors. (Kent, 24)

The explosive growth of manufactured goods brought about by the Industrial Revolution in America created radical changes in the urban household.

Yet, urban consumers were not the only Americans to benefit from this fundamental change in everyday life. The availability of manufactured goods allowed farmers, hunters, and other settlers—far away from population centers—to participate in and benefit from the free market system. Because such common items as kitchenware, precut lumber, nails, canned food, and clothing could be shipped via the ever-improving transportation system at a reasonable cost, isolated settlers need not be completely self-sufficient. Instead, they might concentrate on income-producing endeavors such as lumbering, trapping, or, for the farmer, cash crops (Nye 2003, 58–59). As the century progressed, this tendency away from self-sufficient farms and toward a market economy was fueled by science and technology.

An interesting ancillary to the social impact of the mechanization of agriculture was the effect on farmwives. As the process of planting, cultivating, and harvesting became mechanized, fewer "hired hands" were needed. The farmwife, whose customary job was to prepare several large meals per day for everyone on the labor crew, realized a smaller burden during busy times such as the harvest (Hurt, 201).

LIGHTING THE WAY

Providing artificial light to illuminate the home—whether that home is a cave or a castle—has always been a preoccupation of mankind. In the early nineteenth century, homes were lit at night using a centuries-old technology: the candle. By 1830, oil lamps using whale oil began replacing candles in homes around the world. Unfortunately, the sperm whale was hunted to such an extent that an alternative was sought. At first, scientists and inventors looked for ways to distill a usable lamp oil from hardened oil deposits such as asphaltum and coal. A Canadian, Abraham Gesner, found a way to extract kerosene from coal, and the New York Kerosene Works began production in the late 1840s (Ansell, 485). Not until 1859, when Edwin Drake discovered crude oil in Pennsylvania, did this sort of oil come into common use.

Drake's first well was the beginning of the American oil industry. Using the common drilling practices of the time, Drake's primary innovation was encasing the hole with iron piping to prevent cave-ins and water infiltration (Ansell, 486). The thriving late-century oil industry spawned numerous technical innovations. New drilling methods, new storage techniques, and improvements in transportation—particularly the extensive use of pipelines—all led to an explosive growth in the oil industry. Luckily, this new industry found other uses for its products, as the introduction of new technologies for artificial lighting led to the eventual obsolescence of the oil lamp.

Electricity became an important part of the American household toward the end of the nineteenth century. But before electricity illuminated American homes and cities, gaslights had already found a prominent place in many parts of the country. Although manufactured gas (a by-product of burning coal) was first used for street lighting in Britain, American cities were not far behind. Baltimore became the first American city to illuminate its streets using gaslights in 1816. Imagine—for the first time residents of a major U.S. city could stroll the streets after dark! Gas lighting was a rather messy proposition, however: "Each gaslight had to be individually lighted and snuffed out and its glass globe cleaned" (Jonnes, 58). In addition,

each gas flame flickered and gave off, as it burned, small quantities of ammonia and sulfur, as well as carbon dioxide and water. Over time, these fumes visibly blackened not just the encasing glass globe, but a room's interior décor. Crowded, closed rooms lit by gas could quickly become deficient in oxygen and make people feel ill. (Jonnes, 58)

The discovery of natural gas deposits in New York, Pennsylvania, and throughout the country meant a cheaper and cleaner source of fuel for the rapidly expanding infrastructure. Competing alongside the manufactured gas, natural gas gained a foothold as the fuel of choice in some parts of the country, although it was well into the twentieth century before manufactured gas use began to noticeably decline.

By mid-century, the streets of most of the larger cities in the United States were lit by gaslights. Gas companies formed—more than 400 by 1875 (Marcus and Segal, 143), pipelines were laid, and some homes were supplied with gas for lighting and cooking. However, gas lighting in the 1830s and 1840s was an extravagance only affordable to the wealthier families in a city. As Jack Larkin notes, "Probably nothing could express the inequality of Americans' living conditions more starkly: the poor struggled to see by firelight, while the wealthy could now keep their entire houses ablaze throughout the evening" (Larkin, 143). In spite of the expense, by 1836 Philadelphia's gaslight system had almost 700 customers (Larkin, 142).

THE ELECTRIFICATION OF AMERICA

For the twenty-first century reader, it is probably difficult to imagine what a home would be like without electricity. Appliances that are now taken for granted—television, radio, microwave ovens—would not, of course, be a part of our lives without electricity. Beyond these comforts of modern living, though, are other electrical devices that now seem to be necessities. How different our lives would be without electric lights— bedtime at dark for the whole family! How many American families depend on electric heat in the winter and electric air conditioning in the summer? August in the southern United States was a much different experience before electricity. And electricity is not only necessary to warm us and keep us cool; electric ovens and refrigerators changed the way Americans approached home food preparation. Before looking more closely at the development of the electrical inventions so integral to our lives, let us first briefly address the history of electricity and how it came to be so easily delivered to our homes.

Scientists had long been hopeful that this dimly understood phenomenon called electricity might have important practical applications. It took a series of nineteenth-century discoveries and inventions, however, before this dream materialized. Just before the turn of the century, an Italian by the name of Alessandro Volta invented the battery, thus making it possible to "store" electricity for future use. A little later in the nineteenth century, the English scientist Michael Faraday laid the groundwork for future applications of electricity with work that led directly to the invention of the electric motor and the electric generator. Interestingly, American Joseph Henry concurrently and independently made many of the discoveries attributed to Faraday. Although Faraday is considered the most important figure in the early development of practical electricity, Henry (whose contributions are discussed in Chapter 9) deserves a place in history alongside Faraday.

One of the earliest successes in the application of electricity to an everyday problem was in the illumination of the nation's streets. Although as lighting was in use in many cities, several American inventors, most notably Charles Brush, were determined to use electricity. In the 1870s and 1880s, Brush invented numerous devices that helped make the idea of electric arc lighting a reality. Beginning in the late 1870s, Brush and others established arc lighting as an effective alternative to gas for outdoor illumination. Unfortunately, this form of electric lighting proved much too bright for use indoors, except in large public buildings or factories.

The life story of Charles Brush reads like a romanticized rags-to-riches story so central to the American experience. Born in 1849 on an Ohio farm, young Brush was much more interested in mechanical devices than he was in farming. Thanks to a loan from an uncle, Brush was able to attend the University of Michigan, where he studied mining engineering. This in itself represents quite a departure from the status quo in America. Only a short time before, a young farmer from Ohio would not have had the same opportunities. Public, state-run universities were virtually nonexistent, and science and engineering were seldom offered as fields of study. Since the middle of the century, science had become important enough to everyday life that American colleges made science and engineering an option for those young men who were interested in such careers.

After graduation from the University of Michigan, and brief stints as a chemist and in the iron industry, Brush received his big break when he convinced the Cleveland Telegraph Supply Company to finance his research to develop a practical arc light, along with the electric dynamo he would need to power the light.

Arc lights had been around for some time, but nobody had developed a practical device. Essentially, an arc light worked by creating an electric arc between two carbon electrodes. Unfortunately, the electrodes were slowly consumed in the process and the spacing between the electrodes had to be continually adjusted. Brush developed a regulator that did just that. He also built an improved dynamo to power his arc light and immediately began marketing the lighting system.

Because electricity was virtually unknown to the general public at this time, Brush created quite a stir when he lit the public square of Cleveland with his new arc lights. No one had ever witnessed such a sight, and Brush was soon received requests to install his lights in most other major American cities. Electric lighting had arrived, and the public was enamored with Charles Brush and his accomplishments.

Businesses began using the new technology to draw attention to various outdoor ventures. First with arc lights, and later using the newer incandescent bulbs introduced by Edison, those in business found that Americans were drawn to the electric lighting and began to take advantage of the public's fascination. Part of this fascination with electric lighting came from the fact that, "for the first time in history, light was separated from fire. It needed no oxygen. It was not affected by the wind. It could be turned on in many places simultaneously, at the turn of a switch" (Nye 1994, 176). Entrepreneurs also realized that "in addition to being theatrical, incandescent lighting was superior to gas in other respects: less risk of fire, no danger of explosion, no flickering, and no consumption of oxygen. Electric lighting also offered ease of control, a variety of colors, and immunity to wind or rain" (Nye 1994, 177). The novelty of electric lighting made it a drawing card for promoters of all sorts of events.

Organizers of expositions and fairs were among the first to utilize electric lighting to promote their events. Besides the obvious utility of electric lighting—events might remain open after dark—the lighting itself drew large crowds of curious onlookers. The Louisville Southern States Exposition drew huge crowds for months in 1883, many simply wanting to gaze upon the 4,600 light bulbs installed by the Edison Electric Lighting Company (Nye 1994, 146). Other expositions and fairs found new uses for electric lighting. People attending the 1894 Columbian Exposition in Chicago were stunned by the newly invented Ferris Wheel, covered with light bulbs—not to mention the view of thousands of electric lights from the top of the Wheel (Nye 1994, 148). Amusement parks were built in the late nineteenth century, taking advantage of a growing middle class with money and leisure time to spare, drawing crowds with the creative use of electric lighting.

Another venue that seemed a natural place for exploiting the drawing power of electric lights was the theater. From the first theater to use electric lighting throughout—the Bijou in Boston in 1882—electric lighting spread rapidly to theaters across the country (Nye 1994, 177). By the 1890s, electric lighting had found a place on the biggest stage in American theater—Broadway. In the 1890s, electric lighting was a still a novelty and the electric companies, along with enterprising theater owners, took advantage of the public's curiosity. Promoters were drawn by descriptions such as one offered by the Boston electric company: "How many of us will stop during business hours to read a bill-board advertising somebody's soap? Not one in fifty. How many of us would fail to see and read the same board illuminated at night, cut out in golden radiance and set in a frame of black, the only relief to the eye from a monotony of darkness?" (cited in Nye 1994, 183). The novelty of electric lighting made it a promoter's dream.

Every generation remembers the wonder of a new consumer technology. The first microwave oven purchased by a 1970s family brought with it a reaction of amazement that food could cook at such an incredible speed. By the 1990s, the microwave was commonplace, and busy consumers stood in front of it impatiently waiting for their potato to cook. Electricity, like any other scientific or technological novelty, soon became commonplace:

Electrical novelties faded quickly and became "natural." In 1880, one arc light in a store window drew a crowd; in 1885 a lighted mansion still impressed the multitude; in the 1890s came the first electric signs. Each in turn became normal and hardly worth a glance. (Nye 1990, 57)

Today, any visitor to Broadway finds a landscape awash in electric lighting—so much so that advertisements seem to blend together in a confusing mishmash of color.

This brings us to the story of the development of incandescent lighting. Three men form a triumvirate when it comes to bringing electricity into the American home. Although Thomas Edison, Nikola Tesla, and George Westinghouse came from very different backgrounds and led divergent lives in many ways, their vision, skill, and knowledge made electricity the everyday household convenience that Americans came to take for granted.

The story of Thomas Edison is familiar to every American schoolboy and -girl. The prolific inventor was also an incredible self-promoter. From his headquarters at Menlo Park, New Jersey, Edison and his staff of inventors, mechanics, and technicians turned out a dizzying array of inventions for many decades. Of course, the most famous invention to come out of Menlo Park was the practical incandescent lightbulb. The story of Edison's countless experiments with various materials in his search for a long-lasting and inexpensive filament creates a mythical aura surrounding the inventor. After trying literally hundreds of materials, Edison finally settled upon a filament made from bamboo fibers and began marketing his new invention. His lightbulbs lasted long enough to make them practical and sold for 40 cents each, even though at first it cost Edison much more than that to produce the finished product (de Camp, 181). The manufacturing costs quickly dropped, and before long Edison made a tidy profit on his invention. Edison's lightbulb was on its way to revolutionizing the way Americans lived and worked.

The lightbulb was only a small part of a much larger system envisioned by Edison. With the opening of his Pearl Street Station in New York City in 1882—the first fully functional electric generating plant—Edison's company brought together numerous inventions and innovations—including devices for ensuring even flow of electricity and the first meter for measuring an individual customer's use of electricity—in order to provide, for the first time, a practical means of lighting a large region using electrical power. Edison's dreams were brought to fruition because he understood that industrial progress in a new age required "applied science, a social process, and individual genius" (Billington, 187). Edison and his associates supplied the individual genius and, through many years of laborious experiments, the applied science. Yet, the social process of creating a practical market for the inventions may have been Edison's greatest contribution. Edison's vision of lighting America with the power of electricity proved prophetic.

Thomas Edison was not America's only electricity "prophet." George Westinghouse, like many American inventors of the nineteenth and twentieth centuries, worked in manufacturing shops from an early age—in this

An 1878 illustration titled "Light thrown on a dark subject (which is bad for the gas companies)." The illustration shows Thomas Edison using his electric lightbulb to "throw light" on the gas company monopoly, expressing a general hope of cheaper and more abundant light for the future. Library of Congress.

case his father's agricultural machinery business. Westinghouse became a prolific inventor with important inventions to his credit, ranging from the electric industry to the railroad industry (see Chapter 2). In partnership with Nikola Tesla, Westinghouse helped create the modern American electrical industry.

Westinghouse's vision—that electricity could be produced and delivered to American customers efficiently, cheaply, and safely—was realized through his determination to see his ideas through to their conclusion. One of these visions resulted in the first major hydroelectric plant, built at Niagara Falls, and completed just a few years before the end of the nineteenth century.

Although Edison, Tesla, and Westinghouse all contributed enormously to the electrification of America, throughout their lives the three great visionaries clashed on several aspects of their work. Upon arriving in the United States from his native Croatia, Tesla immediately began working for Edison. It was a short-lived relationship—Tesla and Edison clashed on many subjects, both technical and financial. After leaving the employ of Edison, Tesla soon sold all of his patents to Westinghouse for cash and royalties, and went to work for Westinghouse's company. Many years later Tesla gave up his rights to royalties in order to keep the company profitable, a move that cost the inventor millions of dollars.

Perhaps the greatest battle between the great inventors was over the type of electricity that would be delivered to American homes. Edison championed direct current (DC) while Tesla and Westinghouse were convinced that alternating current (AC) would better fit the electrical needs of the public. A prolonged and ultimately unfriendly conflict erupted. One advantage that DC had over AC was that the DC motor was already well-developed and fully functional. When Tesla finally produced a working AC motor, the fight was on.

Edison and his allies argued that AC was dangerous; Westinghouse, on the other hand, hailed AC as safe and efficient. Both men went to great extremes to sway public opinion, but Edison led a particularly deceptive program trying to discredit AC. In 1887, Edison convinced the state of New York that AC would be an ideal method of executing condemned prisoners. In 1890, the first convict was executed by electrocution. Edison used this fact against AC, employing various scare tactics and even attempting—unsuccessfully—to name the style of execution "Westinghousing." Westinghouse, for his part, safely provided AC electricity to the Chicago Exposition of 1893.

Despite Edison's direct and aggressive attacks on AC (he staged public demonstrations where stray dogs and cats were electrocuted using this "dangerous" form of electricity), Westinghouse and Tesla won the day. Direct current could not be transported great distances because of the energy loss over the electric lines. A DC system required power plants situated close to the electric consumer. Alternating current was the superior product because it allowed efficient transfer of electricity over long distances; this meant large power plants could be built away from population centers. The efficiency of AC electricity was due, at least in part, to the invention of the transformer. A transformer changes an AC to high voltage and low amperage for transmitting across distances, so that the energy losses across those distances are minimized. Then the current is transformed back to a lower voltage and higher amperage nearer the intended customers, where it can be safely used for home applications. Although Westinghouse did not invent the transformer, he adapted and improved the device and used it to safely implement large AC power systems. The efforts of Westinghouse and Tesla resulted in the three-phase, 60-cycles-per-second alternating current still employed in the United States today.

Westinghouse and his engineers continued to find new and innovative ways to bring electrical power to the people of the United States. Before an electric company could be practical—and profitable— Westinghouse engineers had to develop a meter to measure electricity used by individual consumers. With the development of such a meter in 1888, the Westinghouse Electric and Manufacturing Company possessed everything it needed to become dominant in the fledgling industry. Near the end of the century, Westinghouse used the first steam turbines to produce electricity and further cemented his company's position as industry leader.

Although the primary use of electricity in the nineteenth century was for lighting, the success of the first electric companies in bringing electricity into the home paved the way for all of the electrical devices we take for granted today. Once the power line entered the home, it was inevitable that inventors would design washing machines, refrigerators, radios (and televisions), irons, and the multitude of other household appliances that require a dependable source of electricity.

THE SEWING MACHINE

The sewing machine is an icon of nineteenth-century technology and American marketing strategies. The successful design and construction of the first machines, along with the innovative marketing strategies devised by the manufacturers, set the tone for American invention and technology. The sewing machine revolutionized the garment industry by mechanizing factories; at the same time it changed the way American women made their family's clothing at home.

Several European inventors held the first patents on automatic sewing machines. In America, the first patent for a sewing machine was given to Elias Howe in 1846. Although the device worked, his business skills were lacking and the Howe machine was never a commercial success. Following a series of inventions to improve upon Howe's basic idea, the commercialization of the sewing machine followed an elliptical path due to a very confusing patent situation, as described by David Hounshell:

No single inventor or company had gained a patent position sufficiently strong to dominate the industry. In fact, litigation threatened the very existence of the industry. The Great Sewing Machine Combination, the first important patent pooling arrangement in American history, changed all of this. For a fee of $5 on every domestically sold machine and $1 on each exported one Elias Howe contributed to the pool his fundamental patent (1846) for a grooved, eye-pointed needle used in conjunction with a lock-stitch-forming shuttle. Allen B. Wilson, through the Wheeler and Wilson Manufacturing Company, placed his 1854 patent on the four-motion cloth-feeding mechanism into the pool. I. M. Singer & Co., a partnership of inventor Isaac Merrit Singer and lawyer/capitalist Edward Clark, provided a number of its patents, including Singer's monopoly on the needle bar cam (1851). In addition, the Grover and Baker Sewing Machine Company, whose president, Orlando Potter, had been the chief architect of the pool, added some of its patents. Members of the pool could use these patents freely as could any other manufacturer willing to pay a license fee of $15 per machine. In addition to Howe's fee of $4 per machine, a set amount of the $15 (initially $7 per machine) went into a litigation fund actively used to protect the patentees and licensees. The balance was then divided among pool members. (Hounshell, 67–68)

With this arrangement, American sewing machine manufacturers competed freely to see who could build and market the most successful machine. One of the members of the patent pool achieved so much success in doing just this that his name became synonymous with the sewing machine—Singer.

Although not the inventor of the sewing machine, I. M. Singer was the most important figure in the adoption of the new device by thousands of Americans. Singer's machine, which pioneered the now familiar up-and-down motion for sewing, is an American success story on par with Eli Whitney and Henry Ford. Singer's marketing of the sewing machine

"IT STANDS AT THE HEAD"   "THE LIGHT RUNNING"
DOMESTIC SEWING MACHINE.

An advertisement for a "Domestic" sewing machine, circa 1882. Library of Congress.

included demonstrations at county fairs and later at bright new "sewing emporiums" around the country; discounts to certain people who might provide word-of-mouth advertising; and special lease-buy options and other incentives for prospective buyers (Marcus and Segal, 109–10). Singer trained women to "demonstrate to potential customers the capabilities of the Singer machine" (Hounshell, 84). The Singer Company admitted, "a large part of our own success we attribute to our numerous advertisements and publications." The company went on to conclude, "To ensure success only two things are required: 1st to have the best machines, and 2nd to let the public know it" (cited in Hounshell, 85).

Several sewing machine manufacturers competed with Singer for the American market in the nineteenth century. One, Wilcox and Gibbs, was an early pioneer in the American System of manufacture, in which machines were built with specially constructed tools to ensure interchangeability of parts (Hounshell, 121). A second, Wheeler and Wilson, soon followed suit and adopted what was known as the armory system of production for its sewing machines (Hounshell, 121). These two companies remained competitive with Singer through most of the nineteenth century. Although Singer trumpeted his mass production methods as uniquely American, in fact, the Singer Company was a latecomer to the American system of production. In its early years, Singer built his machines using methods more akin to the traditional craftsmanship associated with European manufacturing (Hounshell, 85). Singer slowly mechanized his factories, but it was not until the early 1880s that the Singer Company actually produced sewing machines with interchangeable parts (Hounshell, 91).

The sewing machine became the first mass-produced, mass-marketed product aimed at the middle-class wife. The success of the sewing machine was astounding. In 1853, three years before the patent pool was formed, the major sewing machine manufacturers produced fewer than 2,000 machines. By 1859, three years after the pool formed, this number had risen to more than 32,000 machines. In 1876, a mere 20 years after the formation of this important patent agreement, the three major sewing machine manufacturers in the United States produced more than 380,000 machines (see Table 6.1). By the last quarter of the nineteenth century the sewing machine had become a common item in the American home.

Although today we think of the sewing machine as a small home appliance, the early sewing machines were most important to the large clothing manufacturers:

The sewing machine made possible the wholesale manufacture of all clothing. It came into its own with the Civil War. The great demand at the time was for men's wear, for uniforms for the soldiers, for ready-to-wear-whether-they-fit-or-not. The distinction, the individuality, the "difference" in men's suits subsided, and the standardized suit forthwith was the rule. There was a great benefit to both men and women in the greater quantity of clothes they could have—in underwear, for

Table 6.1
Sewing Machine Production, 1853–1876 (All sources cited in Hounshell, 70, 89)

Year	Wheeler & Wilson	Wilcox & Gibbs	Singer
1853	799	n.a.	810
1854	756	n.a.	879
1855	1,171	n.a.	883
1856	2,210	n.a.	2,564
1857	4,591	n.a.	3,630
1858	7,978	n.a.	3,594
1859	21,306	n.a.	10,953
1860	25,102	n.a.	13,000
1861	18,556	n.a.	16,000
1862	28,202	n.a.	18,396
1863	29,778	n.a.	21,000
1864	40,062	n.a.	23,632
1865	39,157	n.a.	26,340
1866	50,132	n.a.	30,960
1867	38,055	14,150	43,053
1868	n.a.	15,000	59,629
1869	78,866	17,251	86,781
1870	83,208	28,890	127,833
1871	128,526	30,127	181,260
1872	174,088	33,639	219,758
1873	119,190	15,881	232,444
1874	92,827	13,710	241,679
1875	103,740	14,502	249,852
1876	108,887	12,758	262,316

instance—after the sewing machine started mass production, and made life more simply sanitary. (Langdon, 271)

The industrial sewing machine made clothing for all Americans more uniform, although individual dressmakers and tailors continued to produce specially made clothing for the wealthier segments of society.

HOW DID THEY LIVE WITHOUT *THAT*?

In many parts of the country, the beginning of the twentieth century found the typical home without electricity, running water, or many of the other conveniences we have come to expect in our homes. By the end of the twentieth century, the average American home possessed all of these wonders of modern technology, in addition to refrigerators, televisions, and microwave ovens. It was during the nineteenth century, however, that the first inventions intended to ease the burden of housework began to appear on the scene.

The common pin has many uses today; yet, in the nineteenth century its uses were even more numerous. From the seamstress to the office worker to the banker, pins held together fabric, papers, even money. The production of pins was of such importance, even before the nineteenth century, that Adam Smith describes the division of labor used in manufacturing pins in *Wealth of Nations* (Petroski 1994, 53) and Britain passed laws regulating the sale of pins in an attempt to control the pin market (Petroski 1994, 55). Mechanizing the manufacture of pins in the nineteenth century ensured a ready supply of the important little device.

The first successful machine for manufacturing pins was invented by an American physician, John Ireland Howe. With the help of Robert Hoe—whose son's work with printing presses is discussed in Chapter 3— Howe designed and patented a machine for making pins in one operation (Petroski 1994, 54). However, the real bottleneck in pin production was not the manufacture of the pin itself but rather the process of sticking the pins into cards for distribution and sale. This was already the traditional method of distributing the finished product by the time Howe invented his pin-making machine:

The sale of pins on cards came about for several reasons. In the early nineteenth century, people had been used to handmade pins whose quality could vary significantly from piece to piece, some being straighter than others, some having better points than others, some heads being uncomfortably large and others painfully small when holding together (and close to the body) the parts of one's dress. Even after mechanization, by displaying very clearly the head and point of every pin on a card, the manufacturer could demonstrate the uniformly "extra ne plus ultra" quality of the product, and the customer could easily verify that a full count of pins was being bought. Carded pins also were conveniently and safely stored and yet could be at the ready to be picked up when a seamstress might need one in a hurry. (Petroski 1994, 55)

When Howe invented a machine for automating this "sticking" process, the complete pin-making procedure was finally automated.

Howe's pins were used in everyday situations as "bank pins" by businesses to hold together paperwork and as "toilet pins" used by home seamstresses (Petroski 1994, 55). By the end of the century, automation had lowered the price of a half-pound box of bank pins to 40 cents (Petroski 1994, 57). Other inventors worked to improve the pin; changing the shape, the production materials (brass pins and nickel-plated steel pins were made to counter the rusting problems encountered with the traditional steel pins), and working eventually toward the modern paper clip. Each of these improvements were welcomed by consumers as the quality of pins for use in home and office increased at the same time as the price decreased—thanks in part to the mechanization of the pin-making process.

Once the mechanization of pin production was in place, inventors turned their attention to improving the common straight pin. In 1842, a Brooklyn resident by the name of Thomas Woodward patented the forerunner of the modern safety pin. His patent described "a manner of constructing shielded pins for securing shawls, diapers, & c.... It will not become loosened by the motion of the wearer and ... the point of the pin cannot, by any accident, be caused to puncture, or scratch, the person" (Petroski 1994, 93). Woodward's device, which he called "the Victorian shielded shawl and diaper pin" (Petroski 1994, 93), did not catch on, primarily because it lacked the spring needed to hold the pin in its shield.

A few years later Walter Hunt, who invented one of the first sewing machines, also invented the first practical safety pin. Hunt's design corrected the major flaw in Woodward's safety pin by adding a spring mechanism to keep the pin closed (Petroski 1994, 94). Hunt's safety pin was an immediate success and soon became the common household item used today.

Another fastening device deserves mention here, although it did not come into popular use until the twentieth century. The sewing machine pioneer Elias Howe invented the forerunner to the zipper in 1851 (Petroski 1994, 98). Unfortunately, Howe never marketed his device and it was essentially forgotten for several decades. The zipper as we know it (originally called the clasp lock), was invented by Whitcomb Judson in the 1890s. Judson's intention was to replace the difficult-to-handle high-buttoned shoes popular at the time with an easier zipper mechanism (Petroski 1994, 99). He and his partner, Lewis Walker, formed the Universal Fastener Company in 1894 and began trying to market the new invention. It would take improvements, however, by other inventors before a practical and dependable zipper could be successfully marketed.

A myriad of other inventions contributed to fundamental changes in and around the American home. Aqueducts, piping systems, and windmills brought water into the house. Chauncey Jerome mechanized the clock-making industry and was making nearly 300,000 clocks per year in 1850, each brass clock selling for only $1.50. A brass clock on the mantel became a symbol of the American home.

With the development of a stronger and more usable rubber product, the new material became a more common component in everyday products. Rubber shoes and rubber raincoats, in particular, were in common use by the end of the century. In fact, by 1889 there were 11 large factories for manufacturing rubber shoes in the United States, with each factory employing an average of nearly 1,000 workers (Nelson, 121).

There is perhaps nothing in our modern world we take for granted more than plastic. We use it for building materials, in our automobiles, for our recreational activities, and in our furniture—there is hardly a facet of our lives that is not built around plastics. In the nineteenth century this was not the case. When American John Wesley Hyatt invented celluloid while searching for a substitute for the ivory used to make billiard balls, the plastics age began. From billiard balls to dentures, Hyatt pioneered manufacturing processes by using an artificial material to replace natural materials.

At the beginning of the century, the family fireplace was the only source of heat for many American homes. Even with new kinds of stoves—such as the Franklin stove invented by Benjamin Franklin in the previous century— only a few rooms in a house were heated. Bedrooms were often cold retreats; beds were piled high with quilts and heated by rocks or bricks, warmed on a stove or fireplace, wrapped and placed under the sheets. Through much of the nineteenth century, most stoves were of the wood-burning variety.

Several technologies converged to make the home a warmer place to be. Coal-burning stoves, although available in colonial times, awaited more efficient methods for extracting the coal from Middle Atlantic mines. Even if the coal could be profitably mined, improved delivery methods—in particular, the railroad—were required to bring the coal to the outlying regions. Once coal became available, coal-fired stoves began replacing the traditional wood-burning type. Eventually, the coal stove led to a nineteenth-century form of central heating:

The stove had to go [from the various rooms of the house]! It was moved down into the cellar, made bigger and somewhat more complicated; a pipe went up through the walls to every room, emerging through a square hole in the floor covered by ornamental iron work, called a register.... The register was equipped with iron slats behind the grill work which by means of a simple ratchet could be opened or closed to shut it off. The collection of coal stoves, with being moved down into the cellar, had been reduced in number to one, but that one greatly increased in size. The heating of the house had become a system. (Langdon, 224–25)

Improvements were made to the furnace, including using circulating hot water or steam as the heating conduit. Thus, central heating was born.

Although the rough-hewn log cabin was the romantic picture of the American way of life, advances in architecture, materials, and construction techniques found more and more Americans living in "modern" housing. With the rapid growth of cities, new building techniques were needed in order to house large populations in relatively small land areas. New construction techniques such as the balloon frame house and brick row buildings, along with new technologies applied to roads, sewers, and water systems, enabled cities to grow at tremendous rates (Mahoney, 107). Carpets in the American home became more common due in part to mass produc- tion and the use of the power loom. By 1830, approximately one in five American households had purchased the readily available carpets (Larkin, 143). The use of factory-made window curtains also grew, especially in towns and cities, where privacy was a growing concern (Larkin, 143).

The type of clothing worn by typical Americans was greatly influenced by industrialization during the nineteenth century. At the beginning of the century, for instance, wool was a fairly uncommon material for American clothing, with the per capita use limited to less than three pounds (Langdon, 248). By the end of the century, this number had risen to eight pounds per capita (Langdon, 248), an increase that can be attributed to several things, including the proliferation of textile mills and improved transportation to deliver the finished products across the nation.

Cotton was the most common textile in nineteenth-century America. Eli Whitney's cotton gin paved the way for cotton to become the major crop of the South, and the emergence of cotton mills provided a fast, efficient, and inexpensive means of producing large amounts of cotton cloth. Finally, by employing a cylinder press, print patterns were applied in mass to cotton fabrics creating "a boon as it was inexpensive, and so at the command, with little or no financial limitation, of all classes of people" (Langdon, 261).

Factory-made fabrics changed the woman's workload in the home, beginning in the New England states early in the century and progressing through the remainder of the country. The gradual disappearance of spinning and weaving from many Northern households troubled some male, upper-class observers, who feared that farm wives and daughters would have empty time on their hands. In reality, the great majority of women remained hard at work. Some women assumed a larger role in farm work such as dairying, while others began performing "outwork," producing piecemeal clothing for the textile industry. American women and girls actually sewed more as their spinning and weaving declined. Industrial production made far greater quantities of fabric available, and they could make shirts, dresses, curtains, bedspreads, sheets, and towels in greater numbers than their grandmothers. For some women, time that had once been spent making clothes was now available for maintaining higher standards of housekeeping—so they worked harder at keeping their houses clean (Larkin, 50).

Housework was not the only day-to-day activity changed by technology. By the mid-nineteenth century, technology was used to create amusements for people all over the world. From 1850 on, American inventors acquired patents for such things as steam-powered carousels. Carousels became so popular in the nineteenth century that companies produced portable models of the merry-go-rounds in order to offer the thrill of a ride to residents of smaller towns and rural areas (J. Adams, 11).

Originating in France in the early nineteenth century, the roller coaster found its way to the United States later in the century. Originally based on the switchback railways common to mining operations, several inventors capitalized on Americans' growing desire for entertainment by inventing new kinds of roller coaster rides. One of the first roller coasters was built at Coney Island in 1884 and was an immediate success—in the first weeks of operation the ride attracted more than 12,000 riders per day (J. Adams, 14). Soon thereafter, improvements appeared on the roller coasters that made them look like the modern thrill ride we know today. Such innovations as the chain elevator system designed to pull the coaster to the top of the first hill and several safety devices increased the public's fascination with, and confidence in, the rides. These early roller coasters "combined an appearance of danger with actual safety, thrilled riders with exhilarating speed, and allowed the public to intimately experience the Industrial Revolution's new technologies of gears, steel, and dazzling electric lights" (J. Adams, 15).

The first amusement parks began dotting the American landscape late in the nineteenth century. The biggest, most famous, and most popular amusement park in the United States until the mid-twentieth century was Coney Island. Coney Island actually came to include several competing amusement parks, all of which had one thing in common—their use of technology to attract thrill-seeking customers. The machine was the central point of the entire experience:

The essence of Coney Island was its juxtaposition of mechanical amusement devices with an atmosphere of illusion and chaos. The precision and predictability of gears, wheels, and electricity created a fantasyland of disorder, the unexpected, emotional excess, and sensory overload. This brilliant paradox that was Coney, besides generating fun and frolic, allowed members of the growing urban working class, many of whom were immigrants or born of immigrant parents, to assimilate and participate in a culture ever dominated by the machine. (J. Adams, 41)

By the turn of the century, the amusement parks at Coney Island drew up to a million visitors per day to marvel at and enjoy the entertainment brought to them through technology.

Science and technology drove an unprecedented change in everyday life in America in the nineteenth century. In the span of a hundred years, society had changed—from one of self-sufficiency where most, if not all, of the needs and wants of life were grown, built, or made in and around the home—to the beginnings of a mass consumption mindset. The railroad brought an item to the front door of hundreds of thousands, if not millions, of Americans, thus enabling the isolated townspeople and farmers of the West to participate in the new consumerism. That item was the department store catalog. From these catalogs, anyone with available cash could order most of the items that had come to represent "the good life": clothing, building materials, household items, and almost anything else the anxious consumer could imagine could be had from these catalogs:

The arrival at the local railroad station of brown-paper-wrapped Sears and Roebuck and Montgomery Ward packages literally embodied the promise of

American abundance; the two Chicago mail order establishments were modern-day incarnations of the biblical storehouses of plenty. Indeed, in countless rural parlors, the well-thumbed 1,000-page Ward or Sears catalogue offering everything from books, glasses, cutlery, and coffeemakers to buggies, bicycles, wigs, eyebrow pencil, and cherry pitters had a place in family affections rivaling the Holy Bible. (Kent, 23)

The railroad not only brought the catalog, but also the myriad of consumer goods that only a few decades earlier only the wealthiest of urbanites could dream of possessing. The nineteenth century found "the ongoing transformation of North American cities into marketplaces where human interaction would become ever more commodified. Already, the names of companies like Nabisco, Singer, and Kodak and their intensely advertised products were being assimilated into the patterns of popular speech and thought" (Kent, 21).

The typical American home at the close of the nineteenth century was irrevocably changed by science and technology. A housewife from 1800, magically transported to a modern home of 1900, would have found different structures surrounding her, electric lights illuminating the night, new devices for heating the home, and handy devices—from simple pins to complicated sewing machines—designed to make life easier. This same housewife would find that most of the things she and her family used to make, from clothing to soap, could now be purchased at prices affordable to all but the poorest Americans. The turn of the twentieth century revealed an entirely new way of life for Americans at home.

7

Health and Medicine

The nineteenth century witnessed the birth of a medical revolution in the United States (and throughout the world) that would lead to better health, increased life expectancy, and an overall elevated quality of life for most Americans. Although this revolution was still a work in progress by century's end, a new interest in the application of scientific methods to such things as surgical techniques, disease prevention and treatment, and physician training laid the groundwork for modern medicine.

After centuries of medical practices that had changed very little from medieval times, numerous medical milestones occurred in nineteenth-century America. Inoculations helped reduce the threat of some horrible diseases, the use of anesthesia made surgery safer and less painful, and the growing acceptance of the germ theory of disease led to the eventual adoption of antiseptic practices in surgery. Many of the institutions critical to improved health care for the common man formed in the nineteenth century: Modern medical schools emerged, some from the ineffective schools already in existence, whereas others appeared as new experiments in modern medical training; the first woman, Elizabeth Blackwell, received a medical degree from an American college in 1849; the American Medical Association formed in 1847; and the individual states, beginning with Massachusetts in 1869, formed boards of health to monitor medical care. In addition, other institutions related to the overall health of Americans appeared: The first colleges of pharmacology opened; the American Dental Association formed in 1859; and the first dental schools opened after the Civil War.

Each of these institutions resulted in both immediate and long-term health benefits for Americans. Science, and to a lesser extent technology, played an increasingly important role in improving medical care. Ironically, advances in both the theory of medicine and the everyday practice of health care arrived at about the same time that many Americans were becoming increasingly aware of some of the dangers to their health caused by the oncoming Industrial Age. The juxtaposition of the new wonders achieved by science and technology against the societal ills, including issues of health, brought about by some of these same technical advances, continues to be a point of concern for America today.

ANTEBELLUM MEDICAL PRACTICES

Health care in the United States in 1800 was minimal, as it was throughout the world. In a time before the germ theory of disease, before standardized and thorough training for physicians, and before science played a significant role in medicine, the health and welfare of Americans was often more a matter of luck than of medical care. The late nineteenth century witnessed a growing awareness from physicians and the general public alike as to the increasing importance of scientific methods applied to medicine.

The overall health of Americans around the turn of the nineteenth century was much the same as it had been for previous centuries. Simple infections, treated by antibiotics today, often resulted in death. Infectious diseases were not understood and certainly not curable in 1800. Diphtheria, whooping cough, scarlet fever, measles, mumps, typhus, influenza, chicken pox, and smallpox ravaged the population as physicians stood helplessly by. Autopsies performed on victims of an 1820 yellow fever epidemic in Philadelphia represents an unusual instance in which antebellum physicians attempted to use scientific principles to investigate the cause of disease (Shryock 1972, 128). Two diseases in particular caused devastation in the early nineteenth century: malaria, primarily in the South, and tuberculosis, which struck primarily in the crowded cities of the North. In the country, it was difficult for infectious diseases to establish a foothold, whereas in the crowded cities, epidemics were more common. Boston, although relatively healthy as cities go, provided its residents with a life expectancy of five or six years lower than rural Massachusetts (Larkin, 81). New Orleans, with its swampy, semitropical climate, poor sanitation, and plethora of diseases entering from its port, was "very likely the most dangerous place in the United States" (Larkin, 81).

New Orleans was not the only southern locale in which health problems plagued the citizens. Due to factors such as warm weather and low-lying wetlands, malaria and other diseases were more prevalent than in the North (Shryock 1966, 49). The difference in life expectancies was so pronounced that life insurance companies habitually charged more for

Southern policy holders (Shryock 1966, 52). Southerners' health improved with the introduction of vaccinations, new drugs to treat malaria and related fevers, and new and improved techniques for draining wetlands. Unfortunately, the Civil War resulted in a Southern medical infrastructure in disarray (Shryock 1966, 70).

American physicians argued that health and medicine presented unique problems and demands for both the doctor and the citizen. Many of these unique demands were specifically placed on the nervous system: "constant choice and opportunity in business and religion, a lack of standards in personal and social life—all created tension and excitement" (Rosenberg 1966, 140). From school age through adulthood, competition and the hectic pace of life strained the physical and psychological well-being of Americans. The typical American "lived his life at a pace too frenetic for relaxation or rest" (Rosenberg 1966, 140). Especially when compared to Europeans, American religion, politics, and business caused stress. A nineteenth-century commentator on the subject concluded, "The result of this extreme activity, is exhaustion and weakness. Physical bankruptcy is the result of drawing incessantly upon the reserve capital of nerve force" (cited in Rosenberg 1966, 140).

In spite of these sentiments about life in the United States, American physicians were unwilling "to exchange its liberties for the placid tyranny of the Russian or Turkish empires" where politics and religion were seen as comfortable and leading to complacency among their citizens (Rosenberg 1966, 141). For most Americans in the nineteenth century,

> progress and liberty were unquestionably desirable, and the ailments which they induced in American minds were in a sense additional bits of evidence for the superiority of American ways of life. Technological change might be the cause of mental unease, but almost all Americans were relatively sanguine in their attitude toward the future of such material change. Many Americans believed that the very processes of technological change that appeared to threaten mental health would ultimately provide remedies. Such ills that might develop in the interval were those of a transitional period in history and a small price paid for social progress. (Rosenberg 1966, 141)

The type of medicine practiced by the typical nineteenth-century American physician is often referred to as "heroic" medicine, a term implying an aggressive intervention—very often to the disadvantage of the patient—involving bloodletting, the use of purgatives, and other potentially dangerous methods. In a time before medicine was established as a scientific discipline, alternatives to the heroic practice of medicine offered a skeptical, and sometimes desperate, public other opportunities for seeking relief from medical conditions.

American physicians in the nineteenth century often combined "themes of nature, providence, and nationalism to legitimize their efforts"

(Murphy, 76). Popular medical books of the day included herbal remedies, moral aphorisms, and even traditional cures adopted from Native Americans. One of the most popular of these medical books, John Gunn's *Domestic Medicine*, was so widespread that the "typical small library on the southern Indiana frontier, for instance, boasted a Bible and a hymnbook; if there were a third title, it was often Gunn's health manual" (Murphy, 75). Many other herbalist medical manuals gained widespread popularity, such as Samuel Thomson's *New Guide to Health: or, Botanic Family Physician.* The resulting Thomsonian movement affected the healing practices of Americans across the country. Many frontier families looked to these manuals for their health care in lieu of the availability of a local physician. Even trained physicians found use for such "herbals."

Botany and herbal studies seemed a natural fit for the physician, especially the traditional country doctor. Many of America's leading physicians were students of natural history, whether as a subject studied at the university or as a hobby. The latter was especially prevalent, as physicians "concerned with broadening their educational horizons ... acquired practical hobbies in natural history" including the study of such diverse topics as "botany, zoology, geology, mineralogy, chemistry, anthropology, agriculture, and even gardening" (Haller, 204). Country doctors, with the task of traveling many miles between patients, were especially encouraged to fill their time "with quiet contemplation of flowers, trees, and rocks" (Haller, 204). In combination with the popular self-help herbal manuals, nineteenth-century Americans—especially rural Americans—often perceived of medicine as a process of employing nature to help fight sickness and disease.

Medical "movements" outside the medical establishment gained popularity with the common people of the United States who were dissatisfied with the medical treatment offered by conventional practitioners. The list of popular movements is as lengthy as the reasons the American people embraced nontraditional medicine:

The tendency for brinkmanship therapeutics resulted in the spawning of countless system-builders [in medicine], each seeking to replace traditional medicine with a newer mode of treatment. Mesmerism, Thomsonianism, mind-cure, faith-cure, baunscheidtism, Christian Science, electropathy, hydropathy, vitopathy, and chemopathy had all but abandoned the older specifics for promises of quick and harmless cures. These medical heresies rivaled the religious sects, political parties, movements, and fads that emerged, along with the common man, in the early decades of the nineteenth century. Unfortunately, few of the systems did more than compound the errors of the past. (Haller, 100)

Several of these "medical heresies" had a tremendous impact on the common man in America. One such sect was Mesmerism, a hypnotic technique developed by Austrian physician Friedrich Anton Mesmer. Based on the theory that man possessed an animal magnetism, Mesmerism gained the support of many well-known Americans, from respected physicians and professors to college presidents (Haller, 104). Another, phrenology, the belief that the intellect and characteristics of a man could be divined by studying the shape of the head, also attracted a loyal following in the United States.

Homeopathic medicine became very popular by mid-century. This medical sect, founded in Germany and brought to the United States, depended on a philosophy of "likes cure like," with the applications of highly diluted drugs that caused symptoms similar to those experienced by the patient (Shryock 1972, 144). Because of the diluted state in which the drugs were administered, homeopathic physicians tended to cause less harm than their conventional counterparts. By the later part of the century, homeopathy reached such a level of acceptance that its adherents formed their own medical schools and medical journals.

In some ways, improved technologies actually contributed to the declining health of the country. The mail-order business, made possible by faster transportation—especially railroads—and advertised in the new penny papers, "also brought turn-of-the-century Americans, always distrustful of doctors (and carrying a definite streak of hypochondria), access to a new range of quack practitioners and patent medicines" (Kent, 23). Rothstein calls the patent-medicine industry "the single most important long-run alternative to regular medicine" (Rothstein, 158). With the traveling "medicine man" a not-so-happy tradition in isolated settlements, these same predators were now able to advertise and deliver their elixirs from a distance. Gullible Americans with a little cash could order Swamp Root for "weak kidneys caused by overwork, by lifting, or strain," pepsin gum to "cure indigestion and sea sickness," an electric belt "to cure pain and nervous diseases," and "Swift's Specific," which claimed to be "the only hope for cancer" (Kent, 23). One could also order cures for syphilis, rupture, "lost manhood," stomach disorders, and almost any other disease, real or imagined (Kent, 24). Faster communications and transportation fostered a growing market for these miracle cures, just as the Internet today seems to be accelerating the level of awareness of similar miracle drugs.

Medical historian Richard Harrison Shryock notes several contributing factors to the slow improvement of American medicine. The vast size of the country, its regional differences, its heterogeneous population, and even its complex system of government all contributed to the problem (Shryock 1966, 33). In addition, an underlying utilitarian view of scientific research resulted in a nation "to whom technology naturally seemed more significant than 'pure' science" (Shryock 1966, 33). This view of science, coupled with a lack of aristocratic patrons—such as those found in many European countries—interested in funding research, resulted in nineteenth-century America trailing in the types of basic scientific research needed to make great breakthroughs in medicine.

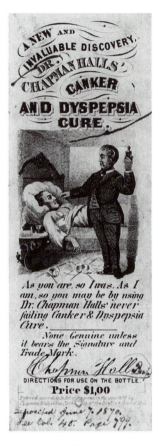

An advertisement for Dr. Chapman Hall's canker and dyspepsia cure, circa 1870.
Library of Congress.

The first nineteenth-century breakthrough attributed to scientific medicine occurred in 1800, when Benjamin Waterhouse began vaccinating
family and friends with Edward Jenner's newly discovered smallpox vaccine. Smallpox had a long history of decimating populations, with a mortality rate of close to 30 percent of those who came down with the dreaded
disease. In fact, smallpox nearly accomplished what many white invaders
tried—the eradication of the Native American population. At the turn of
the eighteenth century, smallpox was a disease dreaded by people all over
the world, and the citizens of the United States were no different.

Enter Benjamin Waterhouse. Waterhouse was an American-born,
European-trained physician who was appointed to one of the first professorships at the Harvard Medical School. In 1800, after reading about
Jenner's recent discovery that cowpox could be used to inoculate humans
against smallpox, Waterhouse wrote to Jenner asking for samples of his
vaccine. To demonstrate his confidence in the safety and effectiveness of

Vaccinating the Baby, 1890. National Library of Medicine.

the smallpox vaccine, Waterhouse's first subjects were his own children, other family members, and household servants. When several of these newly inoculated children were purposely exposed to the smallpox virus with no ill effects, Waterhouse proceeded to persuade others.

In spite of his initial success, it was not smooth sailing for Waterhouse and the smallpox vaccine. Several factors conspired to undermine the public's confidence in the vaccination. Through contamination or spoilage, some of the vaccinations proved ineffective, or worse, actually led to the vaccinated subjects contracting the disease. Waterhouse initially planned to profit from the inoculations by demanding a portion of the profits made by other physicians administering the vaccines. This soured some to Waterhouse and his cause. Yet, properly administered, the results were undeniable. With the support of many powerful people, including President Thomas Jefferson, Waterhouse and others were able to instigate large-scale inoculations that led to significant reduction of smallpox outbreaks in the United States.

Other advances in antebellum medicine helped promote good health and provide relief from, and sometimes even a cure for, disease. Breakthroughs in pharmacology included the isolation of morphine from opium, quinine from cinchona bark, and the introduction of the first hypodermic needles to inject such medicines (Shryock 1972, 131). Morphine became an important—and unfortunately often overused—pain killer, while quinine provided for better control of malaria.

Overall, the health enjoyed by the typical American did not improve to a great degree in the first half of the nineteenth century. Especially in the larger cities, Americans' health may have actually deteriorated. In spite of the continuing health problems, there were indications that things were improving slightly. Life expectancy in Massachusetts, for example, climbed throughout the century (Shryock 1972, 166) and in the 50 years from 1850 to 1900, the nationwide life expectancy climbed from about 50 years to more than 68 years (cited in Shryock 1966, 26). It was the medical advances of the second half of the century—especially the years after the Civil War—that led to a marked improvement in the nation's health. One of the most important developments was an improved system of physician education.

EDUCATING AMERICA'S PHYSICIANS

At the beginning of the nineteenth century, the apprentice system continued to play a primary role in American medical training. Physicians were infrequently educated in the sciences, and medical schools were often disorganized and ineffective. In the first decades of the century, the physician's "training varied enormously—there were men with formal medical education, many who had learned through apprenticeship to another physician, and practitioners who were self-instructed and self-certified" (Larkin, 87). Much medical treatment was based, as it had been for many centuries in Europe, on the "humor" theory of sickness. This theory held that sickness was caused by an imbalance of humors, or fluids, in the body. Thus, "bleeding," or the opening of a vein to draw off blood; "purging," or administering laxatives; and "puking," or administering emetics to induce vomiting, were typical treatments given by physicians (Larkin, 87–88). These treatments usually did more harm than good, and attendance by a physician was really of no more use than being sick without the benefit of a doctor.

Around 1800, only 4 medical schools existed in the United States. By the mid-1820s, this number had grown to 17 (Shryock 1972, 138). It was not until 1825 that Robley Dunglison became the first full-time professor of medicine in the United States at the University of Virginia. Yet, medical training leading to medical degrees did not necessarily ensure qualified physicians. In fact, the public's perception of physicians in antebellum America was much different than today. A practicing physician described the problem:

It is very well understood among college boys that after a man has failed in scholarship, failed in writing, after he has dropped down from class to class; after he has been kicked out of college, there is *one* unfailing city of refuge—the profession of medicine. (cited in Murphy, 104)

Even the president of Harvard, Charles Eliot, lamented the quality of person often found in physicians:

An American physician may be, and often is, a coarse and uncultivated person, devoid of intellectual interests outside of his calling, and quite unable to either speak or write his mother tongue with accuracy. (cited in Murphy, 104)

The reason for such a remarkable disdain for physicians was simple: It was extremely easy to become a "doctor" in the United States. Even in the middle of the century, "almost any man with an elementary education could take a course of lectures for one or two winters, pass an examination, and thereby automatically achieve the right to practice medicine by state law" (Shryock 1966, 152). The education received at American medical schools was sparse, to say the least. How much training, after all, could be obtained in two short terms—the second term being a repeat of the first term, so that students essentially passed through the same training twice? What training that was obtained was usually of low quality. A typical American medical school of the early nineteenth century looked like this:

First, the lecture was the sole pedagogical method used in all courses, except practical anatomy. Clinical, tutorial, or laboratory instruction was rare, even in subjects like chemistry. Second, the quality of instruction, even at the best schools, could be no better than the state of medical knowledge, and was consequently deficient in all aspects. Third, formal medical education complemented rather than replaced the apprenticeship system. Clinical subjects were supposed to be taught by the preceptor, and scientific subjects by the medical school faculty. (Rothstein, 88–89)

With such inadequate training, it is little wonder that an American physician advised, "A boy who proved to be unfit for anything else must become a Doctor" (cited in Murphy, 104).

Several factors contributed to improved medical training in the United States in the later part of the nineteenth century. In the 1870s, American medical schools—beginning with Harvard—began reforming medical training. Many medical schools began replacing the two-term curriculum with an optional three-year graded curriculum (Rothstein, p. 285). Harvard became the first medical school to require a three-year graded curriculum for *all* its medical students (Rothstein, 285). After the Civil War, American medical schools became increasingly aware of the need to train physicians in basic sciences such as physiology, pathology, pharmacology, chemistry, and bacteriology (Stowe, 21). In 1893, the newly established Johns Hopkins Medical School began placing more emphasis on laboratory and scientific education for physicians, a pattern adopted by other medical schools in the years to come (Duffy, 130). Scientific medicine was finally becoming the norm in American medical schools by the end of the nineteenth century.

The opening of the Johns Hopkins Medical School in the early 1890s marked an important turning point in American medical training. Founders planned a medical school to rival the best in Europe—one in which physicians would receive the very best training in the sciences central to medical practice and research. In an address to the graduating class of Johns Hopkins University in 1893, Professor William H. Welch, M.D., laid out a plan for the school that would prove revolutionary for American medicine. Dr. Welch called the school's founding "a great opportunity for medical education," partly due to the cooperation of the university and the medical school (cited in Brieger, 318). The university "provided professorships of chemistry, physiology, and pathology" in support of the medical school, whereas the hospital that would be an integral part of the medical school "had secured a staff of able physicians and surgeons, who received from the university the title of professor" (Brieger, 318). Most importantly, Welch understood that Johns Hopkins established a new kind of medical school, one "unhampered by traditions and free to work out its own salvation" (Brieger, 322). The blueprint upon which the new medical school was built laid a foundation for twentieth-century medical training in the United States.

One of the most important considerations of the founders of Johns Hopkins Medical School was the required training for entering students. As mentioned previously, the education of American physicians lagged far behind that of most university students. Dr. Welch pointed out, "At present in this country, no medical school requires for admission knowledge approaching that necessary for entrance into the freshman class of a respectable college" (Brieger, 319). In Europe, in contrast, requirements for admitting medical students were much more stringent.

Dr. Welch and the founders of the Johns Hopkins Medical School faced a dilemma: "We believe that those who have had a liberal education are best fitted for the study of medicine, but it is important that the study of medicine should begin at an age not exceeding twenty or at the utmost twenty-one years" (Brieger, 319). For this to occur, Welch continued, the university should provide prospective medical students with training in physics, chemistry, biology, French and German, as well as the other liberal arts required for a university degree. Welch believed that to require a four-year course of study for a university degree, followed by four years in medical school and a year or more of special training after, was too daunting a task for most American students: "We fully realize that the number of students who will meet these rigid requirements is not likely to be large" (Brieger, 320).

The fruits of their labors would be great, the founders hoped. Welch hoped, "with improvements in educational methods and systems in this country, there will be corresponding improvements in the character of the training to be required in preparation for the study of medicine" (Brieger, 320). The traditionally low standards of admission that plagued other medical schools would not occur at Johns Hopkins, "for our standard is not only vastly higher than has ever before been attempted in this country, but it is not surpassed in any medical school in the world" (Brieger, 320).

Once a student completed an undergraduate course of study and was admitted to Johns Hopkins Medical School, the student began a regiment of study unheard of in American medical schools. A student's first year of medical school "will be devoted chiefly to the study of anatomy, physiology, and physiological chemistry." After the first year, "there will follow three years of strictly professional, mostly practical, study" including "pathology, pharmacology, and the general principles of medicine and surgery" in the second year and, during the final two years, work that "will be very largely clinical, that is bed-side and dispensary instruction" (Brieger, 321).

In addition to requiring much more training than American medical schools traditionally provided, the Johns Hopkins Medical School would place special emphasis "upon practical work in the laboratories and dissecting room and at the bedside" (Brieger, 321). The emphasis on laboratory work highlights another important innovation envisioned by the Johns Hopkins' founders: that of training doctors to be researchers as well as physicians. Welch drew his address to a close by emphasizing this philosophy:

I believe that there is no one thing so essential as that the teacher should be also an investigator and should be capable of imparting something of the spirit of investigation to the student. The medical school should be a place where medicine is not only taught but also studied. It should do its part to advance medical science and art by encouraging original work, and by selecting as its teachers those who have the training and capacity for such work. (Brieger, 322)

This emphasis on research was a relatively new idea in American higher education—an idea pioneered by Johns Hopkins University itself from its founding two decades before. Although "as late as 1900 there were medical schools which admitted students who could not gain entrance to a good liberal arts college" (Shryock 1966, 152), the tide had turned, and American medical education was increasingly focused on quality applicants and quality graduates.

Johns Hopkins Medical School, as well as many other American schools of medicine, actively attempted to change the culture of medical practice in late nineteenth-century America. It would prove to be a long, slow process, however. A generation of physicians ingrained with the traditional practice of medicine tended to distrust scientific medicine. Even in 1902, a popular book warned physicians:

Do not allow yourself to be biased too quickly or too strongly in favor of new theories based on physiological, microscopical, chemical, or other experiments, especially when offered by the unbalanced to establish their abstract conclusions or preconceived notions, or by those who have blindly identified themselves with the latest medical novelty.

   Also do no allow yourself to be led too far from the practical branches of your profession into histology, pathology, microscopical anatomy, refined diagnostics, bacteriomania ... comparative anatomy, biology, psychology, the arrangements of electrical currents in muscular fiber and analogous wide and digressive subjects that merely interest or create a fondness for the marvelous; else it may impair your practical tendency, give your mind a wrong bias, and almost surely make your usefulness as a practicing physician diminish. (cited in Rothstein, 265–66)

As indicated by this quote, the common person in America could very easily become caught between the traditional physician and the new breed of doctor trained in scientific principles. Change was imminent, however, as better medical training and scientific breakthroughs contributed to improved medical care.

CONTRIBUTIONS FROM SCIENCE

   By the later part of the nineteenth century, Americans were becoming increasingly aware of public health issues. People slowly came to the realization that "good nursing, moderate diet, and rest was usually the best therapy" for treating many ailments (Duffy, 126). Unfortunately, physicians were often the last to see the value in such simple steps, preferring instead to continue aggressive, often harmful, treatments. In fact, whereas "the medical profession might debate whether or not epidemic diseases were the product of meteorological conditions, vegetable and animal putrefaction, or even occult forces ... the public never doubted that these disorders were contagious" (Duffy, 127). Cholera epidemics in the United States in the nineteenth century led to an increased public outcry for health professionals and government agencies to intervene. The result was a new sanitation movement that led to the establishment of more powerful health boards across the nation (Duffy, 128). In 1879, Congress made its first attempt to establish public health policy by creating the National Board of Health. Although the board helped organize and finance various health studies, most particularly studies on yellow fever, it never established a successful track record and was disbanded in 1893.

   Although the germ theory of disease was widely resisted—at least until later in the century—by physicians and common people alike, many physicians and public officials involved in the health of Americans began to realize a connection between cleanliness and health. Sanitary health became an increasingly important part of public policy as the century wore on. The physician who specialized in sanitary health procedures was to be trained in many areas, as witnessed by this 1857 account:

But for the sanitarian physician ... there is especially requisite a knowledge of forensic medicine, or the relations of the science of medicine to law; of meteorology, or the effects of climate and atmospheric influences on the body; of the physical character of dynamics of the atmosphere; of the philosophy and practice of ventilation; of various matters of a mechanical kind, bearing on sewerage, house building, street cleaning, and water supply; of statistics of life and mortality; of the literature of epidemics, and of all sanitary improvements. And, lastly, to be a good sanitarian, requires the possession of sound logical faculties. (cited in Brieger, 232)

The sanitarians were concerned with growing sanitation problems caused by the exploding population of cities across the country. It required a long, slow process—a process that continues today—to incorporate the improvements recommended by the sanitarian physician. The health of average Americans, especially those living in crowded urban conditions, improved slowly as sewer systems improved, houses and streets were cleaned, and safer water supplies became available.

Scientific researchers made great strides in postbellum America in the pathology of disease. Improved microscopic techniques and systematic experimentation with reactions of cells to particular drugs led to medical discoveries and new therapies that would prove vital to improving the health of Americans (Shryock 1966, 27).

Perhaps the most important advance in the history of medicine was the growing awareness of antiseptic methods in the operating room. These methods were tied to the controversial germ theory of disease that did not really inculcate itself in the majority of physicians until very late in the century. One mid-century physician, describing a cholera epidemic, expressed the beliefs of most physicians concerning the germ theory:

I can not imagine and think that the so-called "comma bacillus" is the cause and substance of this dread disease. It is repugnant to my common sense to account for such symptoms as are prevailing in cholera, that this "comma bacillus" could produce such symptoms, as, for instance, the changed voice, the vox cholerica, consisting in nothing but a mere whisper without all tone and strength, the hollow, sunken eye with a black halo, the sharp-pointed ice-cold nose, the continual audible rolling of the gas in the bowels, the cramps in the legs, the asphyate condition of the skin, which will keep standing if elevated, above all, the unquenchable thirst, with a cold-pointed tongue, a continual effort to vomit or purge, of what? Of a rice-water stool, colorless, odorless. No, such grave symptoms are not the result of the "comma bacillus," at least I do not believe it. I cannot adhere to such a doctrine which, if true, has done so far no good at all in promoting a more successful treatment. (cited in Rothstein, 266)

Not only does this passage convey the disdain for the idea that a germ could be the cause of disease, there is also a startling description of the suffering caused by cholera. Even later in the century, opposition was such in the United States that it was not unusual "for well known physicians to get up and leave the hall when medical papers were being read which emphasized the germ theory of disease. They wanted to express their contemptuous scorn for such theories and refused to listen to them" (cited in Rothstein, 205). Those physicians who did embrace the germ theory of disease made great strides towards improving the health of people worldwide.

Louis Pasteur's discovery that living organisms in the air could sour wine led the British surgeon, Joseph Lister, to speculate that these same organisms might be responsible for infection, or "putrefaction," of wounds. Lister, aware that carbolic acid was used to treat sewage, began experimenting with the chemical during surgeries. Although his results were striking, it was some time before physicians around the world became convinced of the efficacy of antiseptic practices in surgery. In 1876, Samuel Gross, an eminent American surgeon, maintained, "little, if any faith, is placed by an enlightened or experienced surgeon on this side of the Atlantic in the so-called carbolic acid treatment of Professor Lister, apart from the care which is taken in applying the dressing, or, what is the same thing, in clearing away cots and excluding air from the wound" (cited in Rothstein, 257).

Even when carbolic acid was used to sanitize wounds, bandages, and the surgeon's hands, other unsanitary practices of the day often interfered with effective treatments. It was not unusual for surgeons to perform surgery in the same clothes they wore to work, use the same instruments on one patient after another without cleaning or sanitizing, or bother to wash their hands between surgeries. Until the germ theory of disease was well understood and universally accepted, it seldom occurred to surgeons that such practices might be the cause of the high mortality rate after surgeries. The result was that even "surgeons using antiseptic measures were rarely able to produce statistics more favorable than those of capable and careful surgeons not using antiseptic measures" (cited in Rothstein, 256–57). With the addition of gloves, masks, and sterilization techniques, surgery in the later nineteenth century was much safer—and had a much lower mortality rate—than it had just a few decades earlier.

In the United States, physicians were slow to embrace Lister's practices. The first hospital in the country to adopt antiseptic surgical practices was Roosevelt Hospital in New York City (Brieger, 249). Sanitizing the surgical process at the hospital was similar to the process first adopted by Lister himself:

The principle, therefore, consists in surrounding a wound from its reception to its cure with an atmosphere charged with the vapor of the [carbolic] acid; and to accomplish this the surgeon operates amid a thin cloud of spray made by atomizing a weak solution, in which his hands, instruments, sponges, are also immersed. The blood vessels are tied by carbolized cords, the edges of the wound closed by carbolized stitches, and, finally, layers of gauze impregnated with carbolic acid and resin are bound over the wound and a considerable part of the adjoining skin, the resin causing the carbolic acid to be evolved slowly, so that the dressing need not be changed for several days (Brieger, 249).

As these and similar antiseptic practices became more common at hospitals around the country, the mortality rate from postoperative infection dropped dramatically.

Another advance in surgical practice came with the discovery of the anesthetic properties of ether, nitrous oxide, and chloroform. The discovery of general anesthetics and their subsequent applications in surgery revolutionized medicine in the United States and throughout the world. Before anesthesia, surgery was a frightening process for the patient and surgeon alike:

In case of amputation, it was the custom to bring the patient into the operating room and place him upon the table. [The surgeon] would stand with his hands behind his back and would say to the patient, "Will you have your leg off, or will you not have it off?" If the patient lost courage and said, "No," he had decided not to have the leg amputated, he was at once carried back to his bed in the ward. If, however, he said "Yes," he was immediately taken firmly in hand by a number of strong assistants and the operation went on regardless of whatever he might say thereafter. If his courage failed him *after* this crucial moment, it was too late and no attention was paid to his cries of protest. It was found to be the only practicable method by which an operation could be performed under the gruesome conditions which prevailed before the advent of anesthesia. (cited in Rothstein, 251)

For obvious reasons, surgeries were delayed until absolutely necessary; often until after it was too late to save the patient.

Although it is difficult to assign credit to one person as the discoverer of anesthetics, several Americans played a seminal role in their discovery and application. Scientists, most notably the Englishman Humphry Davy, had experimented with nitrous oxide since the late eighteenth century. The gas-induced antics of nitrous oxide users provided comical relief for various demonstrations given to the general public in the nineteenth century. In 1844, a Connecticut dentist named Horace Wells witnessed such a show and realized the possible uses for nitrous oxide in dentistry. Wells began administering the gas to his patients, providing pain-free tooth extractions. It's difficult to imagine modern dentistry without anesthesia. For instance, when American George Green patented the first electric dental drill in 1875, such a device would certainly have found limited use in the mouths of an unanesthetized patient. Well's experiments came to a tragic end (at least for Wells himself), when he committed suicide in despondency over a failed demonstration of nitrous oxide to medical students at Massachusetts General Hospital.

Other Americans soon took up the experimental use of general anesthetics in various types of surgeries. Among these early pioneers were Wells's protégé, William Morton, who began using ether to induce sleep before dental procedures (actually, another American, Crawford Long, had used ether in operations as early as 1842—however, he did not publicize his finding for many years); Charles T. Jackson who experimented with the use of several types of anesthetics on himself; and John C. Warren, who also experimented with the use of ether in surgery. Within a few years of these first demonstrations of the power of general anesthesia for surgery, the technique had spread across the country and to Europe, offering a mixed bag of results for physicians and their patients:

The immediate impact of anesthesia was to increase surgical intervention. In the first place, anesthesia removed one of the prime objections to surgery, for even the most callous surgeons could not be completely insensitive to the agony of their patients writhing in the straps of the operating table. In the second place, it provided the opportunity to perform more delicate surgery upon the quiescent patient. The greater number of operations, while they promoted surgical technique and emboldened surgeons to broaden their sphere of action, was not immediately beneficial to patients. In a day when cleanliness in hospitals was a fad adopted by only a few doctors, the net effect was to increase the so-called hospital fevers—gangrene, erysipelas, septicemia, and sot forth. The operations were successful, but there was a sharp rise in the number of patients who died from supervening infections. (Duffy, 122–23)

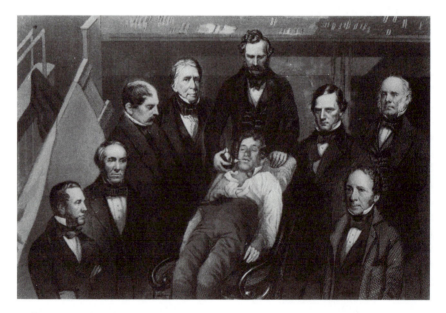

William Morton demonstrating the administration of ether to a patient at Massachusetts General Hospital, 1846. National Library of Medicine.

The use of general anesthesia in surgery allowed surgeons for the first time to operate on the head, chest, and abdomen (Rothstein, 258). However, only when it combined later in the century with a new understanding of antiseptic practices did anesthesia make a significant difference in mortality rates.

Scientific medicine was still in its infancy when the twentieth century began. The nineteenth century found marked improvements in some aspects of medicine, from the nascent germ theory of disease and its applications to antiseptic surgical practices to the discovery of general anesthesia. In addition, a vastly improved educational system for physicians meant better care by more qualified doctors. At the end of the century, these factors contributed to an overall increase in the quality of health and medical treatment for the majority of Americans. Twentieth-century physicians continued the tradition of scientific medicine begun by their nineteenth-century ancestors, completing a revolution in medicine that would culminate in a dizzying array of applications of science and technology to health and medicine.

8

Exploring and Mapping a New Land

Present-day Americans usually don't think of exploration, surveying, navigation, and mapping as everyday activities. In the nineteenth century, however, each played an important role in the everyday life of many Americans. Such activities affected large numbers of Americans on two levels. Many men (and a few women) chose as careers and avocations exploring unknown regions, surveying and mapping new territories, or navigating and mapping the vast American coastline. On another level, even those Americans who did not participate directly in such activities were often deeply affected by their outcomes, as settlers moved west along the trails blazed or coastlines charted by explorers, and settled in towns and territories mapped by pioneer surveyors. The Manifest Destiny mentality of nineteenth-century America meant such pioneers—often driven by and dependent upon scientific advances—were vital members of a growing society.

Explorers and settlers faced many difficulties as they entered the new lands of the United States. Dangers abounded from the land and from the natives who occupied the land. As settlement progressed, new dangers of frontier life arose. Many inventions, some discussed in previous chapters, contributed to the safety and well-being of these early pioneers. Advances in firearms both contributed to the problem of safety as well as to its solution. These new types of firearms were not unknown in the East, but it was in the West that they played their most important role.

NEW WEAPONS FOR AN UNTAMED LAND

Throughout the nineteenth century, American frontiersmen were fond of saying, "God made all men, Colt made all men *equal*." The invention of the Colt revolver is just part of the story, though. Samuel Colt's innovative manufacturing techniques and business practices exemplify the American system of manufacturing.

Although Colt was not the first to envision a revolver type weapon (the American Elisha Collier actually built pistols and rifles with revolving cylinders several decades before Colt), it was Colt who showed the technical expertise and the perseverance needed to manufacture and market the new weapons. Colt first conceived of his radical design while a young man serving aboard a ship bound for East India. After seeing a revolver made by Collier, Colt made a rough wooden model with several improved design features and proceeded to spend the rest of his life perfecting his invention. Upon returning to the United States, Colt made money as a traveling chemistry lecturer while working on his invention, obtaining a patent for a pistol with a revolving cylinder in 1835. In spite of its many advantages over older-style firearms, Colt's first attempts to produce and market the revolver failed. Finally, after winning converts during Indian wars and the Mexican-American war, Colt's new pistol became the most popular weapon in the West.

Many Colt firearms were made at Eli Whitney's armory at New Haven, Connecticut. It had actually been Whitney—of cotton gin fame—who first attempted to manufacture firearms using the concept of interchangeability of parts. Eventually, though, Colt established his own factory in Hartford, Connecticut. Colt had written earlier that he longed to build a gun so that "each arm would be exactly alike and all of its parts would be the same (de Camp, 81). Like Whitney's operation, Colt's armory was a model of nineteenth-century efficiency. The region in which Colt established his factory had a large concentration of skilled mechanics and machinists and already had a history of producing machine-made interchangeable parts. The visionary manufacturer believed that these skilled workers might "by constant practice in a single operation ... become highly skilled and at the same time very quick and expert at their particular task" leading to "better guns and more of them for less money" (de Camp, 81). Colt's experiences with mass production were instrumental in establishing the American System of manufacture as a viable business model. Like many other manufacturers of the time, Colt built an entire town, Coltsville, around his factory, including employee accommodations and public meeting places for religious services, concerts, and lectures. He employed hundreds of workers, including many immigrants, to operate his factory. Colt, like Whitney before him and many others to come, found that one of the advantages of the assembly line method was that unskilled workers could do—for a fraction of the cost—what skilled artisans had done before.

The Colt revolver was not an instant success. One of the first groups to buy the Colt revolver was the Texas Rangers, but sales were so low that, for a time, Colt was forced to stop production. Luckily for Colt, the Rangers found the revolvers quite useful and their requests for more of the guns motivated a new attempt from Colt. The Colt legend grew along with the Texas Ranger legend, as seen in a particular incident involving the lawmen and the new firearm. One afternoon in 1841, Ranger Jack Hayes found himself isolated in a fight with a Comanche war party. Hayes was armed with only a single-shot rifle, but also one of the new Colt revolvers. The Comanches waited patiently, showing themselves as they moved in and out of cover, until Hayes fired his rifle. Their experiences with fighting the Rangers told them that the time was ripe to rush the lone man as he reloaded his weapon. When they did, Hayes opened fire with his Colt revolver. The repeated fire saved his life, as the Comanches retreated under the barrage and other Rangers appeared on the scene. It was episodes such as this that caused the Rangers to request more of the revolvers from Colt.

In spite of its reputation, the Colt revolver was not made with true interchangeable parts. Although mass production guaranteed similarity in

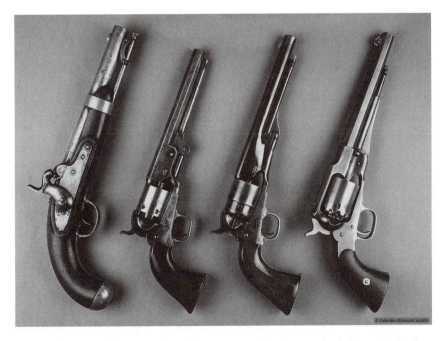

Four common pistols of the nineteenth century. The first on the left is a single-shot pistol, the next two are Colt revolvers, and the fourth is a Remington revolver. Courtesy, Colorado Historical Society.

parts, most still required filing and fitting to work properly. Colt employed a well-known mechanic, Elisha Root, to help mechanize his factory, but even Root showed little interest in the concept of interchangeable parts.

[Root's] tenure at Colt's armory was not distinguished by an aggressive pursuit of interchangeability, with its requisite principles and practices of precision production, but rather by mechanization of work processes. When he moved to Hartford [the location of Colt's factory], Root had had no experience with the model-based gauging techniques used at the national armories to ensure the interchangeability of musket parts. This fact alone may explain why the Colt armory did not use as rigorous a gauging system as, say, the Springfield Armory and also why parts of the Colt revolver, despite the implications of its inventor, did not come close to being interchangeable. (Hounshell, 48)

In spite of Colt's failure to achieve interchangeability, his promotion of the concept and his manufacturing techniques did much to spread the idea, if not the actual practice, of the American system.

Thanks largely to Colt and his factories, the pistol became commonplace on the American frontier. Ownership of a Colt revolver was understood to be a necessity in much of the West. Interestingly, Hollywood dramatizations

Illustration titled "Shooting Buffalos with Colt's Revolving Pistol," 1857. Denver Public Library, Western History Collection, Call No.: Z-3558.

of fast-draw gunslingers "shooting from the hip" are mostly myth. The cost of cartridges precluded extensive practice and the abuse received by Colt revolvers often adversely affected their accuracy (de Camp, 84). Also, most western towns outlawed carrying guns while in town. Of course, this simply led to an increased popularity in smaller Derringer type handguns that could be easily hidden from view. Yet the Colt revolver was far superior to any other weapon in the West. It became the model upon which new guns were designed. Following the Colt revolver, inventors such as B. Tyler Henry, Oliver Winchester, and Christopher Spencer designed repeating rifles; later in the century Richard Gatling invented his famous machine gun.

The emergence of the repeating rifle changed the way of life for several groups who used the new devices. In the West, the repeating rifle became a valued firearm for its ability to fire rounds quickly coupled with the added accuracy over longer distances than a pistol. One of the earliest of these repeating rifles, the Henry repeater, was also one of the first to use self-contained cartridges instead of powder and balls. In addition to the obvious advantage of repeating shots, the cartridge made reloading much easier and was waterproof—a distinct advantage over carrying powder. In one story where the early Henry rifle turned the tide of a battle, a small group of soldiers and civilians from Fort C. F. Smith in Montana was attacked by a much larger group of Sioux Indians. Although the soldiers only had old-fashioned single-shot weapons, one of the civilians carried the new Henry rifle. The barrage of fire that this single rifle was capable of was the difference between life and death for the group. It was said that the civilian with the repeating rifle single-handedly killed 275–300 Sioux Indians in an all-day battle.

The repeating rifle also changed warfare in the United States and around the world. First, used sporadically during the Civil War, the United States Army actually refused to adopt the new rifles until very late in the century. The army continued using muskets and single-shot rifles through the Spanish-American War and the Indian Wars, in spite of the fact that their opponents often carried more firepower after adopting the repeating rifle themselves (Mackey, 326). In fact, Robert Mackey presents a startling look at a familiar battle in American history that may have been decided by the repeating rifle, or lack thereof:

Some historians and archaeologists studying the 1876 Battle of Little Bighorn ("Custer's Last Stand") have discovered mounds of Winchester cartridges surrounding the area where Custer and his men died. This suggests that the Native Americans simply overwhelmed the cavalrymen (who were armed with Civil War-issue repeaters) with firepower from more advanced rifles. (Mackey, 326)

The refusal of the U.S. Army to adopt the most advanced weapons of the time probably cost them many battles and the lives of many soldiers.

Colt and the arms industry were important to American manufacturing as they led the way into mass production and interchangeable parts. On a more immediate level, the guns produced by Colt and his successors proved invaluable to the explorers and settlers who entered the Wild West throughout most of the nineteenth century. The revolver was just one tool of advanced science and technology that would prove critical to the task of settling the new lands.

EXPLORATION

Some of the most important activities undertaken by the scientific community in nineteenth-century America were directly related to exploration. In antebellum America, this usually meant military-directed excursions such as the famous Lewis and Clark expedition. Although the "early relationships between science and the military were extensive and fruitful" they also proved to be "superficial, based upon expediency rather than upon any natural affinity" (Lasby, 255). The military was usually concerned with discipline and security on its expeditions; the scientists, although happy to "utilize the military for protection and transportation," at the same time "voiced a subdued but increasing criticism of the services' control and encroachment in scientific activities" (Lasby, 255).

After the Civil War, civilians and civilian agencies played an expanded role in exploring, mapping, and studying the flora, fauna, and mineralogical traits of the West. Postbellum science increasingly became a point of contention between the military and civilians, with the military often on the losing end:

The greatest blow to the scientific pretensions of the military was the loss of its preeminence in western exploration. To a large extent, this resulted from the fact that gross facts of geography, the very type of information best discovered by the military, were nearly all known. Furthermore, as territories were divided into states, these new jurisdictions usually set up their own fact-finding scientific bodies. The late war had killed off the topographical engineers as a separate group and had hastened the conversion of West Point from a largely engineering school. The Corps of Engineers, with quickly increasing river and harbor appropriations to spend, was being turned into a routine practitioner of civil engineering. (Pursell 1966, 224–25)

After the Civil War, Western exploration became a hodgepodge of government agencies, both military and civilian, vying for funding to complete their own surveys. The Geological Survey, the Coast Survey, the Corps of Engineers, and the General Land Office were all conducting surveys of the West; while at the same time, the soon-to-be famous exploration of the Colorado River and, eventually, much of the Rocky Mountains region, was being conducted under a Congressional bill by John Wesley Powell (Pursell 1966, 225–26).

Powell was one of the strongest advocates of civilian control for scientific work. He argued:

Whenever the scientific works of the General Government fall out of the control of scientific men, and into the hands of officers or functionaries whose interest is not in all research ... science at once becomes severed from the great body of scientific men; it no longer takes a proper part in the great work to be done, and it speedily decays in influence and value. (cited in Lasby, 256)

Powell's concerns echoed throughout nineteenth-century America, and indeed continue to resonate with the concerns of modern scientists who depend on government and/or military funds for their research.

The Lewis and Clark expedition to explore the new lands acquired by President Jefferson is perhaps the most famous journey in American history. Besides exploration and staking claim, as it were, to the new territory, a secondary and little known objective of the expedition was to "enlarge our knoledge [sic] of the geography of our continent ... and to give us a general view of it's population, natural history, productions, soil & climate" (cited in Greene, 196–97). Jefferson hoped that the expedition might discover "further information of the Mammoth, & of the Megatherium," two prehistoric beasts the President believed to be alive in the interior of North America (Greene, 197).

To prepare for the scientific aspect of the journey, Captain Meriwether Lewis, at the request of President Jefferson, embarked on a crash course in botany, zoology, and surveying, as well as mathematics and medicine. Lewis received his training in Philadelphia, the home of the American Philosophical Society and most of the best scientists in America. In the letter to William Clark inviting him to join the epic journey, Lewis emphasized, among other things, the scientific aspect of the trip:

The other objects of this mission are scientific, and of course not less interesting to the U. States than to the world generally, such as the ascertaining by celestial observation the geography of the country through which I will pass; ... the soil and face of the country; it's growth and vegetable productions, its animals; the mineral productions of every description; and in short to collect the best possible information relative to whatever the country may afford as a tribute to general science. (cited in Greene, 198)

The importance to Lewis of the scientific portion of the mission may be gathered from the fact that he carried up to a dozen science reference books through a trip where cargo space was at a premium.

During the course of their epic journey, Lewis and Clark produced maps and drawings of the Missouri River, the Rocky Mountains, and the Columbia River. In addition, they made observations on the flora and fauna of each region, in the process collecting information on and specimens of hundreds of plants, birds, mammals, fish and reptiles, many never before scientifically described. The leaders of the expedition made voluminous notes on meteorology, geological formations, and even attempted to determine the longitude and latitude of various points along their route.

After several delays in publishing their findings (including the death of Lewis in 1809), a report was finally published in 1814 detailing the findings of the expedition. Many of the observations related to natural history found their way into print through the works of American naturalists, while the animal specimens brought back by Lewis and Clark ended up in Charles Wilson Peale's famous museum. Taken together, the scientific findings of the Lewis and Clark expedition influenced many generations of explorers, naturalists, and government officials responsible for expansion policies. Just as importantly, the results of the expedition dispelled some of the myths of the American West and provided a realistic picture, grounded in scientific data, for the multitudes who would soon spill into the new lands.

Although not nearly as famous as Lewis and Clark, William Dunbar and Dr. George Hunter led one of the first expeditions into the new lands acquired by Thomas Jefferson with his Louisiana Purchase. In 1804–1805, the expedition explored several tributaries of the Mississippi River, including the Red, Black, and Oauchita. Dunbar and Hunter, who was a chemist from Philadelphia recommended by President Jefferson, surveyed their route using various astronomical techniques, and made observations and collected specimens of the flora, fauna, and geology of the region. Dunbar even wrote in his report to the President of his discovery of various types of microscopic life in the hot springs at which they camped during the winter (the area which is now Hot Springs National Park, Arkansas).

Other expeditions made important contributions to the knowledge of the world. Charles Wilkes was a United States Naval Lieutenant in charge of the depot of instruments and charts when he was appointed to head an expedition to explore the Southern Seas. The exploration was born when whalers and traders indicated a need for accurate maps of the vast areas little known to sailors. Yet at its completion, the expedition had provided countless other contributions to the expansion of scientific knowledge:

They had explored 280 islands, 800 miles of streams and coast in Oregon, and 1,500 miles of Antarctic coast; cruised the Central Pacific; and brought back hundreds of new species of fish, reptiles, and insects, rich collections in botany, geology, and native artifacts, and a store of charts that served the navy a century later in the Pacific campaigns of World War II. Besides zoology, geology, botany and hydrography, the expedition took account of ethnology, anthropology, meteorology, and physics. (Bruce, 207)

Wilkes brought along many scientists, including James Dwight Dana, who prepared several publications describing the various mineralogical, geological, and zoological specimens he collected during the nearly four-year trip. Dana's work during and after the expedition helped establish him as a preeminent American geologist (Bruce, 209).

This represents only a small sample of the expeditions mounted by the United States during the nineteenth century. Other famous expeditions by such men as John C. Fremont, John Wesley Powell, and Zebulon Pike are important to the history of western expansion. These intrepid explorers paved the way for the surveyors, mapmakers, and settlers who were already pouring into the new regions of the country.

SURVEYING

Surveying was essential for many of the activities preceding and following settlement. Americans armed with scientific techniques provided surveys for building roads, railroads, and bridges; for boundaries between states and counties, as well as between private lands held by farmers, settlers, or land corporations; and for the layout of the new towns appearing all over the landscape. Surveying an unknown wilderness as vast and unyielding as North America proved to be a prodigious task. Some American surveyors were well qualified and accomplished incredible feats of accurate measurement; others were not as talented and made grievous errors in their surveying. Nearly all were hampered by poor-quality equipment and instruments, low pay, little financial support for the surveys, and extremely difficult conditions caused by the size of the land, geographic obstacles, and unfriendly natives. Donald C. Jackson summarizes the main points of colonial American surveying, a science that changed little through the early nineteenth century:

1. The measurement of distance. In the colonial era this was facilitated by use of an iron chain 66 feet long known as Gunter's chain (after Edmund Gunter, an Englishman, who invented it in 1620). Conveniently, eighty chains equaled one mile, and ten square chains equaled one acre. One chain also equaled four poles (or rods), each 16.5 feet long. To calculate the distance between two points, a Gunter's chain was merely stretched out as many times as necessary in order to connect the two points. For example, if it required 4.25 lengths of Gunter's chain to connect two points, then they were 280.5 feet apart.
2. The measurement of direction. This involved the use of magnetic compasses to orient the survey line to a north-south axis (as determined by a region's magnetic declination). Sightings made between two points could provide directional readings by use of a vernier, an instrument that allowed the measurement of horizontal angles. A vernier divided the circular bas of the tripod-mounted sight into 360 degrees and provided a means of determining how much of a sight line diverged from magnetic north-south.
3. The measurement of elevation. The measurement of relative heights was not something that the typical colonial land surveyor needed to worry

about in determining the location and size of various tracts of land. However, for surveyors involved in laying out roads and canals, the measurement of elevations became important. The key to the process lay in using a spirit level that contained an enclosed glass cylinder of water with a small air bubble. By attaching this level to either an open or a telescopic sight, elevation changes could be determined by placing a vertical measuring rod some distance away and then reading through the sight the relative height of the second location. By moving across the terrain and making a series of "backsighting" and "foresighting" readings between evenly spaced points, it was possible for a surveyor to calculate changes in elevation that did not need to be corrected relative to the curvature of the earth. Differences in elevation could also be determined using readings from a "theodolite," an instrument that enabled a surveyor to measure vertical angles; by taking distance and angular measurements between two points, trigonometry could be used to calculate vertical distances. However, in the eighteenth and early nineteenth centuries theodolites were expensive, and they did not find much use among general surveyors. (Jackson, 204–5)

Railroad building would lead to improvements in these techniques out of necessity as tracks were laid into places where roads had never gone. Measuring elevation changes became more important to surveyors. The grade at which a locomotive could climb, or safely descend, was vital and the knowledge of a particular surveyor could mean the difference between a safe railroad and one fraught with dangers.

For the first half of the nineteenth century, surveying and engineering in America usually fell to the Army Corps of Engineers, established at West Point in 1802. The Topographical Engineers, initially a bureau with the Corps of Engineers but later an independent corps, were especially influential in bringing a scientific eye to Western exploration. In antebellum America, the Topographical Engineers, "Armed with more accurate techniques and equipment, consumed by an enthusiasm for inquiry, and fired by the spirit of Manifest Destiny ... provided scientific mapping for half a continent" (Lasby, 253). As early as 1819, the Topographical Engineers participated in explorations involving a great variety of scientists and scientific purposes, as described by an observer to an expedition to explore the headwaters of the Platte and Red Rivers:

Botanists, mineralogists, chemists, artisans, cultivators, scholars, soldiers; the love of peace, the capacity for war; philosophical [scientific] apparatus and military supplies; telescopes and cannon, garden seeds and gunpowder; the arts of civil life and the force to defend them—all are seen aboard. (cited in Lasby, 253)

Whether the job fell to Army Engineers or civilian scientists, surveying the western lands played a critical role in the development of a uniquely American settlement pattern, and scientific surveying became the cornerstone of land distribution in the West. Surveyed and sold in square grids,

A tripod signal erected by the U.S. Coast Survey near Chattanooga, Tennessee, in 1864. Library of Congress.

towns, and farms revealed an organization unknown in Europe and other parts of the world. Surveying and mapping were only the first steps in a process that continued with the purchase of land (or, in many cases, land given away by federal and state government) and subsequent settlement. In the words of Andro Linklater, "The desire to possess land drew people westward, but it was the survey that made possession legal" (Linklater, 166). Thus, the planners "transformed land into a commodity that could be precisely delimited, purchased, and registered in a land office, even if no one had ever seen it" (Nye 2003, 27).

Everywhere the United States acquired new land, and settlers clamored for the right to settle, the same procedure unfolded. The federal government, or in some cases state governments, sent teams of surveyors to lay out the new lands in tidy grids. Then, "When the surveyor's plat was

A man poses with a survey tool used to measure distances, called a waywiser. Part of the Wheeler Expedition in Nevada County, California, 1876. Denver Public Library, Western History Collection, Call No.: Z-7871.

delivered to the district land office, it would show every square of prairie or corner of forest had been given an identity" (Linklater, 168). One farm might be identified as "Section 21, Township 14 North, Range 5 West, Third Principal Meridian" and, once the claim was paid for and the trans-action completed, "the prairie or forest became private property, whose ownership would be protected by the full force of the law" (Linklater, 168). Thousands upon thousands of Americans owed their legal owner-ship of the land, and therefore their right to lawful protection of their possession, to this system.

Interesting results arose from the orderly and seemingly logical method of surveying the land. The 640-acre (one square mile) "sections" were superimposed on the land regardless of natural features. The lines were drawn without regard for meandering rivers and creeks, or hills and mountain ranges. They also ignored important natural resources like water. One section might enclose a river providing plenty of water for the lucky farmer, while another might literally be left high and dry. Through it all, surveyors overcame a myriad of technical problems. One such problem arose when these squares were stacked on each other like blocks as the survey journeyed north. Since the meridians, or lines of longitude converge at the North Pole, boundary lines following carefully surveyed meridians resulted in sections and townships that were narrower at their northern boundary. This was corrected by adjusting the meridian lines at specified distances. This correction presented an interesting problem for nineteenth-century travelers, one that has only worsened with the appearance of faster modes of transportation such as automobiles:

The jog created by these "correction lines," where the old north-south line abruptly stopped and a new one began 50 or 60 yards farther east or west, became a feature of the grid, and because back roads tend to follow surveyors' lines, they present an interesting driving hazard today. After miles of straight gravel or blacktop, the sudden appearance of a correction line catches most drivers by surprise, and frantic tire marks show where vehicles have been thrown into hasty ninety-degree turns, followed by a second skid after a short stretch running west or east when the road heads north again onto the new meridian. (Linklater, 162)

In spite of its numerous inadequacies, the survey of American lands accomplished the goal of partitioning the West with a minimum of cost and effort and made land ownership a basis upon which American culture was founded.

NAVIGATION

While surveyors were organizing the land into manageable pieces ready for private ownership, Americans were performing similar duties at sea. Navigation manuals were centrally important for a nation with extensive seacoasts. Whereas the United States Coast Survey (discussed in Chapter 9), led such efforts after the first quarter of the century, individuals were primarily responsible for advances in navigation from the turn of the century until the 1820s. One of these individuals played a seminal role in navigation, and in American science in general, in the early nineteenth century. His life story serves as an excellent example of how American scientists worked around the turn of the century and what sort of impact they had on everyday life.

Nathaniel Bowditch is the epitome of the American scientist in the early part of the nineteenth century. His life and work not only represent the practical aspects of American science, but also the fruits of his labors influenced seafaring Americans—indeed sailors from around the world—for many years. Bowditch began his career by achieving fame as a practical man of science and ended it by publishing a translation of and commentary on one of the most important theoretical scientific works of the century—all the while applying his innate mathematical abilities in his chosen career as an insurance actuary.

Bowditch was born in Salem, Massachusetts, at a time when the port city played an important role in American sea commerce. At the age of 22 years, Bowditch did what many boys and young men from Salem eventually did: He put out to sea in a merchant ship. While taking part in various capacities in five lengthy sea voyages, Bowditch studied from books brought along on the trip; took meticulous notes concerning the voyage; and became an expert, in fact one might say legendary, navigator. Tales abound concerning Bowditch's navigational prowess. In one such tale, the citizens of Salem were stunned one Christmas day to find Bowditch walking down a misty Salem street, having returned from a long voyage. Bowditch had navigated his way safely into the harbor in a dense fog that no other captain would have dared to challenge (Bowditch, 20–21).

Bowditch also took the opportunity on these long voyages to instruct his fellow shipmates on the art and science of navigation, until he became famous for his crews' ability to navigate a ship, from the captain all the way down to the ship's cook. In spite of the fact that Bowditch never held a teaching position, his successful efforts in teaching navigation to his mates set the stage for a long career committed to disseminating scientific and mathematical knowledge throughout the United States and the rest of the English-speaking world.

One of Bowditch's first discoveries was an improved method for using lunar observations to find longitude. Because chronometers were still undependable and expensive, finding a ship's location by this method was an important tool in navigation. In 1799, Bowditch used his navigation and mathematical talents to edit and correct John Hamilton Moore's *Practical Navigator.* Moore, an Englishman, had composed a guide to navigation that was so full of errors that by the time Bowditch had published a third edition in 1802 it was essentially a new work and was appropriately credited to Nathaniel Bowditch as the author.

The New American Practical Navigator almost instantly became an indispensable guide to navigation on the high seas. Known to seafarers the world over as the "Bowditch," *The New American Practical Navigator* also contained most of the mathematics and astronomy needed by ordinary seamen to find their way by celestial navigation rather than by dead reckoning. It soon became a book that "every British seaman had to read if he hoped to get ahead of the Yankee skippers" (V. W. Brooks, 51). In this monumental work, Bowditch added introductions to basic mathematics like arithmetic, geometry, trigonometry, and the use of logarithms. He also supplied instruction in astronomy, geography, and the basics of navigation. In a foreshadowing of his future career as an actuary, Bowditch included excerpts on marine insurance, adapted to American laws, from a London publication called the *Ship-Masters Assistant.* This discussion on insurance was primarily a legal explanation of insurance policies, not a mathematical evaluation of actuarial questions.

The publication of *The New American Practical Navigator* brought to Bowditch an international reputation that few American authors had achieved. An admiring member of the Royal Society of London called it "the best book on that subject which has ever fallen into my hands." After going through numerous editions, *The New American Practical Navigator* continues to be used today. (In fact, the 1995 edition can be purchased online for around $125.) Reviews of Bowditch's classic work on Amazon. com include comments like "as a first year student in a marine program in Canada I don't know where I would be with out 'Bowditch,'" "One will find this book in every chart room on every U.S. Capital ship, Coast Guard and Navy alike," and "This is the most comprehensive book on navigation ever written." Bowditch's *New American Practical Navigator* became a timeless classic in navigation.

Three aspects of the impact of *The New American Practical Navigator* deserve mention. First, as one would expect in early nineteenth-century America, this contribution to science was important for its utility. No new theories or laws of nature were propounded, and no new conceptual advances were made. Bowditch had created, as the title clearly states, a practical guide; one as indispensable to European sailors as it was to their American counterparts. Second, the work was initially based on a British publication. Despite the fact that voluminous changes made by Bowditch earned him the right to place his name as the author, at a basic level this was not an original work, but rather a derivative one. Finally, much of Bowditch's work on the *Practical Navigator* was done for educational purposes. Bowditch actively participated in the pursuit of educating Americans in science. This dedication to education was essential if the developing nation was to catch up with, and eventually compete with, European science.

The year 1802 was especially significant for Nathaniel Bowditch: Then the *Practical Navigator* was credited to him as author. The importance of this work was not lost on the academic community, for in 1802 Bowditch was given an honorary master of arts from Harvard. It was also in 1802 that Bowditch purchased the first volume of Pierre Simon Laplace's monumental work, *Mécanique Céleste*. Bowditch acquired this important and very difficult treatise just before he was to embark on his last voyage, this time as master of the ship. This position actually required very little of Bowditch, and thus he was able to spend long calm days at sea studying his new acquisition.

After his fifth and last sea voyage, Bowditch was offered, and accepted, the position of president of the Essex Fire and Insurance Company in Salem. Bowditch spent the rest of his life as an insurance company officer, first in Salem and later in Boston. Through it all, he continued his habit of study and research after business hours. Bowditch's reputation was such that, by 1806, he was offered the Hollis Professorship of Mathematics and Natural Philosophy at Harvard. He turned this position down, as he was later to turn down offers from the University of Virginia in 1818 and West Point in 1820.

Although the second major work of Bowditch's career did not have the impact on the common American that his work on navigation had on the country's sailors, it deserves mention as an important part of the fabric of antebellum American science. His work also sheds light on the difficulties encountered by Americans interested in furthering scientific knowledge.

In a time when European (especially British) critics usually degraded American scholarship and American science, Bowditch's translation of and commentary *Mécanique Céleste,* the seminal work of the great French scientist Simon de Laplace, was extremely well received by his European contemporaries. Charles Babbage declared the English translation of *Mécanique Céleste* "a proud circumstance for America that she has preceded her parent country in such an undertaking" (Greene, 155). The *London Quarterly Review,* after Bowditch's publication of the first volume in 1829, called the work "invaluable" to the student of celestial mechanics. The same review called

the idea of undertaking a translation of the whole *Mécanique Céleste* . . . one which, from what we have hitherto had reason to conceive of the popularity and diffusion of mathematical knowledge on the opposite shores of the Atlantic, we should never have expected to have found originated—or, at least, carried into execution, in that quarter. (*London Quarterly Review,* 558)

Bowditch's translation of *Mécanique Céleste* not only supplied the English-speaking world with Laplace's original work, but his voluminous commentary (which more than doubled the length of Laplace's original work) made the text accessible to countless people unable or unwilling to follow Laplace's difficult mathematics. In his introduction to the translation, Bowditch stated that his primary purpose was to reduce the time and labor required to understand Laplace's work even by "persons, who have a strong and decided taste for mathematical studies." Bowditch undoubtedly succeeded in this aim. The Council of the Royal Astronomical Society called Bowditch's translation

unquestionably fitted to bring the *Mécanique Céleste* within the grasp of a number of students exceeding five times, at least, that of those who could master Laplace by themselves. (Greene, 155–56)

Even the noted British mathematician Charles Babbage commented, "I have by its [Bowditch's translation] assistance been relieved from many an hour of weary labor which I have thus been enabled to devote to my own undertakings." Clearly, the commentary added by Bowditch was an important tool utilized by student and professor alike.

How difficult was Laplace's original text? It had been noted in several European publications that hardly 12 persons in all of Britain could read and understand *Mécanique Céleste.* Bowditch himself stated, "Whenever I meet in Laplace with the words 'Thus, it plainly appears,' I am sure that hours, perhaps days, of hard study will alone enable me to discover *how* it plainly appears." This difficulty explains, perhaps even more than the length of the work, the many years that Bowditch spent on the project.

As we have seen, Bowditch's translation of and commentary on *Mécanique Céleste* was very well received by his fellow mathematicians and astronomers in Europe. But to understand the reception of Bowditch and his works by his American and European contemporaries, it is important to remember the perception of American science and scientists in the early nineteenth century. America had no scientists, at least in mathematics and the physical sciences, of the first rank. Although Bowditch was the leading mathematician in America, he realized that he was not of the same caliber as the leading European mathematicians. Bowditch's son, Henry, recorded a conversation he had with his father on this subject. Nathaniel Bowditch stated:

Archimedes was of the same order of talent as Newton, and we honor him much; and Leibniz was equal to either of them. Euclid was a second-rate mathematician, yet I should like to see some of his handwriting. My order of talent is very different from that of Laplace. Laplace originates things which it would have been impossible for me to have originated. Laplace was of the Newton class, and there is the same difference between Laplace and myself as between Archimedes and Euclid. (Berry, 218)

It is especially interesting that Bowditch compared himself to Euclid, while he compared Laplace to Newton and Archimedes. The works of Newton and Archimedes were brilliant but very difficult for most readers, even talented ones. Euclid, in contrast, was more of a compiler than an originator. His *Elements* was more a textbook than original mathematics. These traits of compilation, explanation, and education are very much the same traits as are seen in most of Bowditch's works.

Nathaniel Bowditch left a lasting legacy on American mathematics, astronomy, and science in general. Bowditch, through his publications and correspondence, had a direct influence on the leading American scientists of the day. He encouraged and guided Benjamin Peirce, who would become the leading American mathematician of the next generation. In addition, Bowditch's works continued to influence students of mathematics, astronomy, and navigation for many generations. His *New American Practical Navigator* continues to play a large role in the education and training of mariners all over the world, and his translation of *Mécanique Céleste* also retains an important place in mathematical astronomy. The scientific community in America, in its embryonic stage in the early nineteenth century, owed a significant part of its future development to Nathaniel Bowditch.

Exploration, surveying, and navigation all played a central role in the expansion of the United States in the nineteenth century. In fact, historian Daniel Boorstin assigns to these activities an importance that goes beyond a merely physical presence in an unknown land:

For Americans, then, discovery and growth were synonymous from the very beginning. Old World nations knew—or thought they knew—their extent, their boundaries, their topography, and their resources. Americans expected their nation to grow as they discovered where they were and what they had to work with. If America had not remained a "dark continent" throughout nearly the whole first century of its national existence, it is doubtful whether Americans could have been so vital and so excited. (Boorstin, 223)

Science possessed a dual role in gathering the knowledge about the boundaries, the topography, and the resources of the unexplored lands. First, science and the instruments of science were important tools that made gathering the new knowledge possible. In addition, a plethora of new discoveries added to the storehouse of scientific knowledge. Many of the exploration and surveying parties were accompanied by botanists, geologists, and other naturalists whose purpose was to gather data on the flora, fauna, and geological structures of the new lands. The dissemination, classification, and analysis of this incredible bounty of new information represented the life work of many scientists, both American and foreign, for several generations. Even Americans going about their everyday business were involved in this great expansion of science. Farmers, traders, explorers, trappers, and other travelers collected plants, animals, rocks and minerals, even fossils, many of which made their way to a museum or scientific collection for analysis or classification. Americans of all backgrounds participated in science through their presence in unexplored regions.

9

Scientific and Technical Institutions

In the nineteenth century, a growing number of Americans came to realize the profound impact science and technology had, and would continue to have, on everyday life. Americans from all walks of life embraced science in ways that are foreign to our modern experience. In today's world, where entertainment can be had with the touch of a finger to a remote control; where electronic games are a chief (and cheap) source of diversion for millions of children and adults; and where every newspaper offers a plethora of social and cultural activities for any age, it is difficult to conceive of science as "entertainment." But in a nineteenth-century world where diversions were not as easily obtained, such activities as traveling lectures and scientific demonstrations offered the general public the opportunity to experience new and wonderful things. Although this is a book about the ways in which science and technology affected everyday life in nineteenth-century America, it is impossible to fully understand the relationship between science and the population without at least a cursory understanding of the scientific establishment in the United States.

Scientific and technological developments in nineteenth-century America were more eagerly anticipated and embraced by the general public than they are today. Courses and lectures offered to the public at such places as the Albany Institute in New York or the Franklin Institute in Philadelphia were well attended by artisans, mechanics (an emerging class of skilled laborers who worked with the new machines of the Industrial Age), and others of diverse social and economic backgrounds. Exhibits at museums such as Charles Willson Peale's museum in Philadelphia and the Smithsonian Natural History Museum in Washington, DC, attracted interest from people in all walks of American life. Later in the century, cities began building museums as vessels of public education. The motto of New York's American Museum of Natural History, for instance, was "for the people, for education, for science." Special exhibits such as those found at the 1876 Centennial in Philadelphia drew visitors from all over the country to marvel at scientific and technological wonders from the United States and the rest of the world.

Americans embraced science in the nineteenth century, hoping to attain a higher intellectual plane:

Though abstract science and the institutions which foster it did not flourish in ante-Bellum America, a social climate favorable to its ultimate growth was created.... Americans could view science as an admirable, even socially prestigious, avocation—if not as a practical vocation. Science clubs and botanical and mineralogical trips sponsored by academies and secondary schools all helped to provide young men and even young ladies with a sedate interest in science and left in the minds of a few an inspiration sufficient to encourage the devotion of later years to its pursuit. (Rosenberg 1966, 159)

Because of this heightened interest in science, and the technology produced by science, it is appropriate to close this book with a chapter that looks briefly at the scientific and technical institutions that sprung up all over America in the nineteenth century, as well as the men who contributed to the growth and popularity of science in the United States.

SCIENCE IN GOVERNMENT AGENCIES

In its first century of existence, the United States government struggled to find its place in the support structure of scientific institutions. Only after protracted battles between various factions in and out of government did institutions such as the National Observatory and the Smithsonian Institution arise. As the century progressed, the federal government became more and more involved in supporting institutions of all types, including those dedicated to the idea of employing science for the common good. From exploring and surveying the vast lands of America, to supporting agriculture and science education, by the end of the century the United States government was becoming an important ally in the progress of national science.

The Constitution did not provide for federal funding or sponsorship of science by the government. Most believed that this was one of the many responsibilities of the states; therefore, there was great resistance to the establishment of any federal entity whose purpose was scientific in nature. The first scientific institution established by the federal government was the United States Coast Survey, authorized by Congress in 1807 but not actually established until nearly a decade later. The Coast Survey was created for the very important purpose of charting the country's coast for safer shipping.

The first superintendent of the United States Coast Survey was the Swiss immigrant Ferdinand Hassler. In 1811, Hassler traveled to Europe for the purpose of purchasing scientific instruments needed for the survey. Surprisingly, this buying trip was to last until 1815, in part due to disruptions caused by the War of 1812. After Hassler's return, he was officially named superintendent of the survey. Unfortunately, political infighting led to major delays and eventually to Hassler's departure from the survey. After a long estrangement—when little was done in surveying the coast—Hassler returned as superintendent in 1832 and began anew the serious work at hand.

Hassler was a world-class scientist who demanded that every aspect of the survey be performed to exacting standards. At times, this insistence on methodical surveying did not sit well with an impatient Congress. Through his force of will and a few fortuitous discoveries, Hassler was able to maintain his position and the funding for the Coast Survey. One of these discoveries, a previously uncharted channel leading into the important trading center of New York harbor, served notice to the detractors of the Coast Survey of the importance of their ongoing work.

Upon Hassler's death, Alexander Dallas Bache became the second superintendent of the United States Coast Survey. Bache is one of the most important figures in nineteenth-century American science. From his position at the Coast Survey, he influenced an incredible variety of sciences and scientists. From employing civilian and military scientists as full-time assistants, to assigning special projects to leading scientists in the country not employed by the Coast Survey, Bache used his position to help establish American science as a viable profession.

Bache was well positioned to become a leader of American science in the middle part of the century. The great-grandson of Benjamin Franklin, Bache graduated from West Point at the top of his class and spent the early part of his career as a university professor and administrator. After becoming superintendent of the Coast Survey, Bache expanded on the groundwork laid by Hassler until the Coast Survey was active in every state and in the new territories along the Pacific Coast. Under Bache's leadership, the Coast Survey undertook many important tasks, including determination of longitudes of various locations in the United States; directing magnetic, hydrographical, seismological, topographical, and meteorological studies of various parts of the country; and performing studies of the Gulf Stream and its relationship to navigation. One important outcome of the Coast Survey's longitudinal studies was the development of what became known as the American method for determining differences in longitudes between two locations. This method involved astronomical observations made at the two locations and communicated via telegraph at precise instances. It resulted in dramatic improvements in measuring differences in longitude, especially between points on opposite sides of the Atlantic Ocean after the completion of the transatlantic telegraph. After Bache's death in 1867, Benjamin Peirce was appointed superintendent of the Coast Survey. Peirce was a renowned mathematician from Harvard who had served for many years under Bache making determinations of longitudes.

Besides the important information regarding the physical contours of the coast, the Coast Survey produced an unexpected benefit. At a time when scientific education was difficult to come by anywhere in the country, the Coast Survey provided a training ground for young naval officers with scientific and mathematical interests. Many of these officers went on to important careers in both naval and civilian science.

While the Coast Survey established itself as an important scientific entity, charged with understanding the oceans and coasts of the surrounding the United States, the need to accumulate similar knowledge about the interior of the country led to the birth of several geological surveys. As with the establishment of other government-supported organizations, when it became apparent that a need existed for geological surveys, the authority of the individual states took precedent over that

Alexander Dallas Bache in the field, circa 1858. NOAA Central Library.

of the federal government. Many states established geological surveys from the 1820s onward to document their geological and mineralogical resources. Denison Olmsted carried out the first of these state surveys for North Carolina in 1823.

As the nation grew westward, adding to the land in the public domain and with the discovery of valuable mineral resources on these public lands, it became apparent that the federal government would require the authority to survey, map, and document these lands and their resources. The Corps of Topographical Engineers was established in 1838 to survey these public lands, but it was not until 1879 that the federal government established the United States Geological Survey. Under the leadership of its first two directors, Clarence King and John Wesley Powell, the Geological Survey contributed immeasurably to the settlement and economic vitality of the nation, especially the western lands. This was a demonstrated need, as only 200 million acres of the more than 1.2 billion acres of public lands had been surveyed (Rabbitt). The Geological Survey mapped lands for their mineral content; the type and value of its timber; and its suitability for agriculture, including preparing reports on irrigation of arid and semi-arid lands. All the while, the survey participated in activities that contributed to basic scientific knowledge whenever possible. Through these duties, the United States Geological Survey came to have a great influence over a wide variety of Americans, from farmers to miners, as they struggled to survive and thrive in the American West.

Two events of 1862, one a Presidential mandate and the other an act of Congress, marked a new era of cooperation between science and government. Abraham Lincoln created the United States Department of Agriculture (USDA) in 1862 as a direct descendent of the agricultural division of the Patent Office. As a division of the Patent Office, agricultural researchers in the United States had already established a track record in things such as animal breeding, insect control, soil science, and the use of technology to improve agricultural practices in the country.

The goal of the USDA, in the words of its first commissioner, Isaac Newton (no, not *that* Isaac Newton!), was to help the farmer "make two blades of grass grow where one grew before" (Harding, 27). Toward this goal, the USDA employed entomologists, chemists, botanists, statisticians, and a variety of other scientists to study agricultural issues. During the nineteenth century, the USDA conducted successful studies in plant breeding, fertilizer composition, and food safety, to name a few.

Historian of technology Carroll Pursell summarizes the birth of the complicated interactions between government agency, science, industry, and agriculture:

At the very time that America was being converted into a modern industrial nation, and its farmers were growing restive under the burden of a changing economy which they could neither understand nor control, the Department of

Agriculture evolved into a tool of unprecedented effectiveness for dealing with rural problems. The cutting edge of this tool was to be science, and it was in the future to be directed against specific problems. What in fact happened was that the Department gave birth to that organizational form that was to prove so fruitful for government science in the future—the bureau. (Pursell 1966, 228)

One example of a USDA success story is the work of Charles V. Riley. A disease called cottony cushion scale was ravaging California's citrus crop when Riley, then an entomologist for the USDA, suggested importing a certain species of Australian beetle, a natural predator of the scale. The success of Riley's battle with cottony cushion scale was one of the first major scientific applications of biological controls on agricultural pests.

President Lincoln's creation of the USDA represents an early instance of the executive branch taking an active role in promoting science; the Morrill Act represents the legislative branch's entry into the same movement. The Morrill Act was perhaps the single most influential act of Congress ever devised to aid higher education in the United States. First introduced to Congress in 1857 by Justin Smith Morrill, a Vermont Senator, the Act was vetoed by President Buchanan under pressure from Southern influences. In 1862, with secession eliminating the "Southern influences," President Lincoln signed the Morrill Act into law.

The Morrill Act provided for the use of public lands to help finance new state colleges and universities. The Act provided each state with 30,000 acres of land for every member of Congress in its delegation. These lands could then be sold to finance the establishment of one or more new colleges. The new colleges were to emphasize agricultural and technical education, in stark contrast to the traditional liberal arts education of the established colleges and universities. For the son of a common man, the merchant, artisan or farmer, the Morrill Act provided for:

the endowment, support, and maintenance of at least one college where the leading object shall be, without excluding other scientific and classical studies, and including military tactics, to teach such branches of learning as are related to agriculture and mechanical arts ... in order to promote the liberal and practical education of the industrial classes in the several pursuits and professions in life. (Morrill Act, section 4)

Morrill understood the need for a college education for the children of farmers and the working class. He wanted to establish new colleges and universities throughout the country because, in his own words,

most of the existing collegiate institutions and their feeders were based upon the classic plan of teaching those only destined to pursue the so-called learned professions, leaving farmers and mechanics and all those who must win their bread by labor, to the haphazard of being self-taught or not scientifically taught at all, and restricting the number of those who might be supposed to be qualified to fill places of higher consideration in private or public employments to the limited number of the graduates of the literary institutions. The thoroughly educated, being most sure to educate their sons, appeared to be perpetuating a monopoly of education inconsistent with the welfare and complete prosperity of American institutions. (cited in Struik, 442)

Iowa initiated the remarkable new experiment in education when it opened Iowa State University in 1869. The Morrill Act and the resulting state colleges and universities made higher education a democratic process for the first time.

The Morrill Act was extremely important to agriculture in the United States because it provided for the education of farmers' children. Of equal, and possibly more direct importance to agriculture, was the Hatch Act of 1887. The purpose of the Hatch Act was "to aid in acquiring and diffusing among the people of the United States useful and practical information on subjects connected with agriculture and to promote scientific investigation and experiment respecting the principles and application of agricultural science." These purposes were carried out through the establishment of agricultural experiment stations associated with the various state colleges. By 1893, there were 49 experiment stations created under the Hatch Act throughout the country.

SCIENTIFIC AND TECHNICAL SOCIETIES

"Nothing, in my view, more deserves attention than the intellectual and moral associations in America" (Tocqueville, 517). This line, from the most famous foreign commentator on American democracy, expressed the view that in order to understand nineteenth-century Americans, one must attempt to understand their desire to come together to form clubs, societies, and associations. During his extended tour of America, Tocqueville was struck by the fact that

Americans of all ages, all stations in life, and all types of disposition are forever forming associations. There are not only commercial and industrial associations in which all take part, but others of a thousand different types—religious, moral, serious, futile, very general and very limited, immensely large and very minute. . . . In every case, at the head of any new undertaking, where in France you would find the government or in England some territorial magnate, in the United States you are sure to find an association. (Tocqueville, 513)

Tocqueville realized the power behind these associations. He knew that, in a democracy, such associations spurred action:

As soon as several Americans have conceived a sentiment or an idea that they want to produce before the world, they seek each other out, and when found, they unite. Thenceforth they are no longer isolated individuals, but a power conspicuous from the distance whose actions serve as an example; when it speaks, men listen. (Tocqueville, 516)

These sentiments applied to all sorts of associations, including the many scientific and technological associations formed in the nineteenth century. An understanding of the workings of these associations leads to a better understanding of American attitudes toward the sciences.

The first scientific societies founded in the United States were, for the most part, gathering places for educated Americans to discuss science, as well as other intellectual subjects. They were not scientific societies in terms of the modern definition—organizations of professionals specializing in particular branches of science. Moreover, before the mid-nineteenth century scientific societies were regional, rather than national, in nature. For these reasons, the first societies played a smaller role in the advancement of American science than did organizations established after mid-century.

The American Philosophical Society (APS) was the first learned society of any importance founded in the British colonies of North America. Its incorporation represents America's first sustained attempt to emulate the learned societies of Europe, even before achieving independence. The Society, patterned after the Royal Society of London, published the first volume of its *Transactions* in 1771. The stated purpose of the APS was to extend man's knowledge of science. The knowledge that the Society claimed to target, at least at its inception, was not the esoteric and theoretical knowledge of "pure" science, but rather useful knowledge that might be utilized for the good of the American people.

The American Philosophical Society initially formed six committees with responsibilities in the following areas:

1. Geography, Mathematics, Natural Philosophy, and Astronomy.
2. Medicine and Anatomy.
3. Natural History and Chymistry [sic].
4. Trade and Commerce.
5. Mechanics and Architecture.
6. Husbandry and American Improvements.

Although the founders of the APS initially claimed an almost exclusive interest in practical science, in reality pure science played a small but important role in the pages of the *Transactions* of the Society. For instance, although the subjects of applied mathematics such as surveying, navigation, mechanics, and astronomy dominated the early volumes, a few contributors did write papers on pure mathematics.

Although conceived of as national societies, the American Philosophical Society and others like it remained largely local in scope. The lack of a truly national scientific organization hindered the advancement of science in the United States. This all changed in 1848 when members of the Association of American Geologists and Naturalists formally changed their name to the American Association for the Advancement of Science (AAAS), and in the process changed the scope of the organization to include the promotion of all the sciences in America.

Benjamin Silliman, the first president of the AAAS, was one of the most influential American men of science in the nineteenth century. Silliman, already established as a professor of chemistry and natural history at Yale, was the founder and publisher of the *American Journal of Science*. Under Silliman's guidance, and the guidance of future leaders, the AAAS made many significant contributions to life in America in the nineteenth century, including pioneering support of conservation of natural resources. The original founders of the AAAS conceived of the Association as "a vehicle for influencing national scientific policies and eliminating amateurism in American science" (Sinclair, 250). The AAAS role as promoter of American science, however, resulted in a large membership that included the leading American scientists of the day, as well as a large number of nonscientists from academia, politics, and various walks of life. Although such a membership was rooted in the democratic foundations of the nation, it also led to a dilution of the quality of science presented at the annual meetings and published in the Association's journal, *Science*. Several American scientists, convinced of the importance of including only the scientific elite in shaping the role of science in America, began plans for a new scientific organization sanctioned by the federal government and open to only the best scientists in the nation.

The culmination of a long struggle resulted in the establishment of the National Academy of Sciences (NAS) in 1863. The NAS was the result of years of work and political maneuvering by the leading American scientists of the nineteenth century: Alexander Dallas Bache, Benjamin Peirce, Benjamin Gould, Charles Davies, and Louis Agassiz. These men argued for an organization limited to an elite membership and devoted to advising the federal government on scientific matters. Initially, the Academy was limited to only 50 members. It soon became the most prestigious scientific society in the country, although its goals of serving the government—and reaping financial support for this service—were not realized to the extent its founders had hoped.

In addition to the societies formed by so-called pure scientists, the nineteenth century was extremely important to the development of the engineering profession in the United States, as witnessed by the formation of various engineering societies. The first such society, formed in 1852, was called The American Society of Engineers and Architects (later becoming the American Society of Civil Engineers). This was closely followed by the appearance of The American Institute of Mining and Metallurgical Engineers and other societies for engineering specialties. A rough progression of the application of new science and technology can be seen from these various societies: The need for civil engineers and architects for roads and building construction preceded an increased need for technical expertise in mining and refining the minerals needed for continued progress.

Physicians in America also understood the importance of organization. Building on a foundation of local and state organizations, the American Medical Association (AMA) was founded in 1847. Among its other responsibilities, the AMA helped regulate physician licensing, set standards for medical schools, oversaw a code of conduct for practicing physicians, and established journals for the publication of medical advances.

MECHANICAL AND TECHNICAL INSTITUTES

As Americans became increasingly aware of the role of science and technology in the tremendous changes they observed all around them, informal education in various forms grew in popularity. This increasing role played by science and technology in the minds of the American public was reflected in the "tremendous popularity of public lectures on chemistry, steam engines, geology, and astronomy" (Weiner, 167). The number of lyceums that hosted such lectures grew to 3,000 by 1835 (Weiner, 167).

As American colleges and universities increased in enrollment and prestige, a backlash formed from a large segment of the population who believed the universities were of little help to the common artisan or mechanic. In many instances, concerned citizens formed mechanic's institutes to train and educate the technical workforce in the sciences they believed were crucial to successful and "enlightened" manufacturing. These institutes provided public lectures and various modes of formal education for the sons of local middle class workers. The most famous and most successful of these mechanic's institutes was the Franklin Institute in Philadelphia.

In 1824, the founders of the Franklin Institute intended to provide educational opportunities for working artisans and mechanics, and their children. At various times in its history, the Institute provided evening lectures and formal schools for training in the sciences, technology, architecture, drawing, and many other subjects. No matter the subject or the mode of delivery, the target audience was always the working class rather than the children of the wealthy, who were already served by the colleges and universities. The citizens of Philadelphia and surrounding areas embraced this sort of outreach; by 1839, membership in the Institute had climbed to 2,500 (Sinclair, 240).

An episode occurring in the first years of the Institute's life serves as an example of the original intentions of the founders. In 1830, the Franklin Institute conducted a series of experiments to determine the efficiency of water power, at the time the most important source of power for mills and other manufacturing concerns throughout the nation. Volunteers from the Institute, using money raised from donors such as engineers, mill owners, and other interested parties, performed carefully planned experiments with various types of water wheels and other equipment. The results of the experiments were hailed as an example of the advances that could be achieved when *practical* men of *science* cooperated with private *industry* to find solutions to *technical* problems.

The italicized words summarize the hopes of many leaders of American science and American industry in the nineteenth century. It was strongly held that science could, and should, be practical. This practicality would manifest itself in finding solutions to technical problems in American industry. Part of the Franklin Institute's mission, and the mission of other technical institutes, was to prepare mechanics for the coming revolution in technology by educating them in the methods and theories of science.

Perhaps the most important endeavor undertaken by the Franklin Institute was one that, if successful, might prove the most beneficial to everyday life in America. The study, undertaken in 1830, was intended to determine the causes of boiler explosions on steamboats and to make recommendations as to methods to prevent such explosions. The steamboat, hailed widely as evidence of America's technological abilities and a sign of progress for everyone, was actually a dangerous place in its early days of operation. By 1830, there had been almost 60 explosions taking more than 300 lives in the United States (Sinclair, 171). Although there had been several investigations into the causes of these explosions, including one sponsored by Congress, few conclusions were reached. A special committee of the Franklin Institute, chaired by Alexander Dallas Bache, was appointed to investigate these explosions. In 1835, after years of experiments on boilers, Bache and his committee completed their report.

This study was important for many reasons, not the least of which was calling attention to the continuing tragedies occurring on steamboats across the nation. Besides the obvious benefits, there were other outcomes of the study that established precedents for cooperation among private institutions, business and industry, and the government. Bache's experiments were partially supported by government funding, a novelty in antebellum America (Sinclair, 191). Although funded by government sources, the report was published in the Institute's *Journal*, marking the publication as an important repository for practical scientific information.

Although Bache submitted his report to Congress, with recommendations that legislative action be taken to regulate unsafe practices on steamboats, little was done for years. Even a bill passed by both houses of Congress in 1838 proved ineffectual for controlling the steamboat industry. By 1848, the loss of lives in boiler explosions had risen to more than 2,500 (Sinclair, 190). Finally, in 1852 Congress passed a bill that did prove effective in reducing deaths caused by boiler explosions. There can be no question that in this matter, as well as many other practical matters, the Franklin Institute had a positive impact on everyday life in America—a realization not lost on the many Americans who appreciated the Institute's work.

Other modes of formal and informal education, directed at the common man who might not have the time or the resources to attend college, were prominent in American life. The lyceum movement sprouted throughout the country as lecturers traveled far and wide providing entertaining educational opportunities. Often these lectures addressed scientific topics using laboratory equipment as much for special effect as for education. Many Americans achieved a degree of fame through this informal brand of higher education. Amos Eaton, cofounder of the Rensselaer School in New York, became a noted and wildly popular lecturer on "agriculture, domestic economy, the arts and manufactures," among other topics (Marcus and Segal, 83).

Bringing science directly to the people, in theory, was a good idea. In practice, the preponderance of popular lectures and publications often resulted in misinformation and sensationalism. At the close of the nineteenth century, Robert Simpson Woodward, a physicist at Columbia University, lamented the damage done by unqualified lecturers:

An almost inevitable result of the rapid developments of the last three decades especially is that much that goes by the name of science is quite unscientific. The elementary teaching and the popular exposition of science have fallen, unluckily, into the keeping largely of those who cannot rise above the level of a purely literary view of phenomena. Many of the bare facts of science are so far stranger than fiction that the general public has become somewhat overcredulous, and untrained minds fall an easy prey to the tricks of the magazine romancer or to the schemes of the perpetual motion promoter. Along with the growth of real science there has gone on also a growth of pseudo-science. It is so much easier to accept sensational than to interpret sound scientific literature, so much easier to acquire the form that it is to possess the substance of thought that the deluded enthusiast and the designing charlatan are not infrequently mistake by the expectant public for true men of science. There is, therefore, plenty of work before us; and while our principal business is the direct advancement of science, an important, though less agreeable duty, at times is the elimination of error and the exposure of fraud. (cited in Weiner, 181–82)

America's leading scientists at the turn of the century understood that at least part of their job was to educate the American public in the truths of science.

ASTRONOMICAL OBSERVATORIES

Throughout history, in locations around the world from Persia to Denmark, observatories supported by government or private patrons have provided locations for scientists to gather information and consult among themselves. Many leaders in American science in the early nineteenth century understood the importance of establishing such an observatory. The emergence of a national astronomical observatory occurred only after a protracted fight amongst American politicians and scientists. In fact, legislation to authorize the U.S. Coast Survey specifically forbade the founding of a national observatory. Even with the support of influential leaders in science and politics, including John Quincy Adams, it was many years before such an organization originated.

The United States National Observatory opened in 1844, with Matthew Fontaine Maury, a naval officer with extensive experience in astronomy and hydrography, serving as its first director. Maury already held the position of superintendent of the depots of charts and instruments (later the hydrographical office), a position he continued to hold along with his responsibilities with the observatory. Maury published several scientific works in which he gave an accurate description of the Gulf Stream and suggested the possibility of a transatlantic telegraph cable, among many other scientific subjects.

Although the National Observatory holds a special place in American history, privately funded and operated observatories played a larger role in American astronomy. Under the direction of William Cranch Bond, Harvard opened its observatory in 1839. Bond and his son, George Phillips Bond, made several important contributions to astronomy, including the discovery of satellites of both Saturn and Neptune. Bond was also a pioneer in the use of telescopic photography. He followed the earlier work of another American, John William Draper, by producing a type of early photograph, called a daguerreotype, of the moon.

Only a few years after the opening of the Harvard Observatory, the founding of another privately funded institution illustrates the unique relationship that the American public had with science, scientists, and promoters of popular science. In the first few years of the 1840s, a Cincinnati College professor of mathematics and engineering, Ormsby MacKnight Mitchel, employed a series of spirited astronomical lectures to convince "Cincinnati citizens that national and local honor required them to possess a telescope superior to the finest European instruments" (Miller, 204). The story of Mitchel's successful promotion is an example of how even common Americans could be induced to take an active interest in science:

Mitchel proposed a subscription observatory, and soon walked the streets [of Cincinnati] selling three hundred $25 shares in the Cincinnati Astronomical Society. Membership brought the privilege of viewing the heavens through the best obtainable telescope. Not surprisingly, the local cultural elite responded enthusiastically. What was remarkable was Mitchel's success among ordinary townspeople. Appealing to the same indigenous concern for self-improvement that sustained the lyceum and the mechanic's institute, he enrolled more grocers than physicians, more landlords than lawyers, more carpenters than clergymen. Cincinnati soon possessed the largest telescope in the Western Hemisphere, a twelve-inch refractor of the best German manufacture. In November, 1843, old John Quincy Adams, nearly eighty and racked with fever, made the long journey from Washington to lay the cornerstone. (Miller, 204)

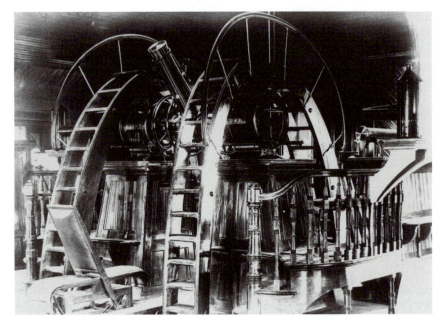

The meridian instrument at the Lick Observatory, 1888. Library of Congress.

Although the Cincinnati Observatory never made an impact as a serious scientific institution, the enthusiastic willingness of grocers, landlords, and carpenters to participate in such a scientific undertaking illustrated, in Mitchel's own words, "what a free people would do for pure science" (Miller, 205).

Later observatories in the United States, such as the Lick Observatory in California and the Yerkes Observatory built in Wisconsin and operated by the University of Chicago, began a tradition of serious scientific work done by astronomers in American observatories. These observatories were of a much different nature than the Cincinnati Observatory; built and maintained for professional astronomers using funds made available by wealthy philanthropists who had at least as much interest in having their names attached to an important scientific project as in some selfless idea of promoting science, the new observatories had little direct affect on the common American.

THE SMITHSONIAN INSTITUTION

When the wealthy Englishman James Smithson, died in 1829, his will stipulated that his vast wealth go to his nephew; however, in the event the nephew died without heirs, the estate would be given to the United States "for the increase & diffusion of knowledge among men." When Smithson's

Smithsonian Institution, Washington, DC, north front, June 1862. Library of Congress.

nephew died in 1835, the United States government found itself with more than half a million dollars and no clear-cut instructions on how the windfall should be spent. A debate raged for more than 10 years over what to do with the gift; some wanted to found a national university or other institution of higher education; others preferred a national observatory (this cause was championed by former president and current congressman John Quincy Adams); while others wanted a library, or a museum, or some sort of research institute. Finally, a compromise was reached and the Smithsonian Institution was established in 1846.

The American physicist and inventor, Joseph Henry, became the first secretary of the Smithsonian Institution primarily because of his reputation as America's greatest living scientist. Henry was best known for his research in electromagnetism, including several discoveries that led directly to Morse's invention of the telegraph. In fact, a dispute arose concerning the true inventor of the telegraph. Henry devised two types of electromagnets, one that produced a higher current than previous devices and another that produced a higher voltage. With these new types of electromagnets and other original inventions, Henry actually constructed a telegraph that he used to demonstrate properties of electromagnetism to his students. However, Henry was never interested in economic exploitation of his inventions, believing as most scientists of the day, that such activities were unbecoming to a scientist whose only interest should be the advancement of knowledge.

In Henry's reticence to seek gain from his discoveries, one can see a basic difference between the scientist and the inventor—a difference that mirrored many of the attitudes of the common American toward science and technology. Henry held similar views as most of his scientific brethren in the United States after the mid-nineteenth century. They held that science was an undertaking of an elite circle of specially trained people whose sole purpose was advancing their discipline through research. These ideas were antithetical to the everyday person in America, where not only the egalitarian ethic led to hate and fear of any sort of elitism, but also the rise of a special form of capitalism led to an emphasis on utility and disdain for science and other "book learning." It is no coincidence that Joseph Henry, one of the leading scientists in the world in the nineteenth century, is often relegated to an historical footnote—if that—while Samuel Morse is known and revered by American school children as the inventor of the telegraph.

Henry's tenure as secretary of the Smithsonian established the nascent institute as America's first and foremost research center. In due time, however, the Smithsonian became much more. Not only did it provide for research in diverse areas of science, it also became a great disseminator of knowledge by publishing research from American scientists, providing public access and programs, and by establishing library and museum space for its great collections. The United States National Museum, assigned to the Smithsonian in 1878 during the tenure of Henry's successor, Spencer Fullerton Baird, grew exponentially as specimens came in from all over the country—many acquired from the various exploring expeditions to the American West. In time, the Smithsonian grew to hold the largest collection of natural history specimens in the country.

SCIENCE IN THE AMERICAN UNIVERSITY

Higher education in the United States changed dramatically during the nineteenth century, and scientific and technological education was at the center of much of this change. At the beginning of the nineteenth century, an American college education meant a traditional classical education in somewhat the same fashion as a European university education. For the most part, a college education "was for the leisure classes, the government leaders, and members of the professions.... A study of such fields as agriculture and the mechanic arts was beneath their [the universities'] academic dignity" (Brunner, 1).

By the end of the century, American universities had become important training grounds for middle-class men (women remained rare in higher education) studying agriculture, engineering, and the sciences. Science and technology began to play a role in the everyday life of more and more Americans as farmers, mechanics, merchants, and even laborers sent their children to American colleges for a practical education.

The perception of the scientific sophistication of the American public in the eyes of college educators was very low in the nineteenth century. Two such educators, one a renowned astronomer and the other a physicist and chemist, both lamented the place of science in American education. Both men were graduates of Harvard's Lawrence Scientific School and the opinion of both on matters of scientific education was well-respected.

In 1874, Simon Newcomb opened his essay "Exact Science in America" with an analysis of the perception of science held by the average "intelligent" citizen:

However strong may be the faith of Americans in the future greatness of their country, their opinion of its present intellectual development is modest in the extreme. To the average intelligent citizen, the idea of this country producing such a mathematician as Le Verrier, or such a physicist as Tyndall, is simply incredible. All he had known of the scientific world leads him to believe that such men are necessarily of transatlantic origin....

Now, while, as we shall presently see, our citizen is quite right in the general belief that we are a generation behind the age in nearly every branch of exact science. (Newcomb, 205)

Newcomb went on to give his reasons for America's lack of standing in the exact sciences such as mathematics, the physical sciences, and astronomy. One of the reasons for scientific shortcomings in the United States was the system of higher education: In America "the universities make the professors" whereas in Germany "the professors ... make the university" (Newcomb, 212). Another shortcoming appeared when Newcomb compared American science to British science and found America lacking in supportive scientific institutions. Whether it was the German university or the British scientific society, science was supported in Europe and virtually ignored in America.

F. W. Clarke, a successful professor and government scientist in the last quarter of the nineteenth century, echoed many of the same thoughts as Newcomb concerning the lack of scientific progress in America. Clarke focused on the shortcomings of the universities, a shortcoming he blamed primarily on the proliferation of second-rate colleges and universities throughout the country. Clarke was very clear concerning his vision of scientific research:

In order that science may flourish in any community, several things are needful. There must be a general appreciation of its true value to the world, clear understanding by men of culture as to the best means for its promotion, facilities for both study and research, and suitable inducements to attract intellectual labor. (Clarke, 229)

Clarke blamed the lack of each of these criteria on the colleges, saying, "The American college system, then, is clearly an impediment in the way of American science" (Clarke, 231). He goes on to give reasons for this indictment of the colleges, including the appearance of too many colleges and subsequent dilution of resources, low pay and prestige for college professors, an outdated curriculum, and an emphasis on practical matters to the detriment of theoretical science.

Higher education in the United States had been, for the most part, concentrated on theology and liberal arts. Colonial colleges required a general and superficial study of science, or natural philosophy as it was then called, but only as a component of a classical education. A serious study of science for the purpose of preparing a student for a career in a scientific field was rare, if not altogether absent. The nineteenth century saw a gradual change to a greater emphasis on science and mathematics, culminating in the appearance of true scientific research universities late in the century. Several events led to this new place for science in higher education.

Almost from its inception, the Military Academy at West Point played a leading role in integrating French learning in mathematics, science, and engineering into the American college curriculum. By the time Sylvanus Thayer became superintendent at West Point in 1817, the Academy had already established a history of employing the best available instructors in mathematics and the sciences. George Baron, the English emigrant who established the first mathematical journal in the United States, was also the first mathematics instructor at the Military Academy from 1801 to 1802. Jared Mansfield, who published an early American work in natural philosophy called *Essays, Mathematical and Physical*, followed Baron. Later mathematics instructors at the Academy included Ferdinand Hassler, the first head of the United States Coast Survey; Andrew Ellicott, an important figure in American science for many decades; and Charles Davies, whose leadership in teaching and translating the newest French mathematical works would influence several generations of American mathematicians.

The year 1816 was especially eventful at West Point, and it proved to be important for American science at large. In 1816, William McRae and Sylvanus Thayer traveled to France to study the methods of instruction at the École Polytechnique in hopes of patterning the Military Academy at West Point after the French military academy. McRae and Thayer returned with more than 1,000 books for the West Point library (Albree, Arney, and Rickey, 1). As superintendent of the Academy, Thayer continued to build the Military Academy's mathematical collections through the 1820s, adding classics in mathematics to the library and acquiring full runs of the leading European mathematics and science journals. To demonstrate further the influence of the French on West Point, by 1830 French titles composed 34 percent of the mathematics collection at the Academy's library (Albree, Arney, and Rickey, 26), whereas in 1803 the mathematics books at the Academy had been almost exclusively British (Albree, Arney, and Rickey, 235–37).

It was also in 1816 that Charles Davies was appointed assistant professor of mathematics at the Academy, becoming a full professor in 1823 and staying at West Point until 1837. Davies, along with engineering professor Claudius Crozet, began teaching the methods of the French and other Continental mathematicians. Crozet introduced descriptive geometry to the cadets at West Point in 1817. He attempted to teach the new mathematical methods to his engineering classes, in spite of the fact the mathematics instructors like Ellicott and Mansfield were still teaching British-style mathematics (Greene, 231). The program of technical education at West Point influenced future scientific schools founded in 1846 at Yale (later named the Sheffield Scientific School) and in 1847 at Harvard (the Lawrence Scientific School). In the process, West Point's program supplied the first engineering professors at these and other American colleges (Albree, Arney, and Rickey, 22).

Before Yale and Harvard founded their science schools, other American educators had attempted to update the mathematics and science curriculum. In the 1820s, Harvard mathematics professor John Farrar translated a series of (mostly French) works. These texts became known as the Cambridge Mathematics Series and the Cambridge Natural Philosophy Series. These texts represent a first attempt to introduce Harvard students to modern science and mathematics.

In 1864, the Columbia School of Mines became one of the first American institutions to concentrate on the training of engineers, in this case mining engineers. This occurred at a time in our history when engineers were trained primarily on the job, not in the colleges and universities. In 1871, approximately 5 percent of American engineers had college training (Marcus and Segal, 169). Even those colleges that offered an engineering education differed as to the best practices for training future engineers. The Massachusetts Institute of Technology, for instance, emphasized hands-on training with practical tools of the trade, while at about the same time Cornell was offering more theoretical and specialized training for engineers.

The watershed year for scientific research (and indeed in other academic disciplines) in American universities was 1876. It was then that Johns Hopkins University opened its doors in Baltimore. Conceived and constructed as the first research university in the United States, Johns Hopkins served as the prototype for future American universities.

The first science professors in America were a diverse group who struggled to overcome many difficulties inherent to the mindset of the time and place in which they worked. Some of them were born in America; some emigrated from Europe; some were born into privileged families; others fought their way to the top from more austere beginnings. Yet, each had something in common—they dreamed of the day that science would gain a legitimate foothold in American society and scientists could pursue their dreams with the support, both financial and psychological, of the American people.

One of the first Americans with an established reputation in science was a Swiss emigrant by the name of Louis Agassiz. When Agassiz came to America in 1846, he already owned a reputation as a preeminent zoologist and geologist. In particular, Agassiz was a leading ichthyologist and had published a multivolume work titled *Research on Fossil Fishes*. He was one of the first scientists to propose that many of the geological features of Europe could be explained by the appearance of a past Ice Age. A brief visit to the United States turned into a permanent move when Agassiz found several opportunities to teach and research in America. By the late 1850s, Agassiz had composed another multivolume work, this one being a scientific survey of his adopted land: *Natural History of the United States*. Agassiz's teaching influenced several generations of Americans who studied natural history at the Lawrence Scientific School at Harvard. He spawned a new generation of teachers and researchers trained in modern scientific methods and who would influence American science through the remaining portion of the century.

By the 1870s, science education had made major advances in American colleges and universities. A growing number of scientists were employed to teach; yet, leading men of science such as Joseph Henry knew that "although *scientists* had found a 'home' in the nation's colleges, *science* itself had not" (Weiner, 178; italics in original). Although science courses had become an important part of the curriculum, Henry and his colleagues "called for improvements in institutions of higher learning, so that they could provide a properly furnished academic home for science, housing scientists who combined teaching and original research" (Weiner, 178). These reforms in higher education in the United States would await the twentieth century.

The scientific landscape in America was profoundly different at the end of the nineteenth century than perhaps anyone could have imagined when the century began. An intellectual backwater in 1800, by 1900 the United States had taken its place among the world's leaders in science. The institutions spawned by a century of struggle set the stage for a twentieth-century America to emerge as the undisputed leader in science and technological innovation. The twentieth century has been called the American Century. Astute observers at the beginning of the twentieth century might have predicted exactly this outcome based on the incredible advances and the groundwork laid during the nineteenth century.

Bibliography

Adams, Judith. *The American Amusement Park Industry: A History of Technology and Thrills*. Boston: Twayne Publishers, 1991.

Adams, Sean Patrick. "Iron." In Paul Finkelman, ed., *Encyclopedia of the United States in the Nineteenth Century*, vol. 2. New York: Charles Scribner's Sons, 2001, 132–36.

Albin, Maurice S. "The use of Anesthetics during the Civil War, 1861–1865." *Pharmacy in History* 42 (nos. 3–4, 2000): 99–114.

Albree, Joe, David Carney, and Frederick V. Rickey. *A Station Favorable to the Pursuit of Science*. Providence, RI: American Mathematical Society, 2000.

Ambrose, Stephen. *Nothing Like it in the World: The Men Who Built the Transcontinental Railroad, 1863–1869*. New York: Simon and Schuster, 2000.

Ansell, Martin R. "Petroleum." In Paul Finkelman, ed., *Encyclopedia of the United States in the Nineteenth Century*, vol. 2. New York: Charles Scribner's Sons, 2001, 485–88.

Ardrey, Robert L. *American Agricultural Implements*, Reprint edition. New York: Arno Press, 1972.

Babbage, Charles. Letter to Bowditch's sons, August 24, 1839, in *Bowditch Collection*, Boston Public Library.

Bain, Barry. "Suburbs." In Paul Finkelman, ed., *Encyclopedia of the United States in the Nineteenth Century*, vol. 3. New York: Charles Scribner's Sons, 2001, 235–36.

Barnhill, Georgia Brady. "Lithography and Prints." In Paul Finkelman, ed., *Encyclopedia of the United States in the Nineteenth Century*, vol. 2. New York: Charles Scribner's Sons, 2001, 223–27.

Bartlett, Irving H. *The American Mind in the Mid-Nineteenth Century*. Arlington Heights, IL: H Davidson, 1982.

Basalla, George. *The Evolution of Technology*. Cambridge: Cambridge University Press, 1988.

Bates, Ralph. *Scientific Societies in the United States.* Cambridge, MA: The MIT Press, 1965.

Bauer, K. Jack. *A Maritime History of the United States: The Role of America's Seas and Waterways.* Columbia, S.C.: University of South Carolina Press, 1988.

Bedini, Silvio A. *Thinkers and Tinkers: Early American Men of Science.* New York: Scribner, 1975.

Berry, Robert Elton. *Yankee Stargazer: The Life of Nathaniel Bowditch.* New York: McGraw Hill, 1941.

Billington, David P. *The Innovators: The Engineering Pioneers Who Made America Modern.* New York: John Wiley and Sons, 1996.

Birr, Kendall A. "Science in American Industry." In David D. Van Tassel and Michael G, Hall, eds., *Science and Society in the United States.* Homewood, Illinois: Dorsey Press, 1966, 35–80.

Bode, Carl, ed. *American Life in the 1840s.* New York: New York University Press, 1967.

Boorstin, Daniel J. *The Americans: The National Experience.* New York: Random House, 2002 (originally published in 1965).

Bowditch, Susan W. *Nathaniel Bowditch, 1773–1838.* Unpublished manuscript-House of Seven Gables, Salem, MA.

Brieger, Gert H., ed., *Medical America in the Nineteenth Century.* Baltimore: The Johns Hopkins University Press, 1972.

Brooks, John. *Telephone: The First Hundred Years.* New York: Harper and Row, 1975.

Brooks, Van Wyck. *The Flowering of New England (1815–1865).* New York: Random House, 1936.

Bruce, Robert V. *Alexander Graham Bell and the Conquest of Solitude.* Boston: Little, Brown and Company, 1973.

Brunner, Henry S. *Land-Grant Colleges and Universities.* Washington, DC: United States Government Printing Office, 1962.

Buel, Jesse. *The Farmer's Companion; or, Essays on the Principles and Practice of American Husbandry.* Boston, 1840. Reprinted in Carl Bode, ed., *American Life in the 1840s.* New York: New York University Press, 1967, 4–13 (page numbers referenced are pages in Bode).

Byington, Margaret. *Homestead: The Households of a Mill Town.* New York: Arno Press, 1969.

de Camp, L. Sprague. *Heroes of American Invention.* New York: Barnes and Noble Books, 1993. Originally published as *The Heroic Age of American Invention,* 1961.

Clarke, F. W. "American Colleges versus American Science." *The Popular Science Monthly* 9 (1876): 476–479. Reprinted in Burnham, John C. *Science in America: Historical Selections.* New York: Holt, Rinehart and Winston, Inc., 1971, 228–39.

Cowan, Ruth Schwartz. *More Work for Mother: The Ironies of Household Technology, from the Open Hearth to the Microwave.* New York: Basic Books, 1983.

Daniels, George H. *American Science in the Age of Jackson.* New York: Columbia University Press, 1968.

———. *Science in American Society; a Social History.* New York: Knopf, 1971.

Davies, John Dunn. *Phrenology: Fad and Science; a 19th-Century American Crusade.* New Haven: Yale University Press, 1955.

Davies, Margery W. *Woman's Place Is at the Typewriter: Office Work and Office Workers, 1870–1930*. Philadelphia: Temple University Press, 1982.

Douglas, George H. *All Aboard! The Railroad in American Life*. New York: Paragon House, 1992.

Dublin, Thomas. *Women at Work: The Transformation of Work and Community in Lowell, Massachusetts, 1826–1860*. New York: Columbia University Press, 1979.

———, ed. *Farm to Factory: Women's Letters, 1830–1860*. New York: Columbia University Press, 1981.

———. *Transforming Women's Work: New England Lives in the Industrial Revolution*. Ithaca, NY: Cornell University Press, 1994.

Duffy, John. "Science and Medicine." In David D. Van Tassel and Michael G, Hall, eds., *Science and Society in the United States*. Homewood, IL: Dorsey Press, 1966, 107–34.

van Dulken, Stephen. *Inventing the 19th Century: 100 Inventions that Shaped the Victorian Age*. New York: New York University Press, 2001.

Dupree, A. Hunter. *Science in the Federal Government, a History of Policies and Activities to 1940*. Cambridge, MA: Belknap Press of Harvard University Press, 1957.

Dwight, Theodore. *Protestants in an Age of Science: the Baconian Ideal and Ante-Bellum American Religious Thought*. Chapel Hill: University of North Carolina Press, 1977.

Eisler, Benita, ed. *The Lowell Offering: Writings of New England Mill Women (1840–1845)*. Philadelphia and New York: J.B. Lippincott Company, 1977.

Endersby, Linda Eikmeier. "Textiles." In Paul Finkelman, ed., *Encyclopedia of the United States in the Nineteenth Century*, vol. 3. New York: Charles Scribner's Sons, 2001, 276–81.

Ess, Daniel R. "Agricultural Technology." In Paul Finkelman, ed., *Encyclopedia of the United States in the Nineteenth Century*, vol. 1. New York: Charles Scribner's Sons, 2001, 32–36.

Fairchild, Louis. "Health Care on the Frontier Plains." *Panhandle-Plains Historical Review* 44 (2001): 1–22.

Fischer, Claude S. *America Calling: A Social History of the Telephone to 1940*. Berkeley and Los Angeles: University of California Press, 1992.

Fleming, James Rodger. "Storms, Strikes, and Surveillance: The U.S. Army Signal Office, 1861–1891." *Historical Studies in the Physical and Biological Sciences* 30 (part 2, 2000): 315–32.

Foner, Philip S. *The Factory Girls: a Collection of Writings on Life and Struggles in the New England Factories of the 1840's by the Factory Girls Themselves, and the Story, in Their Own Words, of the First Trade Unions of Women Workers in the United States*. Urbana: University of Illinois Press, 1977.

Gordon, John Steele. *A Thread Across the Ocean: The Heroic Story of the Transatlantic Cable*. New York: Walker and Company, 2002.

Gordon, Robert B. "Custom and Consequence: Early Nineteenth-Century Origins of the Environmental and Social Costs of Mining Anthracite." In McGaw, Judith A., ed., *Early American Technology: Making and Doing Things from the Colonial Era to 1850*. Chapel Hill: University of North Carolina Press, 1994, 240–77.

Greenberg, Joshua R. "Work: The Workshop." In Paul Finkelman, ed., *Encyclopedia of the United States in the Nineteenth Century*, vol. 3. New York: Charles Scribner's Sons, 2001, 421–22.

Greene, John C. *American Science in the Age of Jefferson*. Ames: Iowa State University Press, 1984.

Gross, Ernie. *Advances and Innovations in American Daily Life*, 1600–1930s. Jefferson, NC: MacFarland, 2002.

Guralnick, Stanley M. *Science and the Ante-Bellum American College*. Philadelphia: American Philosophical Society, 1975.

Hall, Courtney Robert. *History of American Industrial Science*. New York: Library Publishers, 1954.

Haller, John S. *American Medicine in Transition: 1840–1910*. Urbana: University of Illinois Press, 1981.

Harding, T. Swann. *Two Blades of Grass: A History of Scientific Development in the U.S. Department of Agriculture*. Norman: University of Oklahoma Press, 1947.

Harper's Monthly, 1883. "The Brooklyn Bridge Story," reprinted at www.catskillarchive.com/rrextra/bbstory.html

Hasegawa, Guy R. "Pharmacy in the American Civil War." *Pharmacy in History* 42 (nos. 3–4, 2000): 67–86.

Hawke, David Freeman. *Nuts and Bolts of the Past: a History of American Technology, 1776–1860*. New York: Harper & Row, 1988.

Hayter, Earl W. *The Troubled Farmer, 1850–1900; Rural Adjustment to Industrialism*. Dekalb: Northern Illinois University Press, 1968.

Higby, Gregory J. "Chemistry and the 19th-Century American Pharmacist." *Bulletin for the History of Chemistry* 28 (no. 1, 2003): 9–17.

Hounshell, David A. *From the American System to Mass Production: 1800–1932*. Baltimore: The Johns Hopkins University Press, 1984.

Hughes, Thomas Parke. *American Genius: a Century of Invention and Technological Enthusiasm, 1870–1970*. New York: Viking Press, 1989.

Hurt, R. Douglas. *American Agriculture: A Brief History*. Ames: Iowa State University Press, 1994.

Israel, Paul. "Telegraph." In Paul Finkelman, ed., *Encyclopedia of the United States in the Nineteenth Century*, vol. 3. New York: Charles Scribner's Sons, 2001, 264–66.

Jackson, Donald C. "Roads Most Traveled: Turnpikes in Southeastern Pennsylvania in the Early Republic." In Judith A., ed., *Early American Technology: Making and Doing Things from the Colonial Era to 1850*. Chapel Hill: University of North Carolina Press, 1994, 197–239.

Jackson, Richard H, ed. "Transportation in the West." *Journal of the West* 42 (Spring, 2003): 6–101.

Jacobs, David and Neville, Anthony E. *Bridges, Canals & Tunnels: The Engineering Conquest of America*. New York: American Heritage Publishing Co., 1968.

Jamison, David L. "Newspapers and the Press." In Paul Finkelman, ed., *Encyclopedia of the United States in the Nineteenth Century*, vol. 2. New York: Charles Scribner's Sons, 2001, 418–26.

Jenkins, Reese V. "George Eastman and the Coming of Industrial Research in America." In Carroll W. Pursell, Jr., ed., *Technology in America: A History of Individuals and Ideas*. Cambridge, MA: The MIT Press, 1982, 129–41.

———. *Images and Enterprise: Technology and the American Photographic Industry, 1839–1925*. Baltimore: Johns Hopkins University Press, 1987.

Jonnes, Jill. *Empires of Light: Edison, Tesla, Westinghouse, and the Race to Electrify the World*. New York: Random House, 2003.

Keller Jr., Vagel C. "Steel and the Steel Industry." In Paul Finkelman, ed., *Encyclopedia of the United States in the Nineteenth Century*, vol. 3. New York: Charles Scribner's Sons, 2001, 227–32.

Kellogg, Charles Edwin and David C. Knap. *The College of Agriculture: Science in the Public Service*. New York: McGraw-Hill, 1966.

Kent, Noel Jacob. *America in 1900*. Armonk, NY: M. E. Sharp, 2000.

Lacour-Gayet, Robert. *Everyday Life in the United States Before the Civil War*. New York: Ungar Publishing Company, 1969.

Langdon, William Chauncy. *Everyday Things in American Life: 1776–1876*. New York: Charles Scribner's Sons, 1941.

Larkin, Jack. *The Reshaping of Everyday Life: 1790–1840*. New York: Harper and Row, 1988.

Lasby, Clarence G. "Science and the Military." In David D. Van Tassel and Michael G, Hall, eds., *Science and Society in the United States*. Homewood, IL: Dorsey Press, 1966, 251–82.

Lee, Stephen. Letter to William Vaughan (undated), *in Bowditch Collection*, Boston Public Library.

Licht, Walter. *Working for the Railroad: The Organization of Work in the Nineteenth Century*. Princeton, NJ: Princeton University Press, 1983.

———. *Industrializing America: The Nineteenth Century*. Baltimore: Johns Hopkins Press, 1995.

Linklater, Andro. *Measuring America: How and Untamed Wilderness Shaped the United States and Fulfilled the Promise of Democracy*. New York: Walker & Company, 2003.

London Quarterly Review 48 (1832): 558

Lowell National Historical Park Handbook 140. At http://www.nps.gov/lowe/2002/home.htm

Mackey, Robert. "Military Technology." In Paul Finkelman, ed., *Encyclopedia of the United States in the Nineteenth Century*, vol. 2. New York: Charles Scribner's Sons, 2001, 325–8.

Madsen, Troy. "The Company Doctor: Promoting Stability in Eastern Utah Mining Towns." *Utah Historical Quarterly* 68 (Spring, 2000): 139–56.

Mahoney, Timothy R. "Industrialization and the Market." In Paul Finkelman, ed., *Encyclopedia of the United States in the Nineteenth Century*, vol. 2. New York: Charles Scribner's Sons, 2001, 106–10.

Marcus, Alan I. and Segal, Howard P. *Technology in America: A Brief History*. San Diego: Harcourt Brace Jovanovich, Publishers, 1989.

Martin, Albro. *Railroads Triumphant: The Growth, Rejection and Rebirth of a Vital American Force*. Oxford: Oxford University Press, 1992.

Marvin, Carolyn. *When Old Technologies were New: Thinking About Electric Communication in the Late Nineteenth Century*. New York: Oxford University Press, 1988.

McCullough, David. *The Path between the Seas. The Creation of the Panama Canal, 1870–1914*. New York: Simon and Schuster, 1977.

McGaw, Judith A., ed. *Early American Technology: Making and Doing Things from the Colonial Era to 1850*. Chapel Hill: University of North Carolina Press, 1994.

Merritt, Raymond H. *Engineering in American Society, 1850–1875*. Lexington: University of Kentucky Press, 1969.

Miller, Howard S. "Science and Private Agencies." In David D. Van Tassel and Michael G, Hall, eds., *Science and Society in the United States*. Homewood, IL: Dorsey Press, 1966, 191–222.

Montgomery, Scott L. *Minds for the Making: the Role of Science in American Education, 1750–1990*. New York: Guilford Press, 1994.

Morison, Elting Elmore. *From Know-How to Nowhere: the Development of American Technology*. New York: Basic Books, 1974.

The Morrill Act (12 Statutes at Large of the United States of America 503), 1862.

Mulcahy, Richard P. "Mining and Extraction." In Paul Finkelman, ed., *Encyclopedia of the United States in the Nineteenth Century*, vol. 2. New York: Charles Scribner's Sons, 2001, 333–40.

Murphy, Lamar Riley. *Enter the Physician: The Transformation of Domestic Medicine, 1760–1860*. Tuscaloosa: The University of Alabama Press, 1991.

Nelson, Daniel. "Rubber." In Paul Finkelman, ed., *Encyclopedia of the United States in the Nineteenth Century*, vol. 3. New York: Charles Scribner's Sons, 2001, 120–1.

Newcomb, Simon. "Exact Science in America." *North American Review* 119 (1874): 286–308. Reprinted in Burnham, John C. *Science in America: Historical Selections*. New York: Holt, Rinehart and Winston, Inc., 1971, 205–21.

Nye, David E. *Electrifying America: The Social Meanings of New Technology, 1880–1940*. Cambridge, MA: The MIT Press, 1990.

———. *American Technological Sublime*. Cambridge, MA: The MIT Press, 1994.

———. *America as Second Creation: Technology and Narratives of New Beginnings*. Cambridge, MA: The MIT Press, 2003.

Nye, Russel Blaine. *The Cultural Life of the New Nation, 1776–1830*. New York: Harper, 1960.

Oliver, John William. *History of American Technology*. New York: Ronald Press Co., 1956.

Pankin, Mary Faith. "The Yale Scientific Expeditions in Kansas." *Heritage of the Great Plains 35* (Fall-Winter, 2002): 20–35.

de la Pedraja, Rene. "Steam Power." In Paul Finkelman, ed., *Encyclopedia of the United States in the Nineteenth Century*, vol. 3. New York: Charles Scribner's Sons, 2001, 223–27.

Petroski, Henry. *The Evolution of Useful Things*. New York: Vintage Books, 1994.

———. *Engineers of Dreams: Great Bridge Builders and the Spanning of America*. New York: Alfred A. Knopf, 1995.

Plowdon, David. "The Bridges I Love." *American Heritage of Invention and Technology* 18, no. 3 (Winter, 2003): 29–38.

Pursell, Jr., Carroll W. "Science and Government Agencies." In David D. Van Tassel and Michael G, Hall, eds., *Science and Society in the United States*. Homewood, IL: Dorsey Press, 1966, 223–50.

———. "Cyrus Hall McCormick and the Mechanization of Agriculture." In Carroll W. Pursell, ed., *Technology in America: A History of Individuals and Ideas*. Cambridge, MA: The MIT Press, 1981, 71–9.

———. *The Machine in America: A Social History of Technology*. Baltimore: The Johns Hopkins University Press, 1995.

———, ed. *American Technology*. Malden, MA: Blackwell, 2001.

Rabbitt, Mary C. *The United States Geological Survey, 1879–1989*. (U.S. Geological Survey; 1050), 1989.

Razac, Olivier. *Barbed Wire: A Political History*. New York: New Press, 2002.

Reingold, Nathan. *The Sciences in the American Context: New Perspectives*. Washington DC: Smithsonian Institution Press, 1979.

Rosenberg, Charles E. "Science and American Social Thought." In David D. Van Tassel and Michael G, Hall, eds., *Science and Society in the United States*. Homewood, IL: Dorsey Press, 1966, 135–62.

———. *No Other Gods: On Science and American Social Thought* (Revised and expanded edition). Baltimore: The Johns Hopkins University Press, 1997.

Rothstein, William G. *American Physicians in the Nineteenth Century: From Sects to Science*. Baltimore: The Johns Hopkins University Press, 1972.

Rowsome, Frank. *Trolley Car Treasury*. New York: Bonanza Books, 1956.

Saffell, Cameron L. "Meatpacking." In Paul Finkelman, ed., *Encyclopedia of the United States in the Nineteenth Century*, vol. 2. New York: Charles Scribner's Sons, 2001, 274–78.

Sale, Kirkpatrick. *The Fire of His Genius: Robert Fulton and the American Dream*. New York: The Free Press, 2001.

Scharchburg, Richard P. *Frank Duryea and the Birth of the American Automobile Industry*. Warrendale, PA: Society of Automotive Engineers, Inc., 1993.

Shipley, Randolph, ed. *Science and Society in Early America: Essays in Honor of Whitfield J. Bell, Jr.* Philadelphia: American Philosophical Society, 1986.

Shryock, Richard Harrison. *Medicine in America: Historical Essays*. Baltimore: The Johns Hopkins University Press, 1966.

———. *Medicine and Society in America: 1660–1860*, paperback edition. Ithaca, NY, and London: Cornell University Press, 1972.

Sinclair, Bruce. *Philadelphia's Philosopher Mechanics: a history of the Franklin Institute, 1824–1865*. Baltimore: The Johns Hopkins University Press, 1974.

Sloane, Eugene A. *The All New Complete Book of Bicycling*, 3rd ed. New York: Simon & Schuster, 1980.

Smith, Charles. L. "Natural Resources." In Paul Finkelman, ed., *Encyclopedia of the United States in the Nineteenth Century*, vol. 2. New York: Charles Scribner's Sons, 2001, 389–92.

Solbrig, Otto T. and Solbrig, Dorothy J. *So Shall You Reap: Farming and Crops in Human Affairs*. Washington, DC: Island Press, 1994.

Spar, Debra L. *Ruling the Waves: Cycles of Discovery, Chaos, and Wealth from the Compass to the Internet*. New York: Harcourt, Inc., 2001.

Standage, Tom. *The Victorian Internet*. New York: Walker Publishing, 1998.

Stauffer, John. "Popular Culture." In Paul Finkelman, ed., *Encyclopedia of the United States in the Nineteenth Century*, vol. 2. New York: Charles Scribner's Sons, 2001, 526–31.

Stowe, Steven M. "Health and Disease." In Paul Finkelman, ed., Encyclopedia of the United States in the Nineteenth Century, vol. 2. New York: Charles Scribner's Sons, 2001, 17–22.

Struik, Dirk J. *Yankee Science in the Making*. New York: Dover Publications, Inc., 1991.

"Susan." *Lowell Offering*, 4. June, 1844 and August, 1844. Reprinted in Carl Bode, ed., *American Life in the 1840s*. New York: New York University Press, 1967, 28–40.

Theriot, Nancy M. "Negotiating Illness: Doctors, Patients, and Families in the Nineteenth Century." *Journal of the History of the Behavioral Sciences* 37 (Fall, 2001): 349–68.

Thomas, Mary Margaret. *Science, Military Style: Fortifications, Science, and the U.S. Army Corps of Engineers, 1802–1861*. University of Minnesota, 2002.

de Tocqueville, Alexis. *Democracy in America*, 12th edition (1848). Translated by George Lawrence; edited by J. P. Mayer. New York: HarperPerennial, 1969.

Uselding, Paul J. *Studies in the Technological Development of the American Economy during the First Half of the Nineteenth Century*. New York: Arno Press, 1971.

Van Tassel, David D. and Michael G, Hall, eds., *Science and Society in the United States*. Homewood, IL: Dorsey Press, 1966.

"The Virtual Typewriter Museum," www.typewritermuseum.org

Vrooman, John Wright. *The Story of the Typewriter, 1873–1923*. Herkimer, NY: Herkimer County Historical Society, 1923.

Wahl, Jenny Bourne. "Work: Factory Labor." In Paul Finkelman, ed., *Encyclopedia of the United States in the Nineteenth Century*, vol. 3. New York: Charles Scribner's Sons, 2001, 422–25.

Wajda, Shirley Teresa. "Photography." In Paul Finkelman, ed., *Encyclopedia of the United States in the Nineteenth Century*, vol. 2. New York: Charles Scribner's Sons, 2001, 495–99.

Wallace, Anthony F.C. *Rockdale*. New York: Norton Press, 1978.

Ware, Norman. *The Industrial Worker, 1840–1860: The Reaction of American Industrial Society to the Advance of the Industrial Revolution*. Gloucester, MA: Peter Smith, 1959.

Weiner, Charles. "Science and Higher Education." In David D. Van Tassel and Michael G, Hall, eds., *Science and Society in the United States*. Homewood, IL: Dorsey Press, 1966, 163–90.

Wexler, Alice. "Chorea and Community in a Nineteenth-Century Town." *Bulletin of the History of Medicine* 76 (Fall, 2002): 495–527.

Wik, Reynold M. "Science and American Agriculture." In David D. Van Tassel and Michael G, Hall, eds., *Science and Society in the United States*. Homewood, IL: Dorsey Press, 1966, 81–106.

Wolfe, Richard J. *Tarnished Idol: William Thomas Green Morton and the Introduction of Surgical Anesthesia, A Chronicle of the Ether Controversy*. San Anselmo, CA: Jeremy Norman & Co., 2001.

Wyman, Mark. *Hard Rock Epic: Western Miners and the Industrial Revolution, 1860–1910*. Berkeley: University of California Press, 1979.

Zinn, Howard. *A People's History of the United States, 1492–Present*. New York: HarperCollins Publishers, 2001.

Index

About the Author

TODD TIMMONS teaches mathematics, history of mathematics, and history of science at the University of Arkansas–Fort Smith. His professional interests include the history of American science and American mathematics.

The Greenwood Press "Science and Technology in Everyday Life" Series

Science and Technology in Colonial America
William E. Burns